PEOPLE

PEOPLE

Psychology from a
Cultural Perspective

David Matsumoto
San Francisco State University

WAVELAND

PRESS, INC.

Prospect Heights, Illinois

For information about this book, contact:
   Waveland Press, Inc.
   P.O. Box 400
   Prospect Heights, Illinois 60070
   (847) 634-0081
   www.waveland.com

to
Sayaka

Preface

This book is intended for use as a supplemental textbook in introductory psychology courses and, in some cases, as a primary text in lower-division cross-cultural psychology courses. By reviewing cross-cultural research literature in nine popular areas of psychology, this text challenges much of the knowledge that is typically presented in larger, more traditional introductory psychology texts and courses. As a supplement, this text presents a much more detailed discussion of the issues than would be possible in a traditional psychology text. Without considerable changes in content and structure, the latter approach would tend to make the material superficial or tokenistic. In challenging the traditional knowledge, the overall goals of the book are to expose students to psychology from around the world and to provide options from which they can choose the perspective on psychology and human behavior that is right for them.

Below I describe in more detail the rationale for this book as well as its structure and its major themes.

The Purpose of This Book

Psychology from a Limited Perspective

Introductory psychology is one of the most popular courses on college and university campuses across the United States today. In most of these classes, we try to present to students many of the facts, or "truths," that have been gathered through systematic and scientific research in psychology over the years. Armed with a compilation of those facts (the textbook) and the tools with which we can present them (videos, computer disks, instructor's manual, and so on), introductory psychology marches on in teaching students what we know about human behavior.

For many students, most of the information presented in introductory psychology strikes a familiar chord; thus, the nature of the truth that is presented is validated for these students. For many other students, however, much of that same "truth" is just too "foreign." Many of these students leave their classes frustrated or confused, wondering about the relevance of psychology as an academic discipline and a field of study. For them, the truth that was presented is not validated.

These feelings are certainly not limited to students. Many introductory psychology instructors feel the same frustrations as their students. They often wonder about the relevance of the material they have to teach to their students. They also wonder about the relevance of that material to their own lives.

To understand the basis of these frustrations, we need to examine how the truths were produced in the first place. Most, if not all, of the information presented in introductory psychology textbooks is based on findings from research. Until very recently, most of the research conducted in psychology was based on only a single type of person—middle-class Americans of European descent enrolled in introductory psychology classes in American universities, participating in research to fulfill class requirements.

Although there is nothing wrong with most research, and thus its findings, based on this type of sample, there are limitations to the types of knowledge and information that can be gathered this way. For one thing, we wouldn't know whether what we found to be true for this group of people would apply to people of other racial, cultural, or ethnic backgrounds. Do people of *all* backgrounds learn in the same way? Develop in the same way? Express emotions in the same way? React to different psychotherapies in the same way? Common sense says no. Despite the fact, then, that our truths are culture bound (and often gender bound as well), this is often the way our truths are produced. Thus, these truths are limited.

There are probably several reasons why knowledge of psychology has been packaged in such a limited fashion. One of those reasons is that American psychology has been quite ethnocentric. In American psychology, researchers and theorists have been primarily concerned with what has been going on in the United States and much less concerned with people and knowledge outside the United States. By focusing mainly on what other Americans have been doing and the information they have produced, American psychology has fostered, to a large degree, an ignorance of the psychologies of other countries and cultures. It is probably true that the United States is a leader in academic research in psychology; that does *not* mean, however, that we still cannot learn from others about others, as well as about ourselves.

Another reason for the ethnocentrism in American psychology has to do with the funds available for research, which ultimately influence the truths that are produced. For many years, funding agencies were not very concerned with cross-cultural or subcultural research. Instead, most were concerned with advancing mainstream, academic research, which did not include examining cultural, racial, or ethnic differences. Thus, much of the information produced by that "age" of research was limited in terms of its generalizability to different types of people.

Yet a third reason for ethnocentrism involves the lack of subjects of different racial, ethnic, and cultural backgrounds. In the past, many researchers simply did not have access to people of differing racial, ethnic, or cultural backgrounds. Thus, it was more difficult than it is today to study differences even if the researchers wanted to. Even today, researchers in many parts of the United States would find it difficult to study those types of differences across people simply because of the nature of the people that live in the areas where the psychologists work.

A fourth reason for ethnocentrism has to do with the politics of uncovering those differences. When differences are found, it is often politically difficult to make statements about those differences. Even when a statement of differences is made with the most value-free intent, it is difficult not to attribute, or interpret, a value to that statement. To avoid this potential problem, many researchers have, in the past, simply elected not to study the differences.

A fifth and final reason for a lack of knowledge and awareness about ethnic and cultural differences concerns a lack of ethnic and cultural diversity among the researchers themselves. The people doing the research and conducting the studies in years past were, in general, a more homogeneous group of individuals than is the case today. Thus, there was less awareness of ethnic and cultural differences and less concern for studying them.

These are just some of the factors that have contributed to a lack of coverage of issues pertaining to diversity and difference in traditional introductory psychology textbooks. Unfortunately, by presenting psychology from this limited perspective, such textbooks really have done no justice to one of the greatest attributes of people—the individual and collective diversity in thought, feeling, and behavior. This diversity is exactly what psychology is supposed to understand.

The Changing Perspectives of Psychology Today and Tomorrow

Today, there are more reasons than ever to study psychology from a perspective of ethnic and cultural diversity. Among the forces at work in our society today that strongly encourage psychology to deal with human diversity are:

- *The changing demographics of society as a whole.* Not only in the United States, but all over the world, many societies and countries are becoming increasingly pluralistic and multicultural. To function successfully and responsibly in society today, one must be able to recognize, understand, and work with this diversity.

- *The changing demographics of university students.* In addition to the increasing plurality in society as a whole, university students, who are the primary "consumers" of knowledge and information transfer, are also becoming increasingly diverse. Students today come from much more varied backgrounds than ever before. The field of psychology must be able to meet the challenges presented by the changing faces of student consumers. We must teach information that is relevant for as many people as possible, at the same time recognizing important cultural and ethnic differences.

- *The changing demographics of psychology instructors and researchers.* Not only are the demographics of university students changing, but so also are those of university faculty. Recent years have witnessed more women and people from traditionally underrepresented populations becoming university teachers and researchers. The information presented in textbooks must reflect the diversity the instructors themselves bring to their respective positions.

- *An increased awareness of our own ethnocentrism.* In many contexts, the American public as a whole is becoming increasingly more sensitive and aware of cultural, racial, and ethnic differences across people. Today, improving technologies bring people of different national and cultural backgrounds together as never before in many international arenas. Even within the United States, societal thinking has shifted from the concept of this country as a "melting pot" of different races and cultures to the idea of a conglomeration of many different "micro" cultures. Such changing societal emphases and awareness make imperative the study of psychology with a focus on diversity.

- *A recognition of the importance and utility of cross-cultural research.* Shifts have also occurred within the research and academic communities. Cross-cultural psychology in general, and cross-cultural research in particular, used to be viewed as a subfield of psychology reserved for esoteric approaches to psychology, or as a haven for ethnic minority researchers in their individual endeavors. Today, however, there is growing consensus among psychologists and researchers of all backgrounds and disciplines on the importance of cross-cultural psychology to inform and shape the understanding of human behavior in general. Now, many comprehensive approaches to a problem or issue in psychology must incorporate a cross-cultural perspective.

Above all, many people recognize the importance of dealing with issues of cultural, racial, and ethnic diversity *now*. As we end the 20th century and begin the 21st, many of these social changes and issues will become more important, more widespread, more urgent.

Why This Book?

Many of the changes just described force us to ask some very basic, yet extremely important, questions about the nature of the knowledge and information typically taught and learned in psychology classes across America today. These questions concern such topics as the limitations of the information traditionally presented in introductory psychology textbooks and the degree to which this information is applicable to people of different ethnic, racial, or cultural backgrounds. Findings from cross-cultural research can inform us about how studies of people of different cultures, both inside and outside the United States, challenge the traditional information. Then, to the extent that we can find evidence to suggest that the "traditional" information is limited, we need to revise our understanding of that information.

This book is one of our first serious attempts to answer these important questions facing the field of psychology, its teachers, and its students on the introductory level. Indeed, ethnic and cultural diversity has emerged as one of the hottest topics in psychology today. This book is a must for gaining some perspective on the issue of human diversity in the study of psychology.

How Is This Book Organized?

Topics Selected

This book is not intended to replace your introductory psychology textbook. It does not provide a comprehensive review or presentation of the traditional material typically covered in introductory psychology; you should already have that in your regular psychology text. Instead, this book *supplements* psychology textbooks by *re*-presenting some of the same material, but with a multicultural focus.

What material have we chosen to re-present? This was a difficult decision, because many people believe that students should learn *every* major topic and subfield in psychology from a multicultural perspective. However, that is just not realistic. Psychology courses are already pressed for time without rehashing every single topic from a different viewpoint. Thus, we had to choose topics to cover in this book. In making these choices, we tried to follow some basic criteria, which included the following.

1. *The topic had to be typically covered in introductory psychology texts.* In order to address cross-cultural issues taught on the introductory level, topics had to be chosen that are normally covered in introductory psychology texts. Many other topics are interesting, such as culture and gender, culture and health, culture and organizations. But given the supplemental nature of this book, we deemed other topics inappropriate for this edition. By including topics typically discussed in introductory psychology texts, we ensured the coverage of topics in psychology that most psychologists believe are important to learn.

2. *The topics had to be identified by cross-cultural researchers as relevant to presentation in introductory psychology courses.* Because our emphasis is on presenting facts documented through cross-cultural research, we felt it was important to give consideration to topics that the experts—cross-cultural researchers—believe are important. This thinking has guided our selection of the topics presented here.

3. *The topics had to have a substantial cross-cultural research base, so that our reporting could be done with a high degree of certainty.* Above all, we wanted to select topics that have been studied cross-culturally quite extensively. We wanted to make sure that what we tell you in this book goes beyond speculation or impression. To do so, we have included topics with a substantial cross-cultural research base, so that we can be confident that what we tell you has been documented through research, and you can be confident in what you learn.

By applying these three criteria, we decided on eight topics, which we re-present to you with a cross-cultural research focus. These topics are:

- Perception
- Cognition
- Developmental psychology
- Language and language acquisition
- Cognitive development and intelligence
- Emotion
- Abnormal psychology
- Social psychology

In addition, we added a chapter on cultural perspectives on the self to set a conceptual foundation for the rest of the book.

Each of these topics is usually covered in introductory psychology courses and textbooks. Each represents a major subfield of psychology. Each has been identified by cross-cultural researchers as among the most important topics to cover in psychology classes from a multicultural perspective. Finally, each enjoys a rich and substantial cross-cultural research base.

Guiding Themes

Several questions served as guiding themes in writing each of the chapters in this book. These themes included the following:

1. *What is "typically" presented on this topic in traditional introductory psychology?* We introduce, very briefly, some of the most important knowledge typically presented in introductory psychology classes and textbooks. Doing so gives us a basis from which to evaluate the cross-cultural material.

2. *What are the limitations in this knowledge due to the cultural composition of the samples studied in the research that forms the basis of this knowledge? To what degree is this knowledge generalizable to people of other cultural backgrounds?* Students need to know how the information presented to them in psychology was generated and what are some of the limitations of those studies.

3. *How do findings from cross-cultural research challenge traditional knowledge?* We need to look at the cross-cultural research to see whether these findings give us a different picture or understanding of that topic. We also need to examine more closely research in the United States that has used multicultural samples.

4. *Given differences in knowledge from cross-cultural research, how can we, or should we, think about this topic?* This is the key issue. If the cross-cultural studies on this topic suggest that the traditional information presented in most psychology classes is limited and *not* generalizable to people of diverse cultural backgrounds, what are we to make of this? How can we revise our ways of thinking to incorporate these diversities?

In a supplemental text it is impossible to review all of the cross-cultural literature on a topic or to ensure adequate representation of a variety of cultures in the presentation. Instead, we have selected studies that are intended to raise questions about the traditional knowledge and to serve as examples of how that knowledge may be culture bound.

Overall Book Goals

We seek to raise questions about traditional, mainstream knowledge. We want to know whether what is taught is applicable to people of *all* cultural backgrounds. We look for answers to these questions in the cross-cultural literature. If the research suggests that people are different from what is typically presented, we try to find ways of understanding those differences that are better than those available today.

We offer this book as a way to seek alternatives to the material typically presented in psychology. By offering these alternatives, we hope that you will be able to choose a viewpoint or perspective of psychology and human behavior that you believe is right for you. Also, we hope that you will be able to recognize, understand, and most importantly, appreciate the psychology of people of diverse backgrounds, some of which will be very, very different from your own.

Acknowledgments

This book is the product of a collaborative effort by many friends and colleagues. I am in debt to many of them for helping me, directly and indirectly, in making this book a reality.

Paul Ekman, Wally Friesen, Klaus Scherer, Harald Wallbott, and Tsutomu Kudoh have all been direct collaborators in my cross-cultural research program. Much of our collaborative research projects forms the basis for the work reported in the chapter on human emotion. Professor Kudoh has been especially helpful in all of our collaborative research involving Japan.

A number of agencies and institutions have provided support for some of the research reported in this book. Much of our research on the emotions was supported in part by a research grant from the National Institute of Mental Health (MH 42749-01), and an American Psychological Association Minority Fellowship under Clinical Training Grant 5 T01 MH13833 from the National Institute of Mental Health. Our research has also been supported by a Research Fellowship from the Wright Institute (1986–1989) and by President's Research and Professional Development Grants, Affirmative Action Awards, and California State University Awards for Research, Scholarship, and Professional Activity from San Francisco State University (1989–1992).

Over the years, my research laboratory at San Francisco State University, and earlier at the Wright Institute and the University of California, Berkeley, has benefited from the participation of many undergraduate and graduate research assistants. Although there are too many of them to name specifically, I would like to single out one assistant whose aid has been invaluable in the completion of this book. Michelle Weissman first came to my laboratory wanting to become an undergraduate research assistant. Over the years, she has grown to be not only one of my most trusted and valued assistants, but also a good friend. She helped me in all of the organizational and logistic aspects of this book, including the maintenance of correspondence with each of my co-authors and the publisher. Michelle's help was invaluable to the completion of this project.

I am also grateful for having such wonderful author collaborators on this book project. Margaret Lynch, Jeff LeRoux, and Dawn Terrell are fellow faculty members at San Francisco State University. Shinobu Kitayama is a friend and colleague at the University of Oregon, whom I just happened to meet at a convention meeting in 1992. Philip Hull is a colleague from our graduate school days, both of us having received our doctorates from the University of California, Berkeley. All of them produced manuscripts on time, responded to queries, participated in the entire process of producing this book in such a way that it was a true joy to work with each of them.

I am indebted to the wonderful and constructive comments we received from our reviewers: William Dibiase, Delaware County Community College; George Domino, University of Arizona at Tucson; Susan B. Goldstein, University of Redlands; Catherine Hale, University of Puget Sound; G. William Hill, Kennesaw State College; James J. Johnson, Illinois State University; Elizabeth Klonoff, California State University, San Bernardino; Harve E. Rawson, Hanover College; and Yvonne V. Wells, Suffolk University. Their comments, criticisms, and suggestions were invaluable as we revised and polished much of the content of the book. In expressing their concerns, they were also able to convey their support for the project and their agreement on the need for such a resource.

Marianne Taflinger, the editor of this book, has walked me through the process from talking about the idea of a book to the submission of the completed manuscript. She has always been there to answer questions, allay anxieties, and provide any and all kinds of support for this project. I am so grateful that she was the editor for this project. I also extend my gratitude to Ellen Brownstein, Anne Draus, Roy Neuhaus, and Carline Haga for their kind work and patience in completing this book project.

My family has made so many sacrifices over the years, not only in the production of this text, but also during the conduct of the many studies that comprise some of the material in this book. Many early mornings and late evenings have been spent at the computer, phone, or fax in order for our research and this book to proceed. Doing cross-cultural research means extensive travel, taking more time away from home. This book is very much a product of the efforts and sacrifices of my family, without whose patience and understanding none of this could have occurred.

David Matsumoto

Contents

2 *Culture and Self: How Cultures Influence the Way We View Ourselves*   *17*

3 *Perception*   *39*

4 *Cognition*   *51*

7 *Cognitive Development and Intelligence*   *101*

8 *Emotion*   *117*

9   *Abnormal Psychology*   *135*

10   *Social Psychology*   *153*

11   *Conclusion*   *175*

Index   *181*

Introduction

The Nature of Knowledge in Psychology

One of the most important goals of the field of psychology is to understand human behavior. In this sense, psychology is similar to philosophy, which also attempts to understand people. Yet, psychologists are different from philosophers in the way they approach the problem. Psychology relies heavily on scientific *research* about people to generate what knowledge we have about how and why people behave. Typically, before we accept something as a "truth" in psychology (many call these truths "principles"), we have to be assured that the research that produced that truth met some minimal standards for scientific rigor. Thus, the **psychological truth** born from the research could be only that and nothing else.

It follows, then, that what we know as truths in psychology are heavily dependent on how the research that produced those truths was conducted. Because of the nature of research, *all* studies in psychology are conducted under some conditions, within certain parameters and limitations. Thus, to a large extent, all the knowledge generated by psychological research is bounded by parameters and limitations.

What are some of these parameters? Well, in psychological research, there are many parameters and thus limitations. Some have to do with the nature of the *task* that is given to the participants. Suppose, for example, in a hypothetical study subjects were shown a series of facial expressions on slides and were asked to judge what emotion they perceived in those faces. Some of the task-related parameters would include the number and types of expressions that were presented, the length of the presentation, and the type of judgment required (for example, a selection from a list of alternatives or a free response).

Some parameters have to do with the *environment* or *setting* in which the study is conducted. These might include the location of the study (laboratory room, classroom, home), the time of day, the color of the surroundings, and the like.

Finally, some parameters have to do with the nature of the *participants* in the research. Typically, these include the participants' gender, race or ethnicity, socioeconomic status, culture, religious affiliation, and so forth.

All studies in psychology are conducted within a set of specific parameters. For example, the hypothetical study of facial expressions may involve *white*, *middle-class males* and *females* viewing a set of *30* different facial expressions in a *laboratory experiment room* and making a *free-response* judgment of what emotion they perceive in the expressions. Whatever data we obtained from this particular study would constitute some knowledge, and this knowledge would be bounded by the specific parameters under which the study was conducted.

Luckily, most of the material that is typically presented in textbooks is not knowledge that was generated from a single study under its specific parameters. Indeed, the knowledge that we obtain from single studies is rather limited because it was generated only once, under a set of specific parameters. Rather, the material that is presented in textbooks is that which has usually been shown in more than one study—perhaps in two, three, or more. Thus, that knowledge is generally regarded as a "truth" or "principle" in psychology. By relying on such a process of research and repeated research (called *replication*), psychologists can generally accept as "truth" knowledge that weathers the test of time and, more concretely, multiple experiments.

The knowledge generated from our single, hypothetical study, for example, is interesting but still inconclusive. If we found, however, the same results in a *series* of studies where we varied the parameters of the task, environment, and participants, we would begin to consider that the knowledge we have been generating is "truth." If these studies involved people of different races and socioeconomic backgrounds, presented with different numbers and types of stimuli, in different laboratory or natural settings, and we *still* obtained the same findings, we would be fairly well convinced that the knowledge we have obtained is true.

What Is Cross-Cultural Psychology, and How Does It Impact on Psychological Truths?

Cross-cultural psychology is a branch of psychology that is primarily concerned with testing possible limitations to knowledge by studying people of different cultures. In its strictest sense, **cross-cultural research** simply involves the inclusion of participants from different cultural backgrounds and the testing of possible differences among these participants. In its broadest sense, however, cross-cultural psychology is concerned with understanding truth and psychological principles as either universal (that is, true for all people of all cultures) or culture-specific (true for some people of some cultures).

Cross-cultural psychology is not topic-specific. That is, cross-cultural psychologists are interested in a broad range of phenomena related to human behavior, from perception to language, child-rearing to psychopathology. What delineates cross-cultural psychology from "traditional" or "mainstream" psychology, therefore, is not the phenomenon of interest. Rather, it is the testing of limitations to knowledge by examining whether that knowledge is applicable or obtainable in people of different cultural backgrounds. Given this definition of cross-cultural psychology, psychologists can apply cross-cultural techniques in testing the universality or cultural specificity of any and all aspects of human behavior.

Although research in cross-cultural psychology has existed for many years, it has gained in popularity over the past few years. Because of its relative youth in mainstream, academic psychology, there is a relative lack of textbook resources that specifically address cross-cultural issues in psychology and that are geared for university students studying psychology.

The purpose of this book is to provide such a resource. We have chosen some topics in psychology that are very well-established in cross-cultural research and that are also typically covered in mainstream psychology textbooks and courses. In each, we will discuss how cross-cultural research has tested some of the limitations to knowledge generated in single-culture research. Our goals, which we will discuss in greater detail at the end of this chapter, are simply to introduce you, our students, to this major line of inquiry in psychology and to offer you alternatives to what is typically presented as psychological "truth."

Before proceeding further, however, it is important to deal with what we mean when we use the word *culture*.

A Definition of Culture

Despite the fact that most of us probably feel that we know what culture is, culture is a rather difficult concept to define formally. Scholars such as Margaret Mead, Ruth Benedict, Geert Hofstede, and others have offered a number of interesting definitions of culture. For our purposes, we define **culture** as the set of attitudes, values, beliefs, and behaviors shared by a group of people, communicated from one generation to the next via language or some other means of communication (Barnouw, 1985).

This definition of culture is "fuzzy." That is, there are necessarily no hard and fast rules of how to determine what a culture is or who belongs to that culture. In this sense, culture is a sociopsychological construct, a sharing across people of psychological phenomena such as values, attitudes, beliefs, and behaviors. Members of the same culture share these psychological phenomena. Members of different cultures do not.

Culture is not necessarily rooted in biology. That is, culture is not race. Two people of the same race can either share the same values and behaviors—that is, culture—or they can be very disparate in their cultural makeups. Now, it is true that people of the same racial heritage *in general* may share the same socialization processes and may be *enculturated* in similar ways. Thus, we may speak of a Hispanic culture or an African-American culture or an Asian culture. But, it is also true that there need not be a one-to-one correspondence between race and culture. Just because one is born a certain race does not necessarily mean that one adopts the culture that is stereotypic of that race.

Culture is also not nationality. Just because a person is from France, for example, does not necessarily mean that he or she will act in accordance with what one would consider the dominant French culture or with stereotypes of French people. Just as culture does not necessarily conform to race or racial stereotypes, culture also does not necessarily conform to nationality or citizenship. In fact, there is ample and growing evidence to suggest that a small but substantial portion of the population of many different countries do not "match" the dominant cultural stereotype of their country (Triandis, 1992).

In this sense, culture is as much an individual, psychological construct as it is a macro, social construct. That is, to some extent, culture exists in each and every one of us individually as much as it exists as a global, social construct. Individual differences in culture can be observed among people in the degree to which they adopt and engage in the attitudes, values, beliefs, and behaviors that, by consensus, constitute their culture. If you act in accordance with certain shared values or behaviors, then that culture resides in you; if you do not share those values or behaviors, then you do not share that culture.

Etics, Emics, Ethnocentrism, and Stereotypes

One of the major ways of conceptualizing principles in cross-cultural psychology is through the use of the terms *etics* and *emics*. These terms are very related to our previous discussion concerning universality or cultural specificity of knowledge and truths. An **etic** refers to findings that appear to be consistent across different cultures; that is, an etic refers to a universal truth or principle. An **emic**, in contrast, refers to findings that appear to be different across cultures; an emic, therefore, refers to truths that are culture-specific.

The concept of emics and etics is powerful because of their implications about what we may know as truth. If we know something about human behavior and we regard it as a truth, *and* it is an etic (that is, universal), then the truth as we know it is truth for all, regardless of culture. If that something we know about human behavior and regard as truth, however, is an emic (that is, culture-specific), then what we regard as truth is not necessarily what someone from another culture regards as truth. In fact, they may be quite different! Truth, in this sense, is relative, not absolute. This type of definition of truth with regard to emics and etics should force us all to consider whether what we believe is true or not.

There are many examples of both emics and etics in cross-cultural psychology. Indeed, it may be fair to say that one of the major goals of cross-cultural psychology as a discipline is to uncover exactly which aspects of human behavior are emics and which are etics. One of the major goals in each of the subsequent chapters in this book is to present examples of emics and etics that have been generated by cross-cultural research.

In general, most cross-cultural psychologists would agree that there are just as many, if not more, emics as there are etics. That is, people of different cultures actually do find ways to differ with respect to most aspects of human behavior. In a sense, that is not surprising. Each culture evolves in its own distinct way to "manage" human behaviors in the most efficient and appropriate fashion to ensure successful survival. These ways will differ depending on population density, availability of food and other resources, and so on. To the extent that each culture must meet different needs in the environment, each culture will develop differences in the ways in which it impacts on the people within it.

The existence of many emics, or cultural differences, per se is not problematic in and of itself. There is potential for problem, however, when one attempts to *interpret* the reasons underlying or producing those differences. Because we all exist in our own cultures with our own cultural backgrounds, we tend to see things through that background. That is, culture acts as a filter, not only when perceiving things, but also when thinking about and interpreting events. We may interpret someone else's behavior from our own cultural background and come to some conclusion about that behavior based on our own beliefs of culture and behavior. Our interpretation may be wrong, however, if the behavior that we are judging originates from a different cultural orientation than our own. In some cases (more than we all think!), we may be way off in our interpretation of other people's behavior.

For example, suppose you are having a conversation with a person from a culture different from yours. While you are talking to this person, you notice that she does not really make eye contact with you when she speaks. Also, she does not really look at you when you speak. On the few occasions when her eyes look your way, she quickly averts her gaze if your eyes meet. From your cultural background, you may interpret that she does not feel very positive about you or your interaction. You may even feel put off and reject any attempts at future interaction. You may not feel trusting or close to her. But she may come from a culture where direct gazing is discouraged or is even a sign of arrogance or slight. She may actually be avoiding eye contact not because of any negative feelings, but because of deference and politeness to you! Of course, these potential problems have real and practical implications in everyday life. Think about this scenario occurring in a job interview, in a teaching/learning situation at an elementary school, at a business negotiation, or even in a visit with your therapist!

Still, sometimes we cannot separate ourselves from our own cultural backgrounds and biases to understand the behaviors of others. This type of resistance forms the basis of what is known as **ethnocentrism**—the viewing and interpretation of the behavior of others through one's own cultural glasses. All people—students and faculty, laypersons and researchers alike—need to be aware of these biases and tendencies in understanding the behaviors of others of different cultural backgrounds.

Ethnocentrism is closely related to another important topic—stereotypes. **Stereotypes** are fixed attitudes, beliefs, or opinions about people who belong to cultures other than one's own. They may be born of fact. Often, however, stereotypes are combinations of fact and fiction about people from a certain cultural group. Stereotypes may be handy in giving people some kind of basis in judging, evaluating, and interacting with people of other cultures. They can be very dangerous and damaging, however, when people adhere to them inflexibly and apply the stereotypes to all people of that cultural background without recognizing the possible false bases of the stereotype as well as individual differences within that culture.

We often find that we are different from people of other cultures, either through research or through our everyday interactions and experiences. Our discovery of these differences can have severe and serious negative consequences. The potential for misuse occurs when *values* such as good/bad, right/wrong, superior/inferior are attached to the behaviors of others that are different from one's own culture. For example, several years ago a researcher reported that he had found racial differences in IQ (intelligence quotient) tests between African-American and European-American participants. In and of itself this is still "just" a finding. However, some people interpreted this finding as "proof" that European Americans are genetically or biologically smarter than African Americans. As you can imagine, this caused quite a stir. For quite some time, no attention was paid to other interpretations—such as the cultural bias that may be inherent in the actual tests and testing procedures—because of the frenzy caused by the "genetic" interpretation. As it turns out, there is a considerable degree of cultural bias in the intelligence tests that existed at that time, and when those cultural biases were controlled, the racial differences were not replicated.

Emics, etics, ethnocentrism, and stereotypes are all important concepts to learn about and remember. As we progress through our studies of cultural similarities and differences, it is important to have some idea of what the potential pitfalls may be. Needless to say, making value statements and maintaining an ethnocentric attitude are not conducive to progress in this field.

The Need for Incorporating Cross-Cultural Issues in Learning about Mainstream Psychology

There is a lot of information in the field of psychology that American psychologists and students consider as truth. The comprehensiveness of most psychology textbooks and the density of most course syllabi attest to the fact that there is a lot of stuff out there to be learned.

Still, it is vitally important now to incorporate cross-cultural issues into our knowledge of psychology for at least two reasons. The first has to do with what we call "scientific philosophy." The name may look scary, but scientific philosophy simply refers to what we have been discussing all along in this chapter—the need to evaluate our truths in terms of the parameters within which those truths were obtained. More simply put, we need to examine whether the information we have learned (or will learn in the future) is applicable to *all* people of *all* cultures (that is, it is an etic), or whether it is applicable to *some* people of *some* cultures (in which case, it is an emic). Scientific philosophy refers to the notion that we have a duty, an obligation, to ask these questions about the scientific process and about the nature of the truths we have learned, or will learn, in psychology.

The second reason why it is important to incorporate cross-cultural issues in psychology is much more practical. Psychology involves the study of human behavior to improve our understanding of people. One of the goals of this endeavor is to help us in our real-life, everyday interactions and dealings with others. As we have more frequent contact with people of different cultural backgrounds, it becomes increasingly more imperative that we learn about emics and etics in our truths—that is, in the beliefs we hold about people and the way they are. To be ignorant of such emics and etics would make us guilty of ethnocentrism and would hamper our everyday dealings with others.

Incorporating cross-cultural issues in our learning of mainstream psychology means that we need to ask some very basic, yet extremely important, questions about the nature of the truths taught in psychology classes across North America today. Those questions are addressed by cross-cultural psychology. But before we can discuss those more fully, we need to discuss some issues related to cross-cultural research.

Some Special Issues Concerning Cross-Cultural Research Methodology

As we look for answers to our cross-cultural questions, we must turn to cross-cultural research that has been conducted on the various topics. Our reliance on knowledge, and truth, born of systematic research that meets acceptable standards for scientific and methodological rigor ensures that the quality of that knowledge and truth will be upheld. But before we present studies from this literature to you, it is important to discuss some issues that are especially relevant to the conduct of cross-cultural research. These issues include the operational definitions of culture used in the studies, sampling, cross-cultural equivalence, the formulation of research questions and the interpretation of data, language, the research environment, and response sets.

To be sure, most of these issues, with the possible exception of language, are just as salient and important to mainstream psychological research. We discuss them here in terms of their relevance to cross-cultural research, and in terms of what kinds of special problems arise around them, but with no intent of suggesting that they are not important to other research processes as well.

Operational Definitions of Culture

Unfortunately, the field of cross-cultural psychology currently faces a dilemma with respect to methodological operationalizations of culture—that is, how culture is defined and measured in research. As we discussed earlier, most cross-cultural psychologists would agree that culture is the shared conglomeration of attitudes, values, behaviors, and beliefs, communicated from one generation to the next through language. This definition of culture is psychological, not biological, and therein lies the problem.

Despite this definition of culture, cross-cultural researchers have lacked an adequate way of measuring the "sharing" of psychological characteristics in their research. Instead, they have relied on aspects of people that are easier to measure—typically, race (such as European American, Chinese, Mexican, African American) and nationality (American, Japanese, German, Brazilian, and so on). But, as we discussed earlier in this chapter, culture is not necessarily either race or nationality. It is, indeed, a truly sociopsychological construct.

Without a way to measure culture on the sociopsychological level, in accordance with our definition of culture, researchers have had to "trade off" the ability to really study cross-cultural differences. Indeed, most, if not all, of the studies conducted to date, and presented in this book, have measured culture by either race or nationality. Still, we cannot categorically dismiss these studies or their findings. They do provide valuable information about possible cultural differences and limitations to what we know and regard as truth from research in mainstream psychology. Thus, it is still important for us to consider these studies. But we must consider them with caution concerning the discrepancy between our definition of culture and that definition of culture used in the research.

Sampling

In the simplest cross-cultural research design, a researcher obtains a sample of people in one culture, obtains data from them, and compares that data to other data or known values. Let's say, for example, that a researcher obtained a sample of 50 Americans as part of a cross-cultural study. Are the 50 Americans adequate representatives of the American culture? If they were recruited from Beverly Hills in California, would that be the same as recruiting 50 participants from the Bronx in New York? from Wichita, Kansas? If the 50 participants were all of European descent, would they be an "adequate" sample? If not, what percentage of people of different racial and ethnic backgrounds would the researcher need to be satisfied (given that it is too difficult to measure "true" culture)? If the sample required 25% to be of African descent, could *any* African American be recruited to make 25%? What criteria would be used to decide whether the sample of 50 people were adequate representatives of the American culture? What is the definition of the "American" culture, anyway?

These are not easy questions to deal with, and they pertain to any sample of participants in *any* culture. Cross-cultural researchers need to pay particular attention to issues of sampling in the conduct of their research. Aside from being able (or unable) to measure culture on a psychological level, cross-cultural researchers need to ensure that the participants in their studies are adequate representatives of their culture, whatever it is, if the researcher wants to draw conclusions about cultural differences from those samples.

Cross-Cultural Equivalence

Just obtaining samples that are adequate representatives of their culture is not sufficient to conducting valid cross-cultural research. Researchers need to make sure that the samples they compare are somehow equivalent. Say, for example, a researcher is going to compare data from a sample of 50 Americans in Los Angeles with the data from a sample of 50 preliterate members of the Fore tribe in New Guinea. If the Americans and the Fore came from dissimilar socioeconomic classes, or from dissimilar educational levels, or from dissimilar social experiences, how are we to know that any differences, if found, are due to the cultures or to these other dissimilarities? Clearly, comparing data from a sample of respondents in a major, international metropolis with the data from a sample of preliterate tribes with minimal Western contact is very difficult. Perhaps we would obtain the same types of differences if we studied dissimilar socioeconomic classes within the United States? In order to deal with this dilemma, cross-cultural researchers need to establish some basis of equivalence between their samples in order to make cultural comparisons meaningful.

Formulation of Research Questions and Interpretation of Data

In understanding cross-cultural research, it is important to realize that the very questions researchers decide to study are culture bound. Because they are culture bound, the questions may be meaningful in one culture, but not necessarily so in another. Cultural differences found in studies where this disparity exists are confounded by it. That is, it is impossible to know whether one is finding a "true" cultural difference in response, or whether one is merely finding differences due to meaning of the questions being asked.

For example, suppose a researcher decided to study cultural differences in problem-solving ability in the United States and among tribespeople in Africa. To do this, she presented subjects in both cultures with a mechanical contraption that one had to manipulate in some way to obtain a reward such as money. The Americans may be able to approach this task, and be successful in it. The tribespeople from Africa, however, may believe this task to be entirely meaningless, may view the contraption with fear, and may not care one bit about money! In contrast, if the researcher makes the problem-solving task one of tracking different animals through the use of different scents and footprints, the African tribespeople may respond very positively to the task. Imagine American subjects performing such a task.

In addition to the disparity of culture-bound questions, we also have to consider the interpretation of the cross-cultural data obtained. The researchers who are conducting the study are often from a cultural background that is different from that of the subjects in the study. The researchers will inevitably interpret the data they obtain (whether from questionnaires, responses to a task, or whatever) with their own cultural filters on. Their interpretation of the data the subjects produce may not have anything to do with what the subjects actually intended in producing the data. That is, the subjects are operating out of their own cultural background, which may be entirely different from that of the researchers. The interpretation of data obtained in cross-cultural research, therefore, is particularly tricky.

Language and Translation Issues

All cross-cultural research cannot be conducted in English. If you were to compare the questionnaire responses of an American sample to those from Beijing, you would need to have both an English and a Chinese version of the questionnaire. How are we to know that the questionnaires themselves are equivalent? Cross-cultural researchers frequently use a **back-translation** procedure to ensure some type of equivalence in their research protocols. This procedure involves taking the protocol in one language, translating it to the other, and having someone else translate it back to the original. If the back-translated version is the same as the original, then some type of equivalence exists. If it is not, the procedure is repeated until the back-translated version is exactly the same as the original.

Still, even if the *words* being used in the two languages are the same, how do we know that exactly the same meanings, with the same nuances, are attributed to those words in the two cultures? Any differences that we find between the cultures may be due to linguistic or semantic differences in the research protocols used in conducting the study. Cross-cultural researchers need to deal with these issues of language equivalence, so that these issues are not confused with any cultural differences they want to test.

The Research Environment

In many of the universities across North America, students enrolled in introductory psychology classes are required to participate as research subjects in partial fulfillment of class requirements. Because this is an established practice, there is a certain expectation of students to participate in research as part of their academic experience. Many other countries, however, do not have this custom. Just coming to a university laboratory for a psychology experiment can have different meanings across cultures. We may be very accustomed and familiar with this process, but people in other cultures may not be as familiar, and their reactions to just being in the research environment can interfere with cross-cultural comparisons. Cross-cultural researchers need to deal with these types of issues as well.

Response Sets

Another problem that frequently occurs in cross-cultural research has to do with response sets. The issue of response sets really pertains to cross-cultural *findings* and not to the methods by which the study was conducted. **Response sets** refer to a cultural tendency to respond a certain way on tests or response scales that is reflective more of the cultural tendency than of the meaning of the actual scale. For example, participants in the United States and Hong Kong may be asked to judge the intensity of a certain stimulus, using a 7-point scale. When examining the data, the researcher may find that the Americans generally scored around 6 or 7, whereas the people from Hong Kong generally scored around 4 or 5. The researcher may then interpret that the Americans perceived more intensity in the stimulus than did the people from Hong Kong.

But what if the people from Hong Kong actually rate *everything* lower than the Americans do, not just that stimulus? What if they actually perceive a considerable amount of intensity in the stimulus but have a cultural tendency to use the lower part of the scale? This is not as far-fetched as it may seem. Some cultures, for example, encourage their members not to "stick out." Other cultures encourage their members to be unique and very individual. These types of cultural differences may result in different uses of response alternatives on questionnaires or in interviews. Some cultures may encourage extreme responses on a rating scale; others may discourage extreme responses and encourage responses around the "middle" of a scale. Subjects from two cultures may respond in entirely the same way on a questionnaire, except that the data may be located on different parts of the scale.

The issue of response sets, in addition to those other issues already discussed, indicates that cross-cultural research has its own special set of issues that must be addressed for the research to be valid. These and other issues have complicated cross-cultural studies in the past and have probably discouraged some researchers from conducting these types of studies. Recognizing and understanding these issues are important not only to conducting cross-cultural research, but also as first steps in appreciating observed cultural differences.

Despite the difficulty of conducting cross-cultural research properly, many cross-cultural studies have important things to say about the topics in psychology. Those studies that pass muster and that inform us about cultural diversity in human behavior form the basis of this book.

Themes and Goals of the Chapters

We have selected for coverage in this book topics traditionally covered in psychology courses. Each topic is covered in a separate chapter, so that you do not have to worry about learning many different things in a single chapter. We have written each chapter so as to address a standard set of themes or questions. These questions have helped us to write the chapters so they will have the most relevance to you. We hope that these questions help you as you read the chapters and think about the material presented.

What is "typically" presented on this topic in traditional introductory psychology? We introduce, very briefly, some of the most important knowledge typically presented in most introductory psychology classes and textbooks. Doing so gives us a basis from which to evaluate the cross-cultural material.

What are the limitations in this knowledge due to the cultural composition of the samples studied in the research that forms the basis of this knowledge? To what degree is this knowledge generalizable to people of other cultural backgrounds? Students need to know how the information presented to them in psychology was generated and what are some of the limitations to those studies.

How do findings from cross-cultural research challenge traditional knowledge? We need to look at the cross-cultural research to see whether these findings give us a different picture or understanding of that topic. We also need to examine more closely research in the United States that has used multicultural samples.

Given differences in knowledge from cross-cultural research, how can we, or should we, think about this topic? This is the key issue. If the cross-cultural studies on this topic suggest that the traditional information presented in most psychology classes is limited and *not* generalizable to people of diverse cultural backgrounds, what are we to make of this? How can we revise our ways of thinking to incorporate these diversities? In short, what is the truth, and is it an emic or an etic?

After all is said and done, what do we intend that you gain from this book? Well, first of all, we do *not* intend this book to be your primary source of learning basic truths in psychology; that should be accomplished by other texts. Instead, we seek to raise questions about the traditional, mainstream findings. We want to know whether what is told to you in such findings is applicable to people of *all* cultural backgrounds. We want to challenge the traditional by seeking answers to these questions in the cross-cultural literature. If we find that the research suggests that people are different from what is typically presented, we want to find better ways of understanding those differences than are available today.

Although we challenge the traditional, we definitely do not mean to disregard its importance or the work that produced the traditional knowledge. Indeed, to disregard that material or the work that produced it would demonstrate a level of insensitivity that should have no place in academic work. Instead, we offer this book to you, our readers, solely as a way to seek alternatives to the material typically presented in psychology. By offering these alternatives, we can give you two things that were previously unavailable to you.

1. By seeing alternative ways of observing and understanding people, you will have the ability to choose a viewpoint or perspective of psychology and human behavior that you believe is right for you.

2. By being exposed to these alternatives, you will be able to recognize, understand, and most importantly, appreciate, the psychology of people of diverse backgrounds, some of which will be very, very different from your own.

In this book, there should be no right and wrong, no good and bad. We need to remember the dangers and potential pitfalls in making value judgments of good/bad or superior/inferior when cultural differences are observed. Indeed, there are just people—all different kinds of people.

Glossary

Back-translation: A procedure used in cross-cultural research to ensure some type of equivalence in research protocols. This procedure involves taking the protocol in one language, translating it to the other, and having someone else translate it back to the original. If the back-translated version is the same as the original, then some type of equivalence exists. If it is not, the procedure is repeated until the back-translated version is exactly the same as the original.

Cross-cultural psychology: The branch of psychology that is primarily concerned with testing possible limitations to knowledge by studying people of different cultures. In its broadest sense, cross-cultural psychology is concerned with the understanding of truth and psychological principles as either universal (true for all people of all cultures) or culture-specific (true for some people of some cultures).

Cross-cultural research: Research that involves participants from different cultural backgrounds and the testing of possible differences among these groups of participants.

Culture: The set of attitudes, values, beliefs, and behaviors, shared by a group of people, communicated from one generation to the next via language or some other means of communication (Barnouw, 1985).

Emic: Findings that appear to be different across cultures; an emic, therefore, refers to truths that are culture-specific.

Ethnocentrism: The inability to separate ourselves from our own cultural backgrounds and biases to understand the behaviors of others.

Etic: Findings that appear to be consistent across different cultures; that is, an etic refers to a universal truth or principle.

Psychological truth: A statement of fact or knowledge about human behavior that is documented through systematic research and replicated many times.

Response sets: The tendency of members of a culture to use certain response alternatives on a questionnaire or interviews.

Stereotypes: Widely held beliefs that people have certain characteristics because of their membership in a particular group.

References

Barnouw, V. (1985). *Culture and personality.* Chicago: Dorsey Press.

Triandis, H. C. (1992, February). *Individualism and collectivism as a cultural syndrome.* Paper presented at the Annual Convention of the Society for Cross-Cultural Researchers, Santa Fe, NM.

Suggested Readings

Berry, J. W., Poortinga, Y. H., Segall, M. H., & Dasen, P. R. (1992). *Cross-cultural psychology: Research and applications.* New York: Cambridge University Press.

Brislin, R. (1993). *Understanding culture's influence on behavior*. Fort Worth, TX: Harcourt Brace Jovanovich.

Burlew, A. K. H., Banks, W. C., McAdoo, H. P., & Azibo, D. A. (1992). *African American psychology*. Newbury Park, CA: Sage.

Hofstede, G. (1984). *Culture's consequences*. Newbury Park, CA: Sage.

Culture and Self: How Cultures Influence the Way We View Ourselves

with

Shinobu Kitayama
University of Oregon

Hazel R. Markus
University of Michigan

Several months ago, one of us visited Japan and had a series of research meetings with Japanese students. The main purpose of the meetings was to advance specific research goals for our project on self-concept and social thinking. Considerable time was spent explaining some representative studies on self done in the United States. The notion of self was defined according to many Western social psychological textbooks—as an abstract statement or proposition about the self, such as "I am sociable." Each of us, it was explained, creates such abstract knowledge about ourselves by considering our own past behaviors and generalizing from them. This abstract knowledge serves to organize and guide our current and future behaviors. For example, you may refer to this knowledge of "me" as "sociable" to decide whether you would attend a party on Saturday night or visit an old friend on your next trip to, say, New York City or Tokyo.

From the very beginning of the discussion with the Japanese students, however, there was a serious problem. Most of the Japanese students at the meetings did not buy this explanation of self. They insisted that such an oversimplified statement about oneself does not do justice to the full complexity of social life. After all, whether someone is sociable or not might depend on the particular situation. From this perspective, such abstract knowledge about the self is inaccurate at best, and believing it could amount ultimately to self-deception or hypocrisy.

This "misunderstanding" was not due to the students' inability to comprehend or their lack of sufficient intelligence or interest. Indeed, they were students at one of Japan's top schools. It wasn't due to a fail-ure to explain the concept adequately, because the person presenting the topic—a professor at a major American university—had given a number of lectures on the topic without ever encountering such a problem, even at an introductory level. After a lengthy discussion, the skeptical Japa-nese students were persuaded that many Americans indeed held such self-concepts, and find them to be good characterizations of their self-relevant personal experiences. Still, one of the students sighed deeply and said at the end, "Could this really be true?"

This episode illustrates that even though the notion of "self" in its barest form exists almost universally across cultures, what people actu-ally mean and understand by this notion is dramatically different across cultures. In Western, mostly middle-class culture, self is seen as a bounded entity consisting of a number of internal attributes including needs, abilities, motives, and rights. Each individual carries and uses these internal attributes in navigating thought and action in different social situations. A noted anthropologist, Clifford Geertz (1975), ob-served nearly two decades ago that the self is seen as

> . . . a bounded, unique, more or less integrated motivational and cogni-tive universe, a dynamic center of awareness, emotion, judgment, and action organized into a distinctive whole and set contrastively both against other such wholes and against a social and natural background. (p. 48)

Suppose a Caucasian female undergraduate says that she is "so-ciable." She is likely to mean much more than what this single word lit-erally denotes. In fact, a whole array of covert meanings or connotations is probably attached to it. Probably, she is implying that (1) she has this attribute within her, just as she possesses other related attributes such as abilities, rights, and interests; (2) her past actions, feelings, or thoughts have close connections with this attribute; and, moreover, (3) her future actions, plans, feelings, or thoughts will be controlled or guided by this attribute and more or less accurately predicted by it. In short, in her mind her concept of herself as "sociable" may be rooted in, supported by, and reinforced by a rich repertoire of specific information concern-ing her own actions, thoughts, feelings, motives, and plans. As such, the concept of her self as "sociable" may be very central to her self-defini-tion, enjoying a special status as a salient identity (Stryker, 1986) or self-schema (Markus, 1977).

Evidently, however, the Japanese students in the meeting did not fathom this idea implicit in the Western concept of the self. They seemed not to grasp intuitively the idea of an elaborate array of self-rel-evant knowledge underlying the simple summary statement "I am sociable." In fact, it required a considerable stretch of their imaginations to even entertain the possibility that a self-concept could entail such connotations and could guide or organize their behaviors.

By raising the possibility that the Western concept of self may not make much intuitive sense to people of other cultures, we do not wish to imply that students of other cultures, let alone experts in social psychology, fail to understand the foregoing notion of self as a theoretical concept in social psychology. To the contrary, they certainly can and do understand the notion as a theoretical construct. Yet the nature of their understanding is very different from that of the American undergraduate. Non-Westerners may understand Western concepts of self only as much as we Americans may understand four-dimensional space, and vice versa. That is, we may understand concepts of self from other cultures on a theoretical level, but we have almost no experiential basis for understanding them.

In this chapter we will look at different construals, or understandings, of the self. We will contrast the Western construal of self as an independent, separate entity with another construal of self that is more common in many non-Western cultures. According to this latter construal, the person is viewed as inherently connected or interdependent with others and inseparable from a social context. We will illustrate how these divergent forms of self are tied to differences in what people notice and think about, how they feel, and what motivates them. Much of what is mentioned in this chapter will be discussed in more detail in the following chapters. This general introduction, however, should serve as a conceptual foundation upon which more specific information presented later can build.

Two Construals of Self

There are many anecdotes to suggest that construals of self vary widely across cultures. In America, standing out and asserting oneself is a virtue. It is "the squeaky wheel that gets the grease." In many Asian cultures, however, if you stand out, you will most likely be punished—"the nail that sticks up shall get pounded down."

Politics offers another example. American politicians routinely credit success to trust in their instincts, self-confidence, and the ability to make decisions and stick by them. In Japan, political rhetoric sounds very different. A former vice prime minister of Japan once said that in his 30-year career in national politics, he gave utmost importance and priority to interpersonal relations. Similarly, "politics of harmony" was the sound bite that a former Japanese prime minister used to characterize his regime in the 1980s.

Independent Construal of Self

These anecdotes suggest that people may have remarkably different ideas, premises, or construals about self, others, and the relation between the self and others (Markus & Kitayama, 1991a). In many Western cultures there is a strong belief in separateness among distinct individuals. The normative task of these cultures is to maintain the independence of the individual as a separate, self-contained entity.

In American society, many of us have been socialized to "be unique," "express yourself," "realize and actualize the inner self," "promote your own goals," and so on. The culture provides these tasks for its members. Many of the cultural tasks in American culture today have been designed and selected, through history, to encourage the independence of each separate self. With this set of cultural tasks, our sense of self-worth or self-esteem takes on a particular form. When individuals successfully carry out these cultural tasks, they feel most satisfied about themselves. Their self-esteem increases accordingly. Under this independent construal of self, individuals tend to focus on internal attributes such as one's own ability, intelligence, personality traits, goals, preferences, or attributes, expressing them in public and verifying and confirming them in private through social comparison.

The independent construal of self is graphically illustrated in Figure 2.1(a). Self is a bounded entity, clearly separated from relevant others. Note that there is no overlap between self and the others. Furthermore, the most salient self-relevant information (indicated by bold Xs) consists of the attributes that are thought to be stable, constant, and intrinsic to the self, such as abilities, goals, rights, and the like. As such, these attributes are bound to be quite general and abstract.

Interdependent Construal of Self

By contrast, many non-Western cultures neither assume nor value this overt separateness. Instead, these cultures emphasize what may be called the "fundamental connectedness of human beings." The primary normative task is to adjust oneself so as to fit in and maintain the interdependence among individuals. Thus, many individuals in these cultures are socialized to "adjust oneself to an attendant relationship or a group to which they belong," "read others' minds," "be sympathetic," "occupy and play one's assigned role," "engage in appropriate actions," and the like. These are the cultural tasks that have been designed and selected through the history of a given cultural group to encourage the interdependence of the self with others.

Given this construal of the self, one's sense of worth, satisfaction, or self-esteem can have very different characteristics from those familiar to us in the Western culture. The self-esteem of those with interdependent

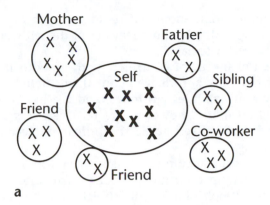

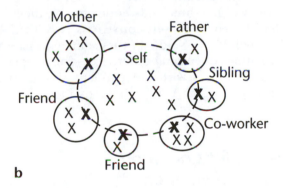

Figure 2.1   **(a)** Independent Construal of Self;
(b) Interdependent Construal of Self. (From Markus,
H., & Kitayama, S. (1991). Culture and the self:
Implications for cognition, emotion and motivation.
Psychological Review, 98, 224–253. Copyright 1991 by
the American Psychological Association. Reprinted by
permission of the authors.)

construals of the self may depend primarily on whether one can fit in
and be part of a relevant ongoing relationship. Under this construal of
self, individuals tend to focus on their interdependent status with other
people and strive to meet or even create duties, obligations, and social
responsibilities. Accordingly, the most salient aspect of the conscious
experience is intersubjective—rooted in finely tuned interpersonal relationships.

The interdependent construal of self is graphically illustrated in Figure 2.1(b). Self is unbounded, flexible, and contingent on context, as indicated by the substantial overlaps between self and relevant others. The

most salient information about self (bold *X*s) concerns aspects of the self-in-relationships—that is, those features of the self related to and inseparable from specific social contexts.

This does not mean, of course, that those with interdependent selves do not have any knowledge about their internal attributes such as personality traits, abilities, attitudes, and the like. They clearly do. These internal attributes, however, are relatively less salient in consciousness and thus unlikely to be the primary concerns in thinking, feeling, and acting.

Of course, any single culture can also have considerable variations among its members in their independent versus interdependent construals of the self. People of different ethnicities within a culture, for example, may have different tendencies with regard to independent versus interdependent self-construals. Men and women have different self-construals. Even within ethnic and gender groups, there can and will be considerable differences in self-construals (Gilligan, 1982; Joseph, Markus, & Tafarodi, 1992). No doubt these differences are also important in our considerations of cultural differences. This chapter describes *general* tendencies associated with independent and interdependent self-construals, acknowledging the limitations in representation within groups.

Consequences for Cognition, Motivation, and Emotion

These different structures of the self across cultures are interesting, and learning about them can be potentially very useful in the modern, increasingly international world. Knowing and understanding people in other cultures from their own perspectives is increasingly important if we are to be effective participants in this world. Studying different cultures, therefore, is important in the discipline of psychology. But many theories in psychology have been examined primarily in the Western culture. They may or may not generalize to other cultures. There can be enormous cultural variations, especially in areas of psychology focusing on social aspects of human behavior, such as social, personality, clinical, and developmental psychology.

In this section we discuss why a cross-cultural approach is indispensable to getting a better theoretical perspective on human social behavior. We do this by examining how two construals of the self affect our thinking, feelings, and behaviors. Cognitive, emotional, and motivational processes can vary dramatically according to the construal of the self shared within a cultural group.

Consequences for Cognition

Self-perception.   Different construals of self have different consequences for how we perceive ourselves. With an independent construal of self, one's internal attributes such as abilities or personality traits are the most salient, self-relevant information. These internal attributes should be relatively less salient for those with interdependent selves, who are more likely to think about the self in particular social relationships (for example, "me" with family members, "me" with my boyfriend) or in specific contexts ("me" in school, "me" at work).

This analysis has received support from several studies. In these studies subjects are asked to write down as many of their characteristics as possible. Subjects typically write several types of responses. One type is abstract personality-trait descriptions of the self, such as "I am sociable." Another type of response is self-descriptions that are situation-specific. Consistent with our views of independent and interdependent selves, studies have shown that American subjects tend to write a greater number of abstract traits than do Asian subjects (Bond & Tak-Sing, 1983; Shweder & Bourne, 1984).

This, of course, does not mean that Americans have more knowledge about themselves than do Asians. Because the most salient information about self for the interdependent selves is context-specific, these individuals must have found it difficult or unnatural to state anything in abstract, noncontextual terms. Instead, those with interdependent selves may be bound to define themselves in very different terms.

Consistent with this analysis, Triandis (1989) and colleagues have shown that individuals from interdependent cultures (such as China, Japan, and Korea) generate many more social categories, relationships, or groups to which they belong. Indeed, in a study done in the People's Republic of China, as many as 80% of all the responses to the self-description task were about their memberships in a variety of groups. This is a strong indication that specific relationships are very important in their self-definitions.

There is yet another interesting implication. We have suggested that interdependent selves find it difficult to describe themselves in terms of abstract internal attributes. That is, they find it artificial and unnatural to make abstract statements such as "I am sociable" without specifying a relevant context. Whether a person is sociable or not depends on the specific situation. If this is correct, interdependent people should be comfortable in describing themselves in terms of abstract, internal attributes once a specific context has been specified.

In a recent experiment, Cousins (1989) provided evidence to support this analysis. He asked American and Japanese respondents to write down who they were in various specific social situations (at home, in school, at work, and so on). This instruction supposedly helped the respondents to picture a concrete social situation, including who was there, what was being done to whom, and the like. The Japanese respondents generated a greater number of abstract internal attributes than did the Americans once the context was specified. The American respondents tended to qualify their descriptions—for instance, "I am more or less sociable at work," "I am sometimes optimistic at home." They seemed to be saying, "This is how I am at work, but don't assume that this is the way I am everywhere." For such a contextualized task, the Americans may have felt awkward in providing self-descriptions because their self-definitions typically are not qualified by specific situations.

Social explanation. Self-construals may also serve as a "cognitive template" for perceiving and interpreting behaviors of other people. Those with independent selves may assume that other people will also have a set of relatively stable internal attributes such as personality traits, attitudes, and abilities. As a result, when they observe the behavior of someone else, they may draw inferences about the actor's internal state, or his or her disposition, that supposedly underlies and even caused that behavior.

Social cognition research done primarily in the West has supported this claim. For example, when subjects read an essay supporting Fidel Castro in Cuba (Jones & Harris, 1967), they inferred that the author must have a favorable attitude toward Castro. Furthermore, it has been amply demonstrated that such dispositional inferences occur even when obvious situational constraints are present. In the original study by Jones and Harris (1967), the subjects inferred the pro-Castro attitude even when they were explicitly told that the author was assigned to write a pro-Castro essay and no choice was given. The subjects ignored these situational constraints and erroneously drew inferences about the author's disposition. This bias to commit an inference about an actor's dispositions even in the presence of very obvious situational constraints has been termed the **fundamental attribution error** (Ross, 1977; see Chapter 10 for a full discussion).

Fundamental attribution error, however, may not be as robust or pervasive among people of interdependent cultures. People in these cultures share assumptions about the self that are very different from those in Western cultures. This construal includes the recognition that what one does is contingent or dependent on, and directed or guided by, situational factors. Thus, these individuals are more inclined to explain another's behaviors in terms of situational forces impinging on the person, rather than on internal predispositions.

In an important cross-cultural study, Miller (1984) examined patterns of social explanation in Americans and Hindu Indians. First, both

Indian and American respondents were asked to describe either someone they knew well who did something good for another person, or someone they knew well who did something bad to another person. After having described such a person, the respondents were asked to explain why the person committed that good or bad action. The American respondents typically explained the behavior of their acquaintances in terms of general dispositions (for example, "she is very irresponsible"). Dispositional explanations, however, were much less common for the Indians. Instead, they tended to provide explanations in terms of the actor's duties, social roles, and the like, which are by definition more situation-specific (see also Shweder & Bourne, 1984).

Some writers (Lively & Bromley, 1973) have suggested another explanation for these results, based on Piaget's theory of intellectual development. In a nutshell, Piaget (1952, 1954) has suggested that humans go through various stages of intellectual development, which generally proceed from "concrete operations" to higher stages of "abstract operations" (see Chapter 7 for a full discussion). Using this theory as a framework, some theorists have suggested that non-Western people (such as the Hindu Indian adults in the study described) are less developed intellectually than American adults. As a result, the Indians used situation-specific, concrete terms whereas Americans used more abstract trait terms in social explanations.

This explanation, however, may be ethnocentric. Whenever we characterize other cultures in a way that places them in an inferior position to our own, we have to be careful. Indeed, the theory may reflect our desire to see ourselves in a favorable light. In this case, our realization of different self-construals accounts for why Indians may not seek to explain social behaviors in abstract terms, even if they are fully capable of abstract reasoning. They find it unreasonable or unnatural to explain others' and their own behaviors in abstract dispositional terms. Still, are there data that rule out differences as a function of cognitive ability?

Fortunately, Miller (1984) collected data from people of different social classes and educational attainment and showed that the Indian tendency toward situation-specific explanations did not depend on these factors. Thus, it is very unlikely that the situational, context-specific thinking common among Indians was due to an inability to reason abstractly. Instead, the context-specific reasoning common in India seems to be due primarily to the cultural assumption of interdependence that is very salient in the Hindu culture. Given the interdependent construal of self, the most reasonable assumption to be made in explaining another's behavior is that this behavior is very much constrained and directed by situation-specific factors.

Consequences for Emotion

Different construals of self have important consequences for emotional experience. In the past few decades, emotion has been studied primarily as an internal mechanism of homeostatic maintenance and regulation of behaviors. This ever-growing line of work has shown a variety of important biological correlates of emotion, including brain mechanisms or facial muscle movements. In addition, several emotion categories—such as joy, fear, sadness, disgust, and the like—are common across cultures (see Chapter 8). Different construals of the self can have several different implications for emotional experience.

Social connotation of emotion.   Kitayama and Markus (in press-a) have distinguished emotions that encourage the independence of the self from those that encourage interdependence. For example, some emotions such as pride or feelings of superiority occur when one has accomplished one's own goals or desires, or has confirmed desirable inner attributes such as intelligence and wealth. The experience of these emotions tends to verify those inner attributes. Similarly, some negative emotions such as anger and frustration result primarily from the blocking of one's own internal attributes (such as goals or desires). Once experienced, the negative emotions highlight the fact that those inner goals or desires have been interfered with.

In both cases, one's inner attributes are made salient and contrasted against relevant social context. These emotions therefore tend to separate or disengage the self from social relationships. They also simultaneously promote the perceived independence of the self from the relationship. Kitayama and Markus (in press-a) have called these types of emotions **socially disengaged emotions.**

By contrast, other positive emotions, such as friendly feelings and feelings of respect, are very different in this regard. They result from being part of a close, more or less communal relationship. Once experienced, they further encourage this interpersonal bond. Some types of negative emotions, such as feelings of indebtedness or guilt, also share similar characteristics. These emotions typically result from one's failure to participate successfully in an interdependent relationship, or from doing some harm to the relationship. Once these emotions are experienced, one is subsequently motivated to restore the harmony in the relationship by compensating for the harm done or by repaying one's debt. These behaviors will further engage and assimilate the self in the relationship and thus enhance the perceived interdependence of the self with the relevant others. These emotions are called **socially engaged emotions.**

The important point to the distinction between socially engaged and disengaged emotions is not that people of independent and interdependent self-construals will have more or less of either type of emotion. Indeed, people with independent self-construals will say that they experience both types, as will people with interdependent self-construals. What is different, however, is the definitions that are associated with social engagement or disengagement, and the social meanings and consequences of the emotions. People of interdependent self-construals will typically experience socially engaged emotions differently than will people of independent self-construals. These emotions may be more intense and internalized for the interdependent selves than for the independent selves, because socially engaged emotions have different implications for interdependent selves as opposed to independent selves. The same is true for socially disengaged emotions.

Social connotation and indigenous emotions.   Although many emotions are common across cultures, there are many emotions that are relatively unique to particular cultures (Russell, 1991). These emotions are called **indigenous emotions.** Several anthropological studies have suggested that the social connotations of emotions, as just outlined, are quite salient in the organization of emotions in some non-Western cultures to a degree that is unheard of in the West. For example, Lutz (1988) has studied the emotions of people on the Micronesian atoll of Ifaluk and suggested that an emotion called *fago* is very central in this culture. According to Lutz, fago can be roughly described as a combination of compassion, love, and sadness. This emotion is likely to motivate helping behaviors and create and enhance close interpersonal relationships. In our terminology, fago is highly socially engaged.

In contrast to fago, another emotion in Ifaluk, *ker*—translated as a combination of happiness and excitement—is perceived as "dangerous, socially disruptive" (Lutz, 1988, p. 145). Ifaluk people thus regard ker as highly socially disengaged.

A similar analysis applies to another non-Western culture, Japan. T. Doi (1973) has suggested that the emotion *amae* is pivotal in understanding the ethos (the "emotional climate") of the Japanese culture. Amae refers to a desire or expectation for others' indulgence, benevolence, or favor. According to Doi, its prototype can be found in a mother/infant relationship, whereby the infant feels a desire for "dependency" on the mother, and the mother in turn provides much needed unconditional care and love to the infant. This prototype is subsequently elaborated to form an adult form of amae, which is much more differentiated and sophisticated. Amae applies in nonkin relationships, such as work relationships between a supervisor and his or her subordinates. For example, the subordinates may feel amae toward the supervisor for his or her favor and benevolence. A reciprocal action from the supervisor would increase and consolidate the affectionate bond between them. However, the supervisor's refusal to reciprocate could lead to negative emotions on both sides. As on Ifaluk, social engagement seems to define this emotion for the Japanese culture.

These anthropological studies fit well with the two construals of the self. For people with interdependent self-construals, public and more intersubjective aspects of the self are more elaborated in conscious experience. For those with independent selves, however, private and more subjective aspects are highlighted. Compare the two diagrams in Figure 2.1. Because social connotation is a relatively public and intersubjective aspect of emotion, this aspect of emotion is especially salient in the emotional experience of non-Western, interdependent people. By contrast, in Western, independent cultures, more internal, private aspects of emotion, such as good or bad feelings or moods, may be more salient (Kleinman, 1988). This is true even though people of independent self-construals recognize the social connotations of different emotions.

Is "happiness" cross-culturally invariant? There are additional cross-cultural differences in emotional experience. One of these concerns the meaning of happiness. "Happiness" refers to the most generic, unqualified state of "feeling good." Emotions such as relaxed, elated, and calm are part of this generic, positive state. People across cultures share the general notion of happiness as defined in this way (Wierzbicka, 1986). But the specific circumstances, and the meanings attached to them, may depend crucially on the construal of the self as independent or interdependent. Specifically, evidence suggests that people experience this most unqualified, good feeling when they have successfully accomplished the cultural task of either independence or interdependence.

Kitayama, Markus, Kurokawa, and Negishi (1993) asked both Japanese and American college undergraduates to report how frequently they experience various emotions. Among them were three types of positive emotions. Some were generic, such as relaxed, elated, and calm. Others had more specific social connotations either as socially engaged (for example, friendly feelings, feelings of respect) or disengaged (pride, feelings of superiority). An interesting cross-cultural difference emerged when correlations among these three types of emotions were examined (see Figure 2.2).

For Americans, generic positive emotions were associated primarily with experiencing the disengaged emotions. That is, those who experience the emotions that signal their success in cultural tasks of independence (socially disengaged emotions such as pride) are most likely to feel

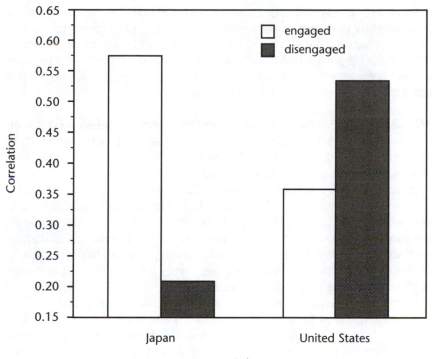

Figure 2.2 Cultural Differences in the Correlation Between General Positive Feelings and Engaged and Disengaged Emotions in the United States and Japan

"generally good." This pattern was completely reversed among the Japanese. Those who experience the emotions that signal success in cultural tasks of interdependence (socially engaged emotions such as friendly feelings) are most likely to feel "generally good." The exact meanings or connotations of "feeling good" were shaped through culture and linked very closely with the cultural imperatives of independence (in the United States) and interdependence (in Japan).

Consequences for Motivation

Cultural differences in self-construals affect motivation as well. As with emotions, Western literature on motivation has long assumed that motivations are basically internal to the actor. One's motives to achieve, affiliate, or dominate are some of the most salient and important features of the internal self—features that direct and energize overt behaviors.

With an alternative, interdependent construal, however, social behaviors are guided by expectations of relevant others, felt obligations to the others, or the sense of duties to an important group to which one belongs, rather than by motivations for "me." This point is illustrated by two topics that have received considerable research attention: achievement motivation and self-enhancement versus effacement.

Achievement motivation.   **Achievement motivation** refers to a "desire for excellence." Such a desire in the broad sense can be found quite widely across cultures (Maehr & Nicholls, 1980). In the current literature, however, this desire for excellence has been conceptualized in a somewhat more specific manner—as individually or personally based, rather than socially or interpersonally rooted. In classic work in this area by McClelland (1961) and Atkinson (1964), for example, the desire for excellence is linked very closely with one's tendency to push oneself ahead and actively strive for and seek individual successes. This notion of achievement, in fact, is quite congruent with an independent construal of the self, shared widely in the West.

From an alternative, interdependent frame, however, excellence may be sought through broader social goals. These social forms of achievement motivation are more prevalent among those with an interdependent construal of the self. Interdependent selves have ever-important concerns that revolve around fully realizing one's connectedness with others. Thus, the nature of their achievement motivation is quite different from that of those with an independent construal of the self.

Discussing this possibility with respect to the Chinese, Yang (1982) distinguished between two forms of achievement motivation: individually oriented and socially oriented (cf. Maehr & Nicholls, 1980). Individually oriented achievement is considered to be common primarily in Western culture. It is for the sake of "me" personally that one strives to achieve. In Chinese society, however, socially oriented achievement is much more common. According to this form of achievement, one strives to achieve for the sake of relevant others, such as one's family members. A Chinese student, for example, may work hard to gain admission to a prestigious university and then eventually to a top company. Behaviorally, there may be no difference between this Chinese individual and an American who also strives to succeed both in school and at work. In the case of the Chinese individual, however, the ultimate goal in doing all this may not be advancement of one's personal career, but rather may be more collective or interdependent in character. The interdependent goals may include enhancing his or her family's social standing, meeting a felt expectation of the family members, or satisfying a sense of obligation or indebtedness to parents who have made enormous sacrifices to raise and support the student. In other words, the Chinese student's desire to achieve is much more socially rooted and may not necessarily reflect his or her desire to advance the quality or standing of himself or herself personally.

In support of this notion, Bond (1986) assessed levels of various motivations among Chinese and found that the Chinese in fact show higher levels of socially oriented rather than individually oriented achievement motivation. Yu (1974) reported that the strength of achievement motive in China is positively related to familism and filial piety. That is, those who are most strongly motivated to excel also take most seriously their duties and obligations to family members, especially parents.

A similar observation is reported in another interdependent culture, Japan. K. Doi (1982, 1985) asked Japanese college students 30 questions designed to measure tendencies to persevere and pursue excellence (that is, achievement tendency). An additional 30 questions measured desires to care for and be cared for by others (that is, affiliation tendency). The results suggested a very close association between achievement motivation and affiliation. Those high in achievement were also high in affiliation, and vice versa. This finding is in stark contrast to many Western findings, which indicate that these two dimensions of motives are typically unrelated (cf. Atkinson, 1964). Both studies of the Chinese and the Japanese indicated that achievement was closely related to their social orientation of being connected and interdependent with important others in life.

Self-enhancement versus effacement.   Since James (1890), psychologists have repeatedly demonstrated what appears to be an extremely powerful motive to have a positive view of self. As early as age 4, American children think they are better than most others. Wylie (1979) found that American adults typically consider themselves to be more intelligent and more attractive than average. Myers (1987), in a national survey of American students, found that 70% of the students thought they were above average in leadership ability; with respect to the ability to get along with others, 0% thought they were below average and 60% thought they were in the top 10%. This tendency to underestimate the commonality of one's desirable traits is called the **false uniqueness effect** and appears to be stronger for males than for females (Joseph, Markus, & Tafarodi, 1992). It is one clear method of enhancing self-esteem. But is it true for people of different cultures?

Maintaining or enhancing self may assume a different form for those with interdependent construals of self. Among those with interdependent selves, positive appraisals of the inner attributes of self may not be strongly linked with overall self-esteem or self-satisfaction. Instead, overall self-esteem or self-satisfaction may be more likely to derive from fulfilling one's interdependence with others.

Overall esteem or satisfaction about the self within an interdependent framework may result from the recognition that one is performing well in the cultural tasks of belonging, fitting in, engaging in appropriate action, promoting others' goals, maintaining harmony, and so on. It may also derive from one's capacity to regulate and coordinate one's inner personal thoughts and feelings so that they can fit into one's pursuit of interdependence with others. For the interdependent selves, viewing oneself as unique or different would be unnecessary to maintain a sense of self-worth. This is because the inner attributes of self contributing to one's perceived uniqueness are less self-defining. Trying to be unique would be undesirable, akin to being the nail that stands out, because it isolates the person from the ever-important relationship.

In an initial examination of cultural variation in the tendency to see one's self as different from others, Markus and Kitayama (1991b) administered questionnaires containing a series of false-uniqueness items to both Japanese and American college students. The questionnaires included a series of questions of the form "What proportion of students in this university have higher intellectual abilities than yourself?" There were three categories of questionnaire items: abilities (intellectual, memory, and athletic), independence (independent, holds more strongly to his or her own view), and interdependence (more sympathetic, more warm-hearted).

The data are summarized in Figure 2.3. The most striking aspect of these data is the marked difference between the Japanese and the American students in their estimations of their own uniqueness. American students assume that only 30% of people on average would be better than themselves in various traits and abilities. The Japanese, however, showed almost no evidence of this false uniqueness. In most cases, they claim that about 50% of students would be better than they are. One might suspect that this occurred because the Japanese students tended to use 50% as their most preferred answer. This was not the case. If anything, the variability in the data was virtually identical for the Americans and the Japanese. Instead, this finding is just what one would predict if a representative sample of college students were evaluating themselves without the need to establish uniqueness.

Conclusion

In this chapter, we suggested that the view that one holds of the self is critical in understanding a variety of individual behaviors. Across cultures, the form of self varies considerably, and various social phenomena and processes also vary accordingly. Indeed, much of the remainder of the book is based on this assumption. Many of the chapters to come

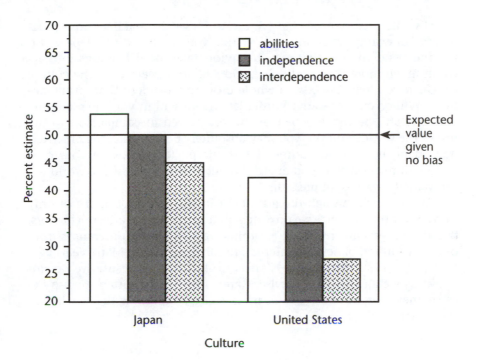

Figure 2.3 Estimates of the Percentage of People Who Are Better Than Oneself in Three Categories of Behavior

take some of the concepts introduced in this chapter—cognitive development, attributions, emotion, and the like—and delve further into the issue of how cultures influence these important processes.

It is very important for psychologists to examine carefully whether and to what extent various social psychological principles—most of which have been advanced in the Western world—can travel across cultural boundaries to account for behaviors of people of other cultures. In so doing, psychologists can identify the phenomena that explain these cultural differences. Self-construal is one such powerful phenomenon, providing a framework by which we can understand and analyze cultural variation in cognition, emotion, and motivation.

Still, this task is not easy. We need to remember that whenever we evaluate cultural influences—whether of our own or of another culture—we look at those influences through our own cultural "eyes." There is an invisible "filter" that is *always* there and *always* influences how we perceive and evaluate things, regardless of whether we are aware of it or not. You are reading this text right now with that filter on! We make judgments about ourselves and others that are totally biased, even if we are absolutely convinced that we are unbiased in making those judgments. For example, you may believe that you are rather interdependent, not independent, and that your behaviors take social relations into account much more than do the behaviors of your peers. Still, the culture in which you live may be as a whole more independent than other cultures. While you are relatively interdependent within your own culture, you may still be *very* independent when viewed in comparison to the rest of the world. And yet, you may absolutely believe that you are interdependent, because you cannot see the implicit standard of your own culture in relation to the standard provided by the rest of the world (cf. Kitayama & Markus, in press-b).

As you work through the rest of this book, it is important not only to consider the evidence we provide about how cultures affect behaviors, but also to remember that we are thinking about these differences from our own cultural biases and internal, implicit standards. Many years ago, Durkheim (1938/1964) wrote, "Air is no less heavy because we do not detect its weight" (p. 5). Likewise, water is no less important to fish because they may not be aware of its existence. Culture is that air for us, and water for the fish.

Glossary

Achievement motivation: Motivation that underlies a "desire for excellence."

False uniqueness effect: The tendency to underestimate the commonality of one's desirable traits.

Fundamental attribution error: A bias to commit an inference about an actor's dispositions even in the presence of very obvious situational constraints.

Independent construal of self: A framework that views the self as a bounded entity, clearly separated from relevant others. The most salient self-relevant information is the attributes that are thought to be stable, constant, and intrinsic to the self, such as abilities, goals, rights, and the like. These attributes are bound to be quite general and abstract.

Indigenous emotions: Emotions that are relatively unique to particular cultures.

Interdependent construal of self: A framework that views the self as influenced by the "fundamental connectedness of human beings." The primary normative task is to adjust oneself so as to fit in and maintain the interdependence among individuals. Self is unbounded, flexible, and contingent on context. The most salient information about self is about aspects of the self-in-relationships—that is, those features of the self related and inseparable from specific social contexts.

Self-perception: How we perceive ourselves.

Social explanation: The process of perceiving and interpreting behaviors of other people; also known as *attributions*.

Socially disengaged emotions: Emotions that tend to separate or disengage the self from social relationships. They simultaneously promote the perceived independence of the self from the relationship.

Socially engaged emotions: Emotions that have high interpersonal meanings, either encouraging or harming interpersonal bonds. By serving as motivators of behaviors that will further engage and assimilate the self into a social relationship, they enhance the perceived interdependence of the self with the relevant others.

References

Atkinson, J. W. (1964). *An introduction to motivation.* Princeton, NJ: Van Nostrand.

Bond, M. H. (1986). *The psychology of the Chinese people.* New York: Oxford University Press.

Bond, M. H., & Tak-Sing, C. (1983). College students' spontaneous self concept: The effect of culture among respondents in Hong Kong, Japan, and the United States. *Journal of Cross-cultural Psychology, 14,* 153–171.

Cousins, S. D. (1989). Culture and self-perception in Japan and the United States. *Journal of Personality and Social Psychology, 56,* 124–131.

Doi K. (1982). Two dimensional theory of achievement motivation. *Japanese Journal of Psychology, 52,* 344–350.

Doi, K. (1985). The relation between the two dimensions of achievement motivation and personality of male university students. *Japanese Journal of Psychology, 56,* 107–110.

Doi, T. (1973). *The anatomy of dependence.* Tokyo: Kodansha.

Durkheim, E. (1964). *The rules of sociological method.* London: The Free Press of Glenscoe. (Original work published 1938)

Ekman, P. (1984). Expression and the nature of emotion. In K. Scherer & P. Ekman (Eds.), *Approaches to emotion* (pp. 319–344). Hillsdale, NJ: Erlbaum.

Geertz, C. (1975). From the natives' point of view: On the nature of anthropological understanding. *American Scientist, 63,* 47–53.

Gilligan, C. (1982). *In a different voice: Psychological theory and women's development.* Cambridge, MA: Harvard University Press.

Harter, S. (1983). Developmental perspectives on the self-system. In E. M. Hetherington (Ed.), *Handbook of child psychology* (Vol. 1, pp. 275–385). New York: John Wiley.

James, W. (1890). *The principles of psychology* (Vol. 1). New York: Holt.

Jones, E. E., & Harris, V. A. (1967). The attribution of attitudes. *Journal of Experimental Social Psychology, 3,* 1–24.

Joseph, R. A., Markus, H. R., & Tafarodi, R. W. (1992). Gender differences in the source of self-esteem. *Journal of Personality and Social Psychology, 63,* 1017–1028.

Kitayama, S., & Markus, H. R. (in press-a). A cultural perspective to self-conscious emotions. In J. P. Tangney & K. Fisher (Eds.), *Shame, guilt, embarrassment, and pride: Empirical studies of self-conscious emotions.* New York: Guilford Press.

Kitayama, S., & Markus, H. R. (in press-b). Culture and self: Implications for internationalizing psychology. In J. D'Arms, R. G. Hastie, & H. K. Jacobson (Eds.). *Becoming more international and global: Challenges for American higher education.* Ann Arbor, MI: University of Michigan Press.

Kitayama, S., Markus, H. R., Kurokawa, M., & Negishi, K. (1993). *Social orientation of emotions: Cross-cultural evidence and implications.* Unpublished manuscript, University of Oregon.

Kleinman, A. (1988). *Rethinking psychiatry: From cultural category to personal experience.* New York: Free Press.

Lively, W. J., & Bromley, D. B. (1973). *Person perception in childhood and adolescence.* London: Wiley.

Lutz, C. (1988). *Unnatural emotions: Everyday sentiments on a Micronesian atoll and their challenge to Western theory.* Chicago: University of Chicago Press.

Maehr, M., & Nicholls, J. (1980). Culture and achievement motivation: A second look. In N. Warren (Ed.), *Studies in cross-cultural psychology* (Vol. 2, pp. 221–267). London: Academic Press.

Markus, H. R. (1977). Self-schemata and processing information about the self. *Journal of Personality and Social Psychology, 35,* 63–78.

Markus, H. R., & Kitayama, S. (1991a). Culture and the self: Implications for cognition, emotion, and motivation. *Psychological Review, 98,* 224–253.

Markus, H. R., & Kitayama, S. (1991b). Cultural variation in self-concept. In G. R. Goethals & J. Strauss (Eds.), *Multidisciplinary perspectives on the self.* New York: Springer-Verlag.

McClelland, D. C. (1961). *The achieving society.* Princeton, NJ: Van Nostrand.

Miller, J. G. (1984). Culture and the development of everyday social explanation. *Journal of Personality and Social Psychology, 46,* 961–978.

Myers, D. (1987). *Social psychology* (2nd ed.). New York: McGraw-Hill.

Piaget, J. (1952). *The origins of intelligence in children.* New York: International Universities Press.

Piaget, J. (1954). *The construction of reality in the child.* New York: Basic Books.

Piaget, J. (1971). Piaget's theory. In P. Mussen (Ed.), *Handbook of child development* (Vol. 1). New York: John Wiley.

Ross, L. (1977). The intuitive psychologist and his shortcomings: Distortions in the attribution process. In L. Berkowitz (Ed.), *Advances in experimental social psychology* (Vol. 10, pp. 174–221). New York: Academic Press.

Russell, J. A. (1991). Culture and the categorization of emotions. *Psychological Bulletin, 110*, 426–450.

Shweder, R. A., & Bourne, E. J. (1984). Does the concept of the person vary cross-culturally? In R. A. Shweder & R. A. LeVine (Eds.), *Culture theory: Essays on mind, self, and emotion* (pp. 158–199). Cambridge, England: Cambridge University Press.

Stryker, S. (1986). Identity theory: Developments and extensions. In K. Tardley & T. Honess (Eds.), *Self and identity* (pp. 89–107). New York: John Wiley.

Triandis, H. C. (1989). The self and social behavior in differing cultural contexts. *Psychological Review, 96*, 506–520.

Wierzbicka, A. (1986). Human emotions: Universal or culture-specific? *American Anthropologist, 88*, 584–594.

Wylie, R. C. (1979). *The self concept: Vol. 2. Theory and research on selected topics*. Lincoln, NE: University of Nebraska Press.

Yang, K. S. (1982). Causal attributions of academic success and failure and their affective consequences. *Chinese Journal of Psychology* (Taiwan), *24*, 65–83. (This abstract only is in English.)

Yu, E. S. H. (1974). Achievement motive, familism, and hsiao: A replication of McClelland-Winterbottom studies. *Dissertation Abstracts International, 35*, 593A (University Microfilms No. 74–14, 942).

Suggested Readings

Berman, J. J. (Ed.). (1989). *Cross-cultural perspectives, Nebraska Symposium on Motivation, 1989*. Lincoln: University of Nebraska Press.

Kitayama, S., & Markus, H. R. (in press). A cultural perspective to self-conscious emotions. In J. P. Tangney & K. Fisher (Eds.), *Shame, guilt, embarrassment, and pride: Empirical studies of self-conscious emotions*. New York: Guilford Press.

Markus, H. R., & Kitayama, S. (1991). Culture and the self: Implications for cognition, emotion, and motivation. *Psychological Review, 98*, 224–253.

Shweder, R. A., & Bourne, E. J. (1984). Does the concept of the person vary cross-culturally? In R. A. Shweder & R. A. LeVine (Eds.), *Culture theory: Essays on mind, self, and emotion* (pp. 158–199). Cambridge, England: Cambridge University Press.

Triandis, H. C. (1989). The self and social behavior in differing cultural contexts. *Psychological Review, 96*, 506–520.

3

Perception

with
Jeff LeRoux
San Francisco State University

When we think of perception, we usually think of being able to see something absolutely factual in the world around us. We think that the things we perceive are real and other things such as ideas and theories are less real. "Seeing is believing," as the old saying goes.

In traditional psychology, sensation and perception have to do with understanding how we receive stimuli from our environment and how we process that stimuli. More specifically, *sensation* usually refers to the actual stimulation of the various sense organs—the eyes (visual system), ears (auditory system), nose (olfactory system), tongue (taste), and skin (touch). **Perception** is generally considered the way in which information from the stimulated organs is processed. This includes how that information may be selected, organized, and interpreted. In short, perception refers to the process by which sensory information is translated into something meaningful.

In this chapter, we ask, How real are our perceptions? Are they more real than theories or ideas? Or are they mental constructions like ideas and theories? And if we decide that our perceptions themselves are not literally true, then what, if any, influences might our cultural backgrounds have on our perceptions?

There is not as much cross-cultural research in the areas of sensation and perception as there is in some of the other areas of psychology such as development, cognitive development and intelligence, emotion, and social psychology (see the other chapters in this book). Of the work that has been done in this area, much has centered on visual perception and our sense of sight. Still, we believe that culture can influence our perceptions of the world around us in the other senses as well. Before we examine the research on cultural differences in visual perception, let's look at some general comments about how cultures can influence perception in the visual as well as other arenas.

Some General Comments about Cultural Influences on Perception

Perception and Reality

One of the first things to realize about perception is that our perceptions of the world do not necessarily match the physical realities of the world or of our senses. Consider how visual perception may not be absolutely factual. We all have a **blind spot** in each eye. This is a spot where there are no sensory receptors because the optic nerve goes through the layer of receptor cells on its way toward the brain. Close one eye and you will probably find that you do not experience the world as missing a part. There is no blind spot in our conscious perception. Even though you have no receptors receiving light from one area before you, you do not "see" that part of your visual field as missing. Your brain fills it in so you think you see everything that is there. Only when something comes toward you from that blind spot can you get some idea that something is wrong with your vision at that particular location. The point here is that our perception of the world as "complete" does not actually match the physical reality of the sensation that we receive in our visual system.

Our everyday experiences with temperature and touch also demonstrate this phenomenon. Fill three bowls with water—one with hot water, one with ice water, and one with lukewarm water. Put your hand in the hot water for a few seconds, and then in the lukewarm water. The lukewarm water will feel cold. Wait a few minutes; then put your hand in the ice water, and then the lukewarm water. The lukewarm water will feel warm. The lukewarm water has not changed temperature. Rather, it is your perception of the water that has changed.

Perception and Experience

Once we begin to question our own senses, we want to know their limits. We want to know how our experiences and beliefs about the world influence what we perceive. We also want to know if other people perceive things the same way we do. If they do not see things as we do, what aspects of their experiences and backgrounds might explain those differences?

One thing we know about our perceptions is that they change. One way in which they change was noted in the experiment with the bowls of water. Our perceptions also change when we know more about some particular thing. We all have experiences in which we are seeing something complex, such as a piece of machinery, for the first time. Can you remember the first time you looked under the hood of a car? To most people it seems like an immense jumble. To those who learn about the engine it becomes familiar and differentiates into specific things—a carburetor, engine block, alternator, and other parts. To those who don't know much about mechanics the engine looks like one big thing.

For a number of years Chase and Simon (1973) have been studying people who are expert in chess or other things. They have consistently found that when people learn more about something, they "see" it in a different way than they did at first. When chess grand masters see a partially completed chess game, they do not see a moderately random scattering of chess pieces across the board. Rather, they see something like the Sicilian defense mounted against a pawn attack.

So, clearly, the way we "see" things changes with our experiences with them. How might someone with a very different background "see" something that is very familiar to us? And how might we "see" something that is very familiar to them and less so to us? A teacher in Australia related an interesting anecdote that highlighted these cultural differences in perception. At a school for aborigine children, she was trying to teach the youngsters to play a schoolyard game called Who Touched Me? In this game, everyone stands in a circle and the person who is "it" is blindfolded. Then another person from the circle quietly walks around the outside of the circle, touches the blindfolded person, and then returns to her or his place. The blindfold is removed, and the person who is "it" has to guess who touched him or her.

The teacher found that the aborigine children didn't really want to play. Even so, they cooperated, because she was the teacher. Later, in the classroom, she found that the students were uncooperative and reluctant to try anything she suggested. They refused to make any effort to learn the alphabet. She started to think that they were being stupid or naughty.

Later, to her surprise, she discovered that all the children thought that *she* was the stupid one. The aborigine children can tell whose footprint is on the ground behind them with a casual glance. So, the teacher had asked them to play a game that seemed completely silly to them; it was so easy that it made no sense at all as a game. When the aborigine children realized that the teacher couldn't tell people's footprints apart, they thought that she was the stupid one. There was no point in paying attention to a stupid teacher, so they just humored her enough not to get into trouble. But they wouldn't take seriously her or her ideas about what they should learn.

Taste Perception

There are four kinds of taste buds: one kind particularly sensitive to sweet, one to sour, one to bitter, and one to salt. We know that newborn babies have very few taste buds, that children from about age 3 to age 10 have the most, and that after age 10 the number of taste buds begins to decline. As we grow older, we have fewer and fewer taste buds. Also, the four different kinds of taste buds dwindle at different rates. The taste buds for bitter and sour disappear at a faster rate than those for sweet and salty tastes.

Most people have experienced changes in their food preferences. In part, these changes may be related to the changing proportions of the different kinds of taste buds in the mouth. We are all familiar with young children's desire for sweets and their pickiness about food in general. These traits are probably due in part to the fact that the same thing tastes different to young children and adults. A chocolate bar may be sickeningly sweet to an older person who has many more sweet taste buds than bitter and sour taste buds. A 3-year-old with many more bitter taste buds than the average adult may think the same chocolate bar has quite a bitter taste.

In the early days of human history one of the likely ways that children learned what is poisonous was by taste. Almost all poisons taste bitter or sour. Thus, avoiding eating bitter and sour things was how children learned not to eat poisonous plants. By the time children lost the ability to finely discriminate bitter and sour tastes, they were old enough to remember which things didn't taste good and which ones did.

Now imagine you are an adult who thinks that children should learn to eat vegetables. You make your children eat their vegetables before they can have dessert. Imagine you are being watched by a bushman from the Kalahari desert. He will probably think you are crazy. He might go home and giggle with his family and friends about the strange Americans who prevent their children from learning about food by preventing them from eating what tastes good to them.

Cultural Influences on Visual Perception

Our discussion so far suggests that different situations and experiences can make things seem very different. This phenomenon, of course, lays the foundation for our understanding of how cultures can influence perceptions. As mentioned earlier in this chapter, there are sporadic studies examining cultural influences on the perception of taste, smell, touch, and hearing. However, the bulk of the research in this area to date has centered on cultural influences on visual perception. These studies are important, because they tell us about how perception differs among cultures in some very basic ways.

The Traditional Knowledge about Visual Illusions

Optical illusions.   Much of the work done in psychology in the area of perception has to do with optical illusions. These are perceptions that involve an apparent discrepancy between how an object looks and what it actually is. Often, optical illusions are based on inappropriate assumptions about the stimulus characteristics of the object being perceived.

One of the most well-known optical illusions is the **Mueller-Lyer illusion** (Figure 3.1). This illusion involves two lines with arrowheads on the ends. On one line, the arrowheads point in, toward the line; on the other line, the arrowheads point out, away from the line. Research has shown that subjects viewing these two figures typically judge the line with the arrowheads pointing in as longer than the other line. This is an illusion, however, because both lines are actually the same length.

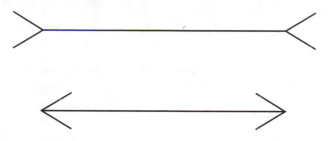

Which line is longer? To most people the top line appears longer than the bottom line. The lines are actually identical in length.

Figure 3.1   The Mueller-Lyer Illusion

Another well-known illusion is the **horizontal/vertical illusion** (Figure 3.2). In this illusion, two lines of the same length are placed perpendicular to each other. When subjects are asked to judge which line is longer, they typically choose the vertical line.

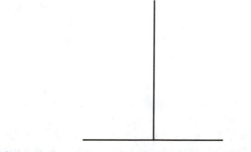

Which line is longer? To most people the vertical line appears longer than the horizontal line although both lines are the same length.

Figure 3.2   The Horizontal/Vertical Illusion

A third well-known illusion is the **Ponzo illusion** (Figure 3.3). In this illusion, two lines are placed horizontally one above the other. Two diagonal lines are drawn over the horizontal lines, closer together at the top than at the bottom. When subjects view this image, they typically report that the horizontal line closer to the top is longer than the other horizontal line. Of course, the lines are actually the same length.

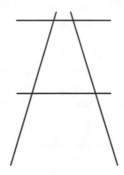

Which horizontal line is longer? To most people the upper line appears longer although both are the same length.

Figure 3.3 The Ponzo Illusion

Prevalent theories about optical illusions. Over the years, three major theories have been developed to account for the effects of optical illusions. Let's examine each one.

The **Carpentered World Theory** suggests that people, such as most Americans, are used to seeing things that are rectangular in shape. We live in a world where many things are made in regular shapes with squared corners. Living in such a squared environment, we unconsciously come to expect things to have squared corners. If we see a house from an angle where the light that reflects off it does not form a right angle on the eye, we still perceive it as a house with squared corners. We have learned that houses in general have squared corners, so we interpret what we see as having squared corners. We have been doing this so long that we are no longer aware of our interpretation of things as being square when the actual stimulation does not form a right angle on our eye. We simply "see" it as square.

In the Mueller-Lyer illusion, we tend to see the figures as square corners that project in depth toward or away from us. We know that things that look the same size to our eyes, but are at different distances, are truly different sizes. We interpret a set length of line as longer when it seems to project away from us and shorter when it seems to project toward us.

The **Front-Horizontal Foreshortening Theory** suggests that we interpret vertical lines on our eyes as horizontal lines that extend into the distance. We then interpret the vertical line in the horizontal/vertical illusion as a line extending away into the distance. Again, we would guess that a line of the same length on our eye would be longer if it is further away in space. Thus, we see the vertical line as longer than the horizontal line, which we do not see as extending away into the distance.

These theories both share some ideas in common. The first is that the way we "see" the world is developed over time through our experiences. Thus, what we see is a combination of the way the object reflects light to our eyes and our learning about how to see things in general. We learn ways to "see" things that are usually correct, but not always. That is, although learning helps us see well most of the time, it is the very thing that causes us to misjudge optical illusions.

The second idea that the theories share is that we live in a three-dimensional world that is projected onto our eyes in two dimensions. Our eyes are nearly flat, so light striking two places on the eye that are right beside each other may be coming from things very different in distance. We interpret distance and depth from cues other than where the light falls on the eye. This happens despite the fact that the light coming to the eye from one thing hits the eye right next to where light coming from another thing hits the eye.

Cross-Cultural Studies on Visual Illusions

A number of cross-cultural studies on visual perception challenge our traditional notions about optical illusions. As early as 1905, W. H. R. Rivers (1905) compared the effects of the Mueller-Lyer and horizontal/vertical illusions on groups from England, rural India, and New Guinea. He found that the English people saw the lines in the Mueller-Lyer illusion as being more different in length than did the two other groups. He also found that the Indians and New Guineans were more fooled by the horizontal/vertical illusion than were the people in England.

These results surprised Rivers and many other people from Europe and the United States. They had believed that the people from India and New Guinea were more primitive and would be more fooled by the illusions than would the more educated and "civilized" people from England. But the results showed that the effect of the illusion differed by culture, and that something other than education was involved in how much people are deceived by illusions. Researchers concluded that there must be some effect of culture on the way the world is "seen." How this difference in perception comes about has been a source of curiosity ever since.

Both the Carpentered World Theory and the Front-Horizontal Foreshortening Theory can be used to explain the results Rivers obtained.

The Carpentered World Theory, for example, would suggest that most Americans and the English people in Rivers' study are used to seeing things that are rectangular in shape. People in India and New Guinea, however, are more accustomed to more rounded and irregular environments. With the Mueller-Lyer illusion, English people would tend to see the figures as squared corners that project in depth toward or away from us. The Indians and New Guineans, however, live in cultures where less of the environment is human-made. They would have less tendency to make the same perceptual "mistake." Thus, the people from England made more errors in interpreting the Mueller-Lyer Illusion than did the people from India or New Guinea.

The Front-Horizontal Foreshortening Theory can also account for the cultural differences obtained in Rivers' study. There are fewer buildings to block the vista of distance in India or New Guinea. Thus, the Indians and New Guineans should rely more on depth cues than do the English and make more errors in judgments of the horizontal/vertical figure. This is, in fact, what Rivers found.

A third theory has been suggested to explain cultural differences in visual perception. **The Symbolizing-Three-Dimensions-in-Two Theory** suggests that in Western cultures, we focus more upon things on paper than do people in other cultures. In particular, we spend more time learning to interpret pictures than do people in non-Western cultures. Thus, people in New Guinea and India would be less likely to be fooled by the Mueller-Lyer illusion because it is more "foreign" to them. They would, however, be more fooled by the horizontal/vertical illusion because it is more representative of their lifestyle.

In order to ensure Rivers' findings held for cultures in general, Segall, Campbell, and Herskovits (1963, 1966) compared people from three industrialized groups to people from fourteen nonindustrialized groups on the Mueller-Lyer and the horizontal/vertical illusions. The results showed that the effect of the Mueller-Lyer illusion was stronger for the industrialized groups than for the nonindustrialized groups. In contrast, the effect of the vertical/horizontal illusion was stronger for the nonindustrialized groups than for the industrialized ones. This supported Rivers' findings.

Segall et al. (1963, 1966) also found some evidence that did not fit with any of the three theories. That is, the effects of the illusions declined and nearly disappeared with age. This presents a problem for all three theories. We might expect the effects of the illusions to *increase* with age because we would expect older people to have learned about their environments better than younger people.

Wagner (1977) examined this problem by using different versions of the Ponzo illusion and comparing the performances of people in both rural and urban environments, some of whom continued their education and some of whom did not. One version of the Ponzo illusion was as shown in Figure 3.3; another version contained the same configuration of lines embedded in a complete picture. Wagner found that with the simple line drawing, the effect of the illusion declined with age for all groups. With the illusion embedded in a picture, he found that the effect of the illusion increased with age, but only for urban people and people who continued their schooling. This offers more direct evidence of the effects of urban environments and schooling on the Mueller-Lyer illusion.

There is also a physical theory that must be considered. Pollack and Silvar (1967) showed that the effects of the Mueller-Lyer illusion are related to the ability to detect contours, and this ability declines with age. They also noted that as people age and are more exposed to sunlight, less light enters the eye, which may affect ability to perceive the lines in the illusion. Pollack and Silvar also showed that retinal pigmentation is related to contour detecting ability. Non-European people have more retinal pigmentation and so are less able to detect contours. Thus, Pollack and Silvar suggested, the cultural differences could be explained by racial differences in retinal pigmentation.

In order to determine which theory—the racial theory or the environmental learning theory—was more correct, Stewart (1973) noted that both race and environment need to be compared without being mixed together as was done in the study by Segall and his colleagues. In order to do this, Stewart tested the effects of the Mueller-Lyer illusion on both black and white children living in one town, Evanston, Illinois. She found no differences between the two racial groups. She then compared groups of elementary school children in Zambia in environments that ranged from very urban and carpentered to very rural and uncarpentered. She found that the effects of the illusion were dependent on the degree to which the children lived in a carpentered environment. She also found that with increased age, the effect declined, suggesting that both learning and heredity played roles in the observed cultural differences.

Hudson (1960) tried to develop a projective test similar to the Thematic Apperception Test for use with Bantu tribesmen in South Africa. He had an artist draw pictures that the psychologists thought would make the tribesmen think of their deep emotions. They were surprised to find that the tribesmen often saw the pictures in a very different way than anticipated. The tribesmen often did not use relative size as a cue to depth. In the picture depicted in Figure 3.4, for example, we tend to see the hunter as preparing to throw his spear at the gazelle in the foreground, while an elephant stands on a hill in the background. Many of the Bantu tribesmen, however, saw the hunter in a similar picture as preparing to stab the baby elephant.

What is the hunter's target? Americans and Europeans would say it is the gazelle in the foreground. The Bantu tribesmen in Hudson's (1960) research, however, said it was the elephant.

Figure 3.4 Hudson's (1960) Picture of Depth Perception

In another picture, an orator who we would see as waving his arms dramatically with a factory in the background was seen as warming his hands over the tiny chimneys of the factory.

Hudson (1960) found that these differences in depth perception were related to both education and exposure to European cultures. In other words, Bantu people who were educated in European schools, or who had more experience with European culture, saw things as Europeans did. Bantu people who had no education and little exposure to Western culture saw the pictures differently.

Conclusion

The bulk of the work reviewed in this chapter centers on how cultures help to mold or construct the way in which we perceive our environment visually. The work done to date, especially on the so-called optical illusions, is clear in suggesting that perception is a process of construction—of putting the pieces of sensory information together to be meaningful in some way. Because it is a process of construction, it is learned as we progress from birth through childhood, adolescence, and adulthood. Because it is learned, it can be shaped, molded, and influenced by the culture in which we are raised. Thus, the way we perceive the world around us, especially as adults, is influenced by the ways in which culture has helped us to learn how to construct meaning and understanding from sensory information we receive via our senses.

That the bulk of the work in this area of psychology exists in the area of visual perception—or, more precisely, in the area of optical illusions—is not to suggest that no work exists in other areas. Indeed, there are some, albeit sporadic, studies that strongly indicate the existence of cultural differences in perception of pain (Laguerre, 1981; Weisenberg, 1982). There are many anecdotal and experiential data that would support this conjecture, especially in relation to cultural beliefs concerning pain and body mutilation, cultural differences in rituals, and cultural differences in values such as stoicism and perseverance.

Some cross-cultural work also exists in other areas of perception, such as constancies, perception of form, and binocular disparity (see Deregowski, 1980, for a review). Cross-cultural research on color perception and categorization is yet another important area of research, where more than just a few studies are available. This line of research is reviewed in Chapter 6, on language and language acquisition, because of its relevance to categorization.

In any case, it seems clear that, whereas perception is influenced by a number of factors—including age, maturation, environment, and situation—cultural background is still a large determinant of one's perception of the world. Although most Americans believe in the axiom "seeing is believing," the material we have reviewed here suggests that we may not be able to trust absolutely what we see, because it could be different from what the world is like in an absolute sense. It is also very likely to be different from what a person from a different culture or environment will see and believe. Such cultural influences on perception raise questions about beliefs that one's own culture has a better grasp of the absolute truth than does another culture.

Glossary

Blind spot: The part of the visual field that corresponds to the part of the back of the eye (retina) through which the optic nerve passes and which has no light receptors.

Carpentered World Theory: The belief that living in a world where much of our environment is made by humans and has squared corners affects the way we perceive lines in general.

Front-Horizontal Foreshortening Theory: A theory that suggests we tend to see vertical lines as extending in space whereas we see horizontal lines as lying in the plane of the page.

Horizontal/vertical illusion: An illusion that a vertical line and a horizontal line of the same length placed close together are actually different in length.

Mueller-Lyer illusion: An illusion in which angled extensions to a line make the line appear either longer or shorter depending on the angle of the extensions.

Perception: The act of putting together information from memory organs into a whole that we can understand.

Ponzo illusion: An illusion of length seen when horizontal lines are embedded in a field of radiating lines.

Symbolizing-Three-Dimensions-in-Two Theory: The conjecture that we perceive the world differently because of our frequent experience of looking at two-dimensional representations of three-dimensional objects such as pictures and drawings.

References

Chase, W. G., & Simon, H. A. (1973). The mind's eye in chess. In W. G. Chase (Ed.), *Visual information processing*. New York: Academic Press.

Deregowski, J. B. (1980). Experienced and inexperienced model makers: Model-making and drawing in Rhodesia. *Journal of Cross-Cultural Psychology, 11*, 189–202.

Hudson, W. (1960). Pictorial depth perception in subcultural groups in Africa. *Journal of Social Psychology, 52*, 183–208.

Laguerre, M. S. (1981). Haitian Americans. In A. Harwood (Ed.), *Ethnicity and medical care*. Cambridge, MA: Harvard University Press.

Pollack, R. H., & Silvar, S. D. (1967). Magnitude of Mueller-Lyer illusion in children as a function of the pigmentation of the fundus oculi. *Psychonomic Science, 8*, 83–84.

Rivers, W. H. R. (1905). Observations on the senses of the Todas. *British Journal of Psychology, 1*, 321–396.

Segall, M. H., Campbell, D. T., & Herskovits, J. (1963). Cultural differences in the perception of geometric illusions. *Science, 193*, 769–771.

Segall, M. H., Campbell, D. T., & Herskovits, J. (1966). *The influence of culture on visual perception*. Indianapolis: Bobbs Merrill.

Stewart, V. (1973). Tests of the "carpentered world" hypothesis by race and environment in America and Zambia. *International Journal of Psychology, 8*, 83–94.

Wagner, D. A. (1977). Ontogeny of the Ponzo illusion: Effects of age, schooling and environment. *International Journal of Psychology, 12*, 161–176.

Weisenberg, M. (1982). Cultural and ethnic factors in reaction to pain. In Al-Issa (Ed.), *Culture and psychopathology*. Baltimore, MD: University Park Press.

Suggested Readings

Goldstein, E. B. (1980). *Sensation and perception*. Belmont, CA: Wadsworth.

Segall, M. H., Campbell, D. T., & Herskovits, J. (1963). Cultural differences in the perception of geometric illusions. *Science, 193*, 769–771.

4

Cognition

with
Jeff LeRoux
San Francisco State University

In the last chapter, we saw how the basic process of perception can make the world seem very different to people in different cultures. This is so in part because people's basic perceptions of the world are different, and in part because people are socialized to pay attention to different things in their everyday world. But what happens after something is perceived? How do we think about the world around us? What processes do our minds go through to remember things, solve problems, and categorize objects or events?

Questions such as these fall within the purview of what is known as *cognition*. Actually, **cognition** is a general term that encompasses all mental processes that transform sensory input into knowledge. These processes involve perception, rational thinking and reasoning, language, memory, problem solving, decision making, and the like. Some aspects of cognition are actually covered in other parts of this book. Perception, for example, was covered earlier in Chapter 3. Language is covered later in Chapter 6. Cognitive development is covered in Chapter 7.

In this chapter, we will look at several aspects of cognition: categorization, memory, and problem solving. Although we assume that all human beings have similar basic mental processes, you will see that people from different cultures differ in the manner in which they organize, transmit, and act upon information. They also differ in the degree to which they have developed certain practical abilities and in the training, or lack, of European-style formal education. Although it is impossible to cover in one chapter all the topics that typically fall within the purview of cognitive psychology, we hope that you get a taste of how cultures influence our thinking processes.

Categorization and Concept Formation

The Traditional Knowledge

We have probably all seen imported, handmade, brass pitchers of various designs and sizes. Once, after dinner with a Persian friend at an American's home, we all gathered in the living room. After a moment, our Persian friend turned red, giggled, and looked embarrassed, but didn't say anything. When the host left the room a few minutes later, the Persian pointed out a large ornate brass pitcher with a long spout that was sitting on a coffee table as a decoration. It had been made in the Middle East where toilet paper is scarce and people clean themselves after going to the bathroom by using such pitchers to pour water on themselves. So what was a prized decoration for our host was an object of embarrassment to my friend. What was going on? Although both the Persian friend and the host probably had very similar visual images of the brass pitcher, they had very different reactions to it. That is, they each thought of the pitcher as a member of a different category.

One of the most basic mental processes is the manner in which people group things together into categories. People **categorize** on the basis of similarities and attach labels—namely, words—to groups of objects that are perceived to have something in common. In so doing, people create categories of objects that share certain characteristics. For instance, a bean-bag chair, a straight-backed dining room chair, and a seat in a theater differ in appearance from one another, but all belong to the basic category "chair." All these things can be grouped together under the label "chair" because all share a common function. When we say "That thing is a chair" in our culture, we mean that the item can and should be used as something for people to sit on (Rosch, 1978). In this example, function is the primary determinant of the category.

Function, however, is not the only consideration that determines whether or not an object is labeled a chair. One way people decide whether something belongs in a certain group is by comparing it to the most common or representative member of that category. When we judge whether something is a chair, for instance, we compare it with our idea of the best example of an ordinary chair. Within the chair category, some things will be considered better examples of chairs than others. Although we would judge a bean-bag chair to be a chair because people sit on it, we would regard a dining room chair as a better example of a chair because it more closely resembles the **prototype** of a chair in our culture. Thus, the boundaries as to what can or cannot be called a chair will be determined in comparison to the most chairlike example. Objects that people often sit on in other cultures (for instance, pillows, hammocks, or carpets) are excluded from the chair category in the West because they do not look at all like the best example of a chair in our society. One can imagine how people from different societies might group similar sorts of things.

Cross-Cultural Studies on Categorization

Some universal aspects of categorization.   Although the grouping of many things differs from culture to culture, as with the brass pitcher, cross-cultural research indicates that some categories used in thinking and conveying information are less dependent on culture than others. For example, facial expressions that signal basic emotions—happiness, sadness, anger, fear, surprise, and disgust—are placed in the same categories across cultures (see Chapter 8 on emotion).

Likewise, there is widespread agreement across cultures as to which colors are primary and which are secondary. The way in which people select and remember colors appears to be largely independent of both culture and language. Regardless of whether people speak a language that has dozens of words for colors or a language that distinguishes colors only in terms of bright and dark, individuals from both cultural extremes group colors around the same primary hues. They also remember primary colors with greater ease when they are asked to compare and recall colors in an experimental setting. For example, an individual from a culture with only one word for red/yellow/white will select the same kind of red as the best example of this category as graduate students at Harvard will. Also, both groups of people will remember that particular color of red more easily than they will a shade such as lilac or orange-pink, despite having a very different set of names for colors. (See Chapter 6 on language for a full discussion of color perception and the categorization of colors.)

People across cultures also tend to categorize shapes in terms of the best example of basic forms (perfect circles, equilateral triangles, and squares), rather than forming categories for irregular geometrical shapes. These cross-cultural parallels suggest that physiological factors influence the way in which humans categorize certain basic stimuli. That is, people seem to be predisposed to prefer certain shapes, colors, and facial expressions.

Some culture-specific aspects of categorization.   In looking at categorization, then, we have seen that in areas in which experience is somewhat the same—such as colors, shapes, and facial expressions—people make similar groupings and judgments. When cultural experiences are different, however, people of different cultures will make very different judgments about things, such as in the example of our Persian friend and the host. From this we can infer that the underlying processes of categorization must be the same, while the experiential bases by which we categorize are quite different. Only by studying mental processes across cultures can we see both the similarities and the differences in mental processes.

Researchers have used **sorting tasks** as another way of studying how people's minds group things together. When presented with pictures that could be grouped in terms of either function, shape, or color, children in Western cultures tend to group by color at younger ages. As they grow older, they group by shape and then by function (cf. Bruner, Oliver, & Greenfield, 1966). Consequently, adults in Western cultures group by function more often than by color or shape. This means that Western adults tend to put all tools into one group and all animals in another rather than put all red things or all round things together in groups. Researchers had assumed that this age trend was a function of basic human maturation. But, given similar sorting tasks, adult Africans were found to show a strong tendency to group objects by color rather than by function (Suchman, 1966; Greenfield, Reich, & Oliver, 1966). This shows that something besides simple maturation must be responsible for the change.

One hypothesis about this difference in grouping attributes it to education. In Western societies where nearly everyone goes to school, there would be no practical way of separating the effects of education from those of aging. Evans and Segall (1969) attempted to separate the effects of maturation from those of schooling by comparing children and adults in Uganda. Some of the subjects had received formal schooling, while others had not attended school. The researchers gave sorting tasks to all their subjects and found that a preference for color grouping is most common among people who have had little or no formal schooling.

Thus, there appear to be universal processes in categorization and concept formation. These universals have been typically found around those objects or events that have commonality in experience across cultures, such as colors or facial expressions. Some evidence has been found for cultural differences in categorization as well, particularly related to sorting tasks. Follow-up studies, however, make it difficult to disentangle these cultural differences from the effects of European-style formal education. Thus, it is not clear at this time whether cultural differences in sorting tasks and categorization are best attributed to differences in cultural heritage or to differences as a function of having received formal schooling.

Memory

The Traditional Knowledge

Another major intellectual task we all share in dealing with the world is that of remembering things. We have agonized over the task of trying to memorize for tests and noticed the difficulty with which we memorize lists of dates or names or other similar things. Whenever we can, we use memory aids such as shopping lists and calendars to help us remember things that we know, from experience, we are likely to forget.

We know that there are various types of memory, such as sensory memory, short-term memory, and long-term memory. **Sensory memory** refers to the retention of original information in the sense organs for a brief period of time after it is received, usually only a fraction of a second. **Short-term memory** refers to a limited capacity of memory, where information can be retained for slightly longer periods of time, usually from 20 to 30 seconds. **Long-term memory** refers to the encoding of information that can be retrieved for considerably longer periods of time.

Rehearsal is a convenient means by which information can be stored in short- and then long-term memory. Also, chunking—the grouping of bits of information into meaningful and manageable clusters—aids the retention and retrieval of information.

Two of the most widely noted aspects of memory in experimental psychology are the serial position effects involving primacy and recency (Hovland, 1938). The **primacy effect** is the tendency we have to remember the first things in a given context better than things in the middle. The **recency effect** is the tendency we have to remember better the things that have happened more recently than things previous to them. After watching a movie, all other things being equal, we are more likely to remember the opening and ending scenes than any scenes in between.

Cross-Cultural Studies on Memory

We have probably all heard the claim that individuals from nonliterate societies develop better memory skills because they don't have the capacity to write things down to remember them (Bartlett, 1932). Is it true, then, that our memories are not as good when we habitually use lists and the like as aids in remembering?

Ross and Millson (1970) suspected that reliance on an oral tradition might make people better at remembering. They compared the memories of American and Ghanian college students in remembering stories that were read aloud. They found that, generally, the Ghanian students were better than the Americans at remembering the stories. Thus, it seemed that cultures with an oral tradition were better at remembering things. Cole and his colleagues (Cole, Gay, Glick, & Sharp 1971), however, found nonliterate African subjects did not perform better when they were tested with lists of words instead of stories. Their findings imply that cultural differences in memory as a function of an oral tradition may be limited to meaningful material.

Although serial position effects are well-established in the United States, Cole and Scribner (1974) found no relationship between serial position and the likelihood of being remembered in studying the memories of Kpelle tribespeople in Liberia. Wagner (1981) suggested that the primacy effect is dependent on rehearsal or the silent repetition of things one is trying to remember. He further suggested that this is a memory strategy that is related to schooling. Wagner compared groups of Moroccan children who had gone to school with those who had not, and found indeed that the primacy effect was much stronger in the children who had attended school. Wagner suggested that the process of memory has two parts: a **"hardware"** part that is the basic limitation of memory, which does not change across cultures, and a **"software"** or programming part that has to do with how one goes about trying to remember, which is learned. It is this second, "software" part that varies across cultures.

In examining this idea, Scribner and Cole (1981) found that students in Quranic schools in Liberia who are required to memorize immense passages of the Quran use a special set of skills for memorizing the Quran but do not use them in other memory tasks. These findings support Wagner's ideas and suggest that we learn specific memory skills in different contexts that change our memory performance.

In particular, a person's ability to remember unconnected information appears to be influenced not so much by culture, but by whether the person has had the experience of attending school. In a classroom setting, children are expected to memorize letters, multiplication tables, and other basic facts. Subjects who have been to school, therefore, have had more practice at memorizing than have unschooled individuals. They are also able to apply these skills in test situations that resemble their school experience. A study by Scribner (1974) with educated and uneducated Africans supports this idea. Educated Africans were able to recall lists of words just as well as American subjects could, whereas uneducated Africans remembered fewer words.

Thus, cross-cultural research on memory has shown that people in cultures with oral traditions are better at remembering things than are people in cultures with written traditions. This effect, however, seems localized to meaningful material as conveyed in stories, rather than lists of items. Other cross-cultural research has documented cultural differences in serial position effects. But the effects of culture on the findings to date cannot be separated from the effects of European-style schooling. Thus, it is not clear now whether culture or schooling, or both, contribute to the observed differences.

Problem Solving

The Traditional Knowledge

Problem solving refers to the process by which we attempt to discover ways to achieve goals that do not seem readily attainable. Different types of problems lead to different types of problem solving. Some problems are related to structure; people need to discover relationships among the various components or elements involved in the problem. Other problems are related to arrangement, where people need to discover ways in which the various components or elements can be arranged in a manner that addresses the problem or part of it. Finally, there are problems of transformation, where people need to carry out sequences of steps in order to achieve goals or solve problems.

A number of factors contribute to the difficulty of problem solving. For example, people can be led astray by irrelevant information. Or they may have certain mental sets that represent ways in which similar problems were solved in the past but which would be incorrectly applied to the current problem. Another obstruction to problem solving involves our inability to think of uses of objects or elements of the problem in ways other than their traditional uses.

Problems are typically solved in a number of ways. For example, people can go through a trial-and-error process, attempting various solutions until one seems to work. They may go through a means/end analysis, identifying ways in which the current situation can be changed to match end-state goals. They may work backward on a problem, starting with the end state and working systematically backward to the current state of affairs. Of course, there is always the chance of insight—a sudden discovery of a solution, often occurring after trial and error.

Cross-Cultural Studies on Problem Solving

Behavioral problems.   Cultural differences in problem solving are difficult to measure in natural settings because they can be hard to distinguish when people are making logical deductions and when their behavior reflects their cultural backgrounds. For example, a hunter who successfully tracks an animal might be said to have logically deduced the animal's direction, speed, and condition from the shape and spacing of its tracks. It could also be argued, however, that the hunter's previous experience and training have taught him to follow traditional procedures and to expect certain animal behaviors.

Psychologists have tried to isolate the process of problem solving by asking people from different cultures to solve unfamiliar problems in artificial settings. One such experiment (Cole et al., 1971) consisted of instructing American and Liberian subjects on the use of an apparatus that contained various buttons, panels, and slots. In order to open the device to obtain a prize, subjects had to independently combine two different procedures—first pressing the correct button to release a marble, and then inserting the marble into the appropriate slot to open a panel.

American subjects under the age of 10 were generally unable to obtain the prize. Older American subjects, however, combined the two steps with ease. Liberian subjects of all ages and educational backgrounds, in contrast, experienced great difficulty solving the problem; less than one-third of the adults were successful. One might conclude from this experiment that Americans are better at advanced problem solving than are Liberians, and that the Liberian culture produces adults who seem to lack a capacity for logical reasoning.

However, this experiment may have been biased toward the Americans, despite its apparent objectivity. That is, the American subjects may have benefited from the hidden advantage of living in a technological society. As Americans, we are accustomed to mechanical devices; buttons, levers, dials, and slots on machines are common in our daily environment. But, in some non-Western cultures, people seldom operate machines and the unfamiliarity of the apparatus may have influenced the outcome by intimidating or bewildering the Liberian subjects. (Remember the first time you ever worked on a computer?)

In fact, Cole and his colleagues repeated their experiment with materials familiar to people in Liberia, using a locked box and keys instead of the mechanical contraption. In the new version of the two-step problem, the Liberian subjects had to remember which key opened the lock on the box, and which matchbox container housed the correct key. Under these circumstances, the great majority of Liberians solved the problem easily.

The success of the Liberians in solving a two-step problem with a familiar set of materials brings us back to the question of whether the experiment tested their ability to think logically or their ability to solve the problem on the basis of previous knowledge and experience with locks and keys. In an attempt to clarify this issue, the researchers designed a third experiment, combining elements from both the first and second tests. Liberian and American subjects were again presented with a locked box, but the key that opened the box had to be obtained from the apparatus used in the first experiment. To the surprise of the researchers, the third test produced results similar to those of the first experiment. Americans solved the problem with ease, whereas most Liberians were not able to retrieve the key to open the box.

Cole and his colleagues concluded that the ability of the Liberians to reason logically to solve problems depends on context. When presented with problems that employ materials and concepts already familiar to them, Liberians drew logical conclusions effortlessly. When the test situation was alien to them, however, they had difficulty knowing where to begin. In some cases, the problem went beyond confusion; uneducated Liberians appeared to be visibly frightened by the tests that employed the strange apparatus. Indeed, they were reluctant to manipulate it. Although adult Americans did very well in these experiments in comparison to the Liberians, one might wonder how average Americans might react if placed in a similar experimental situation, requiring the use of wholly unfamiliar concepts and technology. Such an experiment might involve requiring American subjects to track animals using smells and the appearance of animal footprints!

Word problems.   The ability to solve word problems is yet another aspect of logical reasoning that has been studied cross-culturally. One type of word problem used to measure ability to reason logically is the syllogism—for example, all children like candy; Mary is a child; does Mary like candy?

In wide-ranging studies of tribal and nomadic peoples in East and Central Asia, Luria (1976) documented sharp differences in the way people approached verbal problems of this nature. As with other cultural differences in cognition and thought, the ability to provide the correct answer to verbal problems was found to be closely associated with school attendance. Individuals from traditional societies who were illiterate were generally unable to provide answers to syllogisms that contained unfamiliar information. Individuals from the same culture, and even the same village, however, who had received a single year of schooling could respond correctly.

Various explanations have been proposed to account for the inability of uneducated people to complete word problems. Luria (1976) concluded that illiterate people actually think differently from those who are educated. According to this hypothesis, logical reasoning is essentially artificial, because it is a skill that must be learned in a Westernized school setting.

Studies that might appear to lend support to this interpretation have examined how and when schoolchildren first begin to use formal logic. In one such study, Tulviste (1978) asked schoolchildren in Estonia from the ages of 8 to 15 to solve verbal problems and to explain their answers. Although the children were able to solve most of the problems correctly, they explained their answers by citing the logical premises of the problem only in areas where they did not have firsthand knowledge. Elsewhere, their answers were justified with appeals to common sense or statements about their personal observations. Thus, the capacity to reason logically would appear to be a skill that children first acquire and use in the classroom and only later begin to apply to their everyday lives.

Scribner (1979) questioned whether illiterate subjects are truly incapable of thinking logically and looked more closely into the reasons why uneducated people fail to give correct responses to verbal problems. When uneducated peasants were asked to explain illogical answers to syllogism problems, they consistently cited evidence that was known to them personally or stated that they didn't know anything about the subject, ignoring the premises given to them. For example, in response to the word problem cited earlier, subjects might shrug their shoulders and comment, "How would I know whether Mary likes candy—I don't even know the child!" or "Maybe she doesn't like candy; I've known children who didn't." These subjects appear to be unable or unwilling to apply concepts of scientific thinking to verbal problems. But this is not because they lack the capacity to reason logically; rather, they do not understand the hypothetical nature of verbal problems. People who have attended school have had the experience of answering questions posed by an authority who already knows the correct answers. Uneducated people, however, have difficulty understanding that questions need not be requests for information.

Schooling would seem to affect people's ability to solve verbal problems because in a school setting people become accustomed to answering questions that would be silly in most social settings. They also are trained to respond in a particular way to the authority figures—teachers—in the school setting. Students learn about matters beyond their own everyday experience and are coerced into remembering and using what they have learned in ways that are very similar to experimental tasks used by psychologists.

Conclusion

In this chapter we discussed several basic mental processes and how these processes differ, to some extent, across different cultures. Categorization was found to be similar across cultures when experience was similar—such as with colors, facial expressions, and geometric shapes. From this we inferred that the basic process was similar in all people. We also found categories to be dissimilar when people had different backgrounds of cultural experience. In sorting tasks, we found an effect of schooling, which would not have been discovered had the problem not been examined cross-culturally.

In discussing memory, we learned that people from cultures with oral traditions did better in remembering some oral materials than did people from our own culture, which focuses on written communication. We also found some limits to the notions of serial position effects in memory that depended on culture. In discussing problem solving, we found cultural familiarity to have an effect on ability to solve problems. Further cross-cultural studies on logic and problem solving showed that what we thought were processes of maturation were, instead, effects of schooling on the students' perceptions of what is socially appropriate in a school setting.

As we were in the last chapter, we are left now with a sense that the world is more varied and complex than our conception of it. Cross-cultural research has been able to demonstrate some of the limits and boundaries of our thinking processes. In discovering these, we have also uncovered what may be some cross-cultural universals, as well as cultural differences, in concept formation, memory, and problem solving. However, the cross-cultural differences that we have discussed also highlight the considerable effects of schooling on cognition and thinking processes. Much of the research we have reviewed left open the question of whether cultural differences are due solely to effects of schooling, culture, or both. Also, when cultural differences do occur, they appear not to be differences in cognitive abilities or capacities; rather, they may be differences in preferences for certain cognitive styles. Future controlled studies examining the dual influence of and interaction between culture and education will shed more light on this issue.

Glossary

Categorization: The process of associating similar things with each other and, sometimes, of giving the groups of associated objects a name.

Cognition: A general term for any sort of mental processes.

Hardware: In information-processing jargon, this refers to the physical machine that is processing the information, which is usually a computer.

Long-term memory: The memory storage system in which things may last as long as we are alive and which seems to have no limits to its capacity.

Primacy effect: The fact that the first few items in a list tend to be better remembered than items in the middle of the list.

Prototype: The best example of a category.

Recency effect: The fact that the last few items in a list tend to be better remembered than the items in the middle of the list.

Sensory memory: A very short-term storage for information in a partially processed state; it has a large capacity, but from it information is quickly lost.

Short-term memory: A memory system in which things last for only a minute or two; it has a usual capacity of about seven plus or minus two pieces of information.

Software: In information-processing jargon, this refers to the programs that a computer runs, which are distinguished from the machine that runs them (hardware).

Sorting task: A task of putting things into categories, usually used in order to see the mental processes that underlie the sorting.

References

Bartlett, F. C. (1932). *Remembering.* Cambridge, England: Cambridge University Press.

Bruner, J. S., Oliver, R. R., & Greenfield, P. M. (1966). *Studies in cognitive growth.* New York: John Wiley.

Cole, M., Gay, J., Glick, J. A., & Sharp, D.W. (1971). *The cultural context of learning and thinking: An exploration in experimental anthropology.* New York: Basic Books.

Cole, M., & Scribner, S. (1974). *Culture and thought: A psychological introduction.* New York: John Wiley.

Evans, J. L., & Segall, M. H. (1969). Learning to classify by color and function: A study of concept discovery by Ganda children. *Journal of Social Psychology, 77,* 35–55.

Greenfield, P. M., Reich, L. C., & Oliver, R. R. (1966). On culture and equivalence II. In J. S. Bruner, R. R. Oliver, & P. M. Greenfield (Eds.), *Studies in cognitive growth* (pp. 270–318). New York: John Wiley.

Hovland, C. I. (1938). Experimental studies in rote learning. *Journal of Experimental Psychology, 23,* 172–190.

Luria, A. R. (1976). *Cognitive development: Its cultural and social foundations* (M. Lopes & L. Solotaroff, Trans.). Cambridge, MA: Harvard University Press. (Original work published 1974)

Rosch, E. (1978). Principles of categorization. In E. Rosch and B.B. Lloyd (Eds.), *Cognition and categorization* (pp. 28–48). Hillsdale, NJ: Lawrence Erlbaum Associates.

Ross, B. M., & Millson, C. (1970). Repeated memory of oral prose in Ghana and New York. *International Journal of Psychology, 5,* 173–181.

Scribner, S. (1974). Developmental aspects of categorized recall in a west African society. *Cognitive Psychology, 6,* 475–494.

Scribner, S. (1979). Modes of thinking and ways of speaking: Culture and logic reconsidered. In I. O. Freedle (Ed.), *New directions in discourse processing* (pp. 223–243). Norwood, NJ: Able.

Scribner, S., & Cole, M. (1981). *The psychology of literacy*. Cambridge, MA: Harvard University Press.

Suchman, R. G. (1966). Cultural differences in children's color and form perception. *Journal of Social Psychology, 70*, 3–10.

Tulviste, P. (1978). On the origins of the theoretic syllogistic reasoning in culture and in the child. *Acta at commentationes Universitatis Tortuensis, 4*, 3–22.

Wagner, D. A. (1981). Culture and memory development. In H. C. Triandis & A. Hernon (Eds.), *Handbook of cross-cultural psychology: Volume 4* (pp. 187–232). Boston: Allyn & Bacon.

Suggested Readings

Bartlett, F. C. (1932). *Remembering*. Cambridge, England: Cambridge University Press.

Cole, M., & Scribner, S. (1974). *Culture and thought: A psychological introduction*. New York: John Wiley.

Rosch, E. (1978). Principles of categorization. In E. Rosch and B. B. Lloyd (Eds.), *Cognition and categorization* (pp. 28–48). Hillsdale, NJ: Lawrence Erlbaum Associates.

5

Developmental Psychology

with

Margaret Lynch
University of California, Davis

Developmental psychology is the area of psychology that is concerned with change in behavior over time. As we grow, we are not only able to do more things, but we can do them in different ways at different points in time. The task of the developmental psychologist is to define and explain the course of developmental change. What changes occur with time and what causes these changes?

Many developmental changes occur because of an interaction between biological growth and the environment in which the individual lives. In early research, developmental psychologists often debated whether biology or environment is more important to growth. More recently, however, developmentalists have increasingly come to realize that the two are inseparable. That is, development as we know it does not occur without the close interrelationship between biology and the environment. For example, consider children beginning to talk and using more and more words. As children grow and develop, their language changes not simply because they can say more, but because they are able to understand and use words in increasingly complex and different ways. In only five years, children's language develops from baby noises to almost adult speech. These changes occur because of an interaction between biological growth and the environment in which the children live. Certainly, children's brains undergo a biological process of growth and change; but during that time children live in an environment in which they hear language spoken and used in particular ways.

Many different topics fall within the purview of developmental psychology: prenatal and neonatal development; motor development; the development of temperament, attachment, and personality; the development of aggression or altruism; cognitive and socioemotional development; family structure and parenting styles; moral reasoning; and the like. In recent years, developmental psychologists have studied the entire life span, and an increasing number of researchers have concentrated their attentions on adolescence or young, middle, or older adulthood.

In this chapter we discuss four areas of development from a cross-cultural viewpoint: temperament, attachment, parenting styles and family structures, and moral reasoning. The focus in this chapter is on the developing child rather than on later years of development. This is not to say that cross-cultural research on other topics of development is nonexistent or not important. Indeed, other topics of development are very important and are covered in other areas of this book (for example, cognitive development in Chapter 7 and language acquisition in Chapter 6). The goals in this chapter are merely to challenge some of the traditional knowledge typically described concerning developmental psychology and to raise awareness of sociocultural issues in development.

Before we turn our attention to the specific content areas, however, let's look at some general concerns about the nature of the knowledge about development that has been generated to this point.

Some General Concerns about Our Knowledge in Developmental Psychology

Recently Michael Lamb (1992) commented, when discussing some of his cross-cultural work, that one of the constraints on some of the developmental research reviewed for reanalysis was that the samples were markedly skewed because many of the subjects were children of college professionals. That is, many of the subjects involved in developmental studies were the offspring of the researchers and their friends! This is not at all uncommon in psychological research, because it is often very difficult to obtain research subjects, especially minors. So, university students, friends of the researchers, and their children often represent the bulk of subject populations on which psychological "truths" are formed. To be sure, just because the research samples are comprised in this manner does not necessarily mean that the findings are entirely false. Rather, we merely need to raise caution flags regarding the generalization of those "truths."

This is especially true for research in child development. Childhood is a period of considerable change and flux. It is a period that is probably subject to more cultural and environmental influences than any

other in the lifespan. Thus, researchers and the consumers of that research—students—need to be particularly concerned about the nature of
the samples involved in the generation of knowledge concerning child
development.

Throughout the world, people emerge from childhood with a wish
to become happy, productive adults. The various ways in which children
develop along the same trajectory are evidence of the ability to achieve
positive outcomes that account for survival while socializing children to
the culture in which they live. Cultures differ, however, in exactly what
they mean by "happy" and "productive." Thus, despite the similarities
among cultures in the overall goals of development, there still also exists a tremendous amount of variability.

Each culture has knowledge of the adult competencies needed for
adequate functioning (Ogbu, 1981). But these competencies differ by
culture and environment, and children are socialized in ecologies that
promote their specific competencies (Harrison, Wilson, Pine, Chan, &
Buriel, 1990). For example, if you need a formal education to succeed in
your culture, you are likely as a child to be exposed to these values early.
You may receive books and formal instruction at a young age. In contrast, children in other parts of the world may have to do spinning and
weaving as part of their adult livelihood. These children are likely to be
familiarized with such crafts early in childhood.

Because of the difficulties of research, samples in developmental
studies are often small. In some cases, research findings using small
samples form the basis for an enormous amount of subsequent research—as if a huge pyramid is balanced upside down on its apex! Much
of our knowledge in our own culture is based on small, somewhat limited samples and studies. The same is often true of what we know of
other cultures. Furthermore, even what we learn about other cultures is
constrained by the fact that the "data" are often interpreted by researchers who are not from those cultures.

The gist of this discussion is that we cannot assume that the research
conducted in the somewhat restricted and homogeneous ecologies will
have the same relevance to other cultures. This is applicable to all areas
of psychology, not just development. Still, what is available in the cross-
cultural research literature on specific topics in development is revealing.

Temperament

The Traditional Knowledge

Any parent can tell that no two babies are alike. It is not simply that
they look different, but they are different from the very beginning in
what is called temperament. Each baby has his or her own way of being

in the world—easygoing or fussy, active or quiet. These qualities of responsiveness to the environment that we call temperament exist from
birth and evoke different reactions by people in the baby's world. **Temperament** is generally considered to be a biologically based style of interacting with the world that exists from birth.

Thomas and Chess (1977) have described three major categories of
temperament: easy, difficult, and slow-to-warm-up. **Easy temperament**
is defined by a very regular, adaptable, mildly intense style of behavior
that is positive and responsive. **Difficult temperament** is an intense, irregular, withdrawing style that is generally marked by negative moods.
Slow-to-warm-up infants need time to make transitions in activity and
experiences. Although they may initially withdraw or respond negatively, given time and support they will adapt and react positively.

The interaction of children's temperament with their parents seems
to be a key to the development of personality. This is a concept known
as **"goodness of fit."** Parental reactions to their children's temperament
can promote stability or instability in their children's temperamental responses to the environment. The interaction of the parent's responses
to their children's temperament will also affect their subsequent attachment.

Cross-Cultural Studies on Temperament

One question that cross-cultural researchers have asked concerns whether
or not children of non-American cultures have different general styles of
temperament than that described for American infants. Freedman (1974),
for example, found that Chinese-American babies were calmer and more
placid than Caucasian-American babies or African-American babies.
When a cloth was placed on their faces covering their noses, the Chinese-
American babies lay quietly and breathed through their mouths. The
other babies turned their heads or tried to pull off the cloths with their
hands. Freedman also found similar differences in Japanese-American
and Navaho babies when compared to Caucasian-Americans. Likewise,
Chisholm (1983) also extensively studied Navaho infants and found that
they were much calmer than Anglo infants.

Chisholm (1983) argues that there is a well-established connection
between the condition of the mother during pregnancy (especially high
blood-pressure levels) and irritability of the infant. This connection between maternal blood pressure and infant irritability has been found in
Malaysian, Chinese, Aboriginal and white Australian infants as well as
Navaho (Garcia Coll, 1990). Garcia Coll, Sepkoski, and Lester (1981)
found that the differences in the health of Puerto Rican mothers during
pregnancy were related to differences in their infants' temperaments
when compared to Caucasian-American or African-American infants.

The Puerto Rican babies were alert and did not cry easily; the African-American babies scored higher on motor abilities—behaviors involving muscle movement and coordination. Therefore, the temperament difference we find as characteristic of a cultural group may reflect differences in genetics and in reproductive histories.

The interaction between parents' responses and infant temperament may also be an important factor in cultural differences. The quiet temperament and placidity that is notable in infants from Asian and Native American backgrounds is probably further stabilized in later infancy and childhood by the response of the mothers. Navaho and Hopi babies spend long periods tightly wrapped in cradle boards; Chinese parents value the harmony that is maintained through emotional restraint (Bond & Wang, 1983).

These types of differences that occur from birth contribute to differences in personality in adults of different cultures. It is important to realize the magnitude of these contributions as building blocks in the development of adult members in cultures around the world.

Attachment

The Traditional Knowledge

Attachment refers to the special bond that develops between the infant and caregiver. Many psychologists feel that the quality of attachment has lifelong effects on an individual's relationships with loved ones. Attachment provides the child with emotional security. Once attachment is established, babies are distressed by separation from their mothers (called separation distress or anxiety).

The studies on attachment in rhesus monkeys by the Harlows (Harlow & Harlow, 1969) highlighted the importance of contact and physical comfort in the development of attachment. Bowlby (1969) concluded that infants must have a preprogrammed, biological basis for becoming attached to their caregivers. This program includes behaviors such as smiling and cooing that will, in turn, elicit physical, attachment-producing behaviors on the part of their mothers.

Ainsworth, Blehar, Waters, and Wall (1978) have delineated three different styles of attachment: secure, avoidant, and ambivalent. Mothers of **securely attached** babies are described as warm and responsive. Mothers of **avoidant** children, who shun their mothers, are suspected of being intrusive and overstimulating. **Ambivalent** children are uncertain in their response to their mothers, going back and forth between seeking and shunning their attention. These mothers have been characterized as insensitive and less involved.

Attachment underpins the concept of basic trust. Erikson (1963) described the formation of basic trust as the important first step in the life-long process of psychosocial development. Poor attachment is a component of mistrust—the unsuccessful resolution of the needs of the infancy stage. Basic trust is presumed to affect later relationships and also the subsequent stages of development. Erikson described the other stages that occur in childhood as ones involving the tasks of establishing autonomy, initiative, and competency. All of these are parts of the developing self and are influenced by how mothers and important others in the child's life respond to him or her.

Cross-Cultural Studies on Attachment

One of the assumptions about the nature of attachment in the United States is that secure attachment is the ideal. In fact, the very choice of term that Ainsworth used to describe this type of attachment, and the negative terms selected to describe others, reflects this underlying bias. Cultures differ, however, in their notions of "ideal" attachment. For example, German mothers value and promote early independence and therefore regard avoidant attachment as the ideal. German parents see the "securely" attached child as "spoiled" (Grossmann, Grossmann, Spangler, Suess, & Unzner, 1985). Of Israeli children that are raised on a kibbutz (collective farm), half display anxious ambivalent attachments and only a third appear to be securely attached (Sagi et al., 1985). Children raised in traditional Japanese families are also characterized by a high rate of the anxious, ambivalent type of attachment, with practically no avoidant types (Miyake, Chen, & Campos, 1985). These traditional mothers seldom leave their children and foster a strong sense of dependence in their children. This supports the traditional cultural ideal of family loyalty. In nontraditional Japanese families where the mother may have a career, attachment patterns are found to be similar to those in the United States (Durrett, Otaki, & Richards, 1984).

Some cross-cultural studies also challenge the notion that closeness to the mother is necessary for secure and healthy attachment. Indeed, this notion is a very prevalent one in traditional theories of attachment based on research in the United States. Studies involving an African tribe of forest-dwelling foragers known as the Efe (erroneously referred to by most people as the Pygmies—a name they do not like) show a very different situation than what psychologists have come to accept as part of healthy attachment (Tronick, Morelli, & Ivey, 1992). Efe infants spend most of their time away from their mothers and are cared for by a variety of different people. They are always within earshot and sight of about ten people. They have close emotional ties to many people other than their mothers and spend very little time with their fathers. The researchers found the children to be emotionally healthy despite having multiple caregivers.

Although this study demonstrated that closeness or proximity to mothers is not necessary for healthy attachment, this is not necessarily the case for children of other cultures. It is certainly not comparable to U.S. children that attend day-care centers. The Efe have large, extended families, and these families are permanent parts of the growing Efe children's lives. In day-care centers in the United States, staff turnovers are typically high, and relationships with children are not usually long term. What the Efe may be revealing is that multiple caregivers who remain stable in a child's life are a healthy alternative to our traditional ideas.

There is still much to be done to understand the attachment patterns in other cultures. The studies that do exist to date, however, are clear in suggesting that we cannot assume that what is seen most often in Anglo-American culture is best, or most descriptive, for all. Notions concerning the quality of attachment, and the processes by which it occurs, are qualitative judgments made from the perspective of cultures, each of which has values different from, and not necessarily better than, others.

Parenting, Families, and Socialization

The Traditional Knowledge

Clearly our parents play an important, if not the most important, role in our development. Parenting styles can differ dramatically. Baumrind (1971) has identified three major patterns of parenting. The **authoritarian parent** expects unquestioned obedience and views the child as needing to be controlled. **Permissive parents**, in contrast, allow children to regulate their own lives and provide few firm guidelines. The **authoritative parent** is firm, fair, and reasonable. This style is seen as promoting psychologically healthy, competent, independent children who are cooperative and at ease in social situations. Other researchers (Maccoby & Martin, 1983) have identified a fourth type of parenting style called "uninvolved." **Uninvolved parents** are often too absorbed in their own lives to respond appropriately to their children and often seem indifferent to them.

Much of the influence on our development occurs in our relationships with people other than our parents. As children grow out of early childhood, friendships change. These changes are in great part due to cognitive development. The new abilities to think about themselves and others and to understand their world allow children to develop peer relationships that have more depth and meaning.

In school a major portion of a child's life is spent away from parents. The socialization process that has its basis in the primary relationship with the parent continues with peers in play situations and school. Socialization is the instrumental process by which the child internalizes cultural values and attitudes. School institutionalizes these standards and is a significant contributor not only to the intellectual development of the child but, just as importantly, to social emotional development.

Cross-Cultural Studies on Parenting, Families, and Socialization

Parenting and the economic environment. One of the first things we in the United States need to consider is that parenting and child rearing often occur in very different conditions in many other countries and cultures. These conditions, in turn, produce socialization processes that vary extremely from culture to culture. Child-rearing practices may differ not merely because of difference in beliefs, but also because of very marked differences in standards of living. Using a yardstick that we might apply to evaluating parenting in the United States could lead to harsh conclusions about parenting in different countries and cultures.

Parenting and child-rearing are affected, sometimes severely, by conditions of poverty or poor economic conditions. The slum-dwelling Brazilian mother who leaves her three children under the age of 5 locked in a bare, dark room for the day while she goes out to obtain food and clothing could be viewed quite harshly by our standards. However, is it fair to judge her by our standards? Even when economic conditions are not as harsh as they are in this example, how do we evaluate child-rearing practices in other cultures? Certainly, the answer to this question is that they should *not* be judged by accepted practices in this, or any single, culture.

It is common folklore in Western cultures that picking up a baby and bringing the child to the shoulder reduces bouts of crying. Babies who are ignored and allowed to cry for fear of spoiling actually cry more. However, in remote rural river regions of China, week-old infants are left for long periods of time while their mothers work in the fields. They are placed in large sacks of sand that support them upright and act as an absorbent diaper. Quickly these babies cease to cry because they learn early that it will not bring any response.

If a society has a high rate of infant mortality, parenting efforts may concentrate on meeting basic, physical needs. Parents may have little choice but to disregard other developmental demands. Sometimes the response to harsh and stressful conditions brings about changes that we might consider positive. In the Sudan, for example, the mother traditionally spends the first 40 days after delivery entirely with her baby. She rests and her relatives tend to her as she focuses all her energy on her baby (Cederblad, 1988).

Levine (1977) has theorized that the caregiving environment reflects a set of goals that are ordered in importance. First is physical health and survival; next is the promotion of behaviors that will lead to self-sufficiency; and last are behaviors that promote other cultural values such as morality and prestige. Many families in the United States are fortunate in that they can turn their attention to meeting the second and last goals. In many countries, the primary goal of survival is all-important and often overrides the other goals in the amount of parental effort exerted. Indeed, this is true in many areas of the United States as well.

Parenting and extended family structure. Aside from the general environment in which children are raised, the structure of the family also has a large impact on child-rearing and caregiving. Again, we can find many important cultural differences that affect child-rearing. In many non–Anglo-American cultures, extended families are prevalent. In the United States in 1984, for example, 31% of African-American children lived in extended families, while only 19.8% of children of other races lived in such families (U.S. Bureau of the Census, 1985). Extended families are a vital and important feature of child-rearing, even when resources are not limited. Many cultures, in fact, view extended-family child-rearing as an integral and important part of their cultures. It can provide a buffer to stresses of everyday living. It is also an important process by which cultural heritage is transmitted from generation to generation.

Extended families can support and facilitate child-rearing in ways that are completely different from the traditional Anglo-American nuclear family. Research on parenting tends to assume a nuclear family structure when delineating the style of parenting (for example, authoritarian, permissive, authoritative, neglectful). In the United States, ethnic-minority families have been characterized as extended and generally more conservative than Caucasian-American families. For example, Japanese-American families have been categorized as extended with strict age and sex roles, and as having an emphasis on children's obedience to authority figures (Trankina, 1983; Yamamoto & Kubota, 1983).

Even though mothers are still seen as the primary caregivers, children experience frequent interaction with grandparents, godparents, siblings, and cousins in an extended family situation. Godparents are seen as important models for children in Hispanic and Filipino families. They are also sources of support for the parents. Sharing households with relatives, characteristic of extended families, is seen as a good way of maximizing the family's resources for successful child-rearing.

We need not look outside the United States to recognize the importance of extended families. In the United States, however, participation in child-rearing through extended families is often seen as a consequence of poor economics rather than a desirable state of affairs. Limited resources are a reality for many; 11.2 million children in the United States were living below the poverty level in 1990. Of such children many are born to single mothers; thus, the extended family plays an important role in the child-rearing process. Grandmothers are more actively involved with their grandchildren when they live with their single adult daughter. These children possibly experience a greater variety of main caregivers and have different social interactions than their traditional Caucasian-American counterparts.

Teenage parenting also forces us to think differently about traditional notions of parenting. The presence of the maternal grandmother in these families has been found to nullify some of the negative results associated with teen mothering (Garcia Coll, 1990). The grandmother often serves as a valuable source of information about child development. She also tends to be more responsive and less punitive with her grandchildren than the teen mother. The grandmother in these three-generation households has a very important role as a teacher and role model to her daughter, and she can provide favorable, positive social interaction for her grandchild.

Extended family situations differ in their composition from one culture to another, but they have in common the sharing of resources, emotional support, and caregiving. The experiences of a child growing up in these situations can be quite different from those of a child in a traditional Caucasian-American household. In addition, we need to be aware that the "traditional," two-parent household composition is changing in many Caucasian-American homes. Future studies will undoubtedly change the way we view parenting in this culture as well.

Parenting and sleeping arrangements.   Of the many different child-rearing behaviors people of different cultures engage in, one of the most representative of cultural differences concerns sleeping arrangements. One of the single, greatest concerns of urban-dwelling, Western parents—especially Americans—is getting their baby to sleep through the night and to do so in a room separate from the parents'. In the United States, we shun co-sleeping arrangements, with the underlying assumption that sleeping alone will help develop independence. Some assistance is offered to the child by way of "security objects," such as a special blanket or toy.

This value is not shared by many other cultures. In rural European areas, for example, infants sleep with their mothers for most, if not all, of their first year. This is also true in many other cultures. Comfort objects and bedtime rituals are not often found in other cultures. Mayan mothers allow their children to sleep with them for several years because of a commitment to forming a very close bond with their children.

When a new baby comes along, older children move to a bed in the same room or share a bed with another member of the family (Morelli, Oppenheim, Rogoff, & Goldsmith, 1992). In traditional Japanese families the child sleeps with the mother, with the father either on the other side or in a separate room by himself.

Sleeping arrangement is just one of the many ways in which cultures differ in child-rearing practices. As we have discussed, different cultures place different values on parenting styles, and child-rearing often occurs in family structures and economic environments that differ from what we would consider a middle-class, American way of life. In many ways, child-rearing and parenting reflect a process that prepares children to live within the context of their culture. Just as those cultural contexts differ dramatically for adults, the parenting and child-rearing practices they experienced in childhood differ dramatically as well.

Moral Reasoning

The Traditional Knowledge

Children develop increasingly complex ways of understanding their world. These cognitive changes also bring about changes in their understanding of moral judgments. Why something is good or bad changes from the young child's interpretation of reward and punishment to principles of right and wrong.

The dominant theory of moral reasoning in developmental psychology is that proposed by Kohlberg (1976, 1984). Kohlberg's theory, in turn, was based on Piaget's earlier work on cognitive development. Kohlberg's theory suggests that there are three general stages of development of moral reasoning skills. Each of these three general stages, in turn, can be further subdivided into two stages each, for a total of six substages of moral development. The three general stages of moral reasoning according to Kohlberg are:

1. **Preconventional morality**, with an emphasis on compliance with rules to avoid punishment and get rewards

2. **Conventional morality**, with an emphasis on conformity to rules that are defined by others' approval or to society's rules

3. **Postconventional morality**, with an emphasis on moral reasoning according to individual principles and conscience

In the last decade, work by Gilligan and her colleagues (Gilligan, 1982) has challenged Kohlberg's theory by suggesting that the six substages of Kohlberg's theory are biased toward the particular way in which males, as opposed to females, view relationships. Gilligan argues that male moral reasoning is equated with justice, whereas female moral reasoning is equated with obligations and responsibilities. Despite the fervor of the debate, however, reviews of the research seem to indicate that sex differences in moral reasoning have not been found (Walker, 1984). Cross-cultural research may yet shed more light on this issue.

Cross-Cultural Studies on Moral Reasoning

The universality or cultural specificity of moral principles and reasoning has been an area of interest for anthropologists and psychologists alike. A number of anthropological ethnographies, for example, have examined the moral principles and domains of a number of different cultures (see review by Shweder, Mahapatra, & Miller, 1987). Many of these works have challenged traditional American views of morality.

Likewise, in psychology, a number of cross-cultural studies on moral reasoning raise questions about the universal generalizability of Kohlberg's ideas. One of the underlying assumptions of Kohlberg's theory is that moral reasoning according to individual principles and conscience, regardless of social laws or cultural customs, represents the highest level of moral reasoning. This underlying philosophy is very related to the cultural milieu in which Kohlberg developed his theory, which had its roots in studies involving American males in the Midwestern section of the United States in the 1950s and 1960s. While democratic notions of individualism and unique, personal conscience may have been appropriate to describe his samples at that time and place, it is not clear whether those same notions represent universal moral principles that are applicable to all people of all cultures.

In fact, some researchers have indeed criticized Kohlberg's theory for harboring such cultural biases (Bronstein & Paludi, 1988). Miller and Bersoff (1992), for example, compared how subjects in India and the United States responded to a moral judgment task. The researchers reported that the Indian subjects, children as well as adults, considered it a moral transgression *not* to help someone more than did the American subjects, regardless of whether the situation was life-threatening or whether the one in need was related. The researchers interpreted the cultural differences as being related to values of affiliation and justice, suggesting that Indians are taught a broader sense of social responsibility—the individual responsibility to help a needy person.

The issue of interpersonal responsiveness that Miller and Bersoff (1992) raised is related to Gilligan's (1982) claims of gender bias in U.S. studies. It is entirely possible that Gilligan's findings are just as influenced by cultural, as well as gender, differences.

Snarey (1985) completed a review of moral reasoning studies involving subjects from 27 different countries. Snarey concluded that moral reasoning is much more culture-specific than Kohlberg originally suggested. Kohlberg's theory, as well as the methodology for scoring moral stages according to verbal reasoning, may not recognize higher levels of morality as defined in other cultures.

Conclusion

Developmental psychology is an exciting area in which cross-cultural research can have a particularly important impact. As seen in this chapter, our notions of temperament, attachment, parenting, child-rearing, family structures and environment, and moral reasoning should all be tempered by the cultural context within which that development is occurring. Cross-cultural research on development grounds us in recognizing many of the roots of cultural differences we observe in our adult lives.

Still, we have much more work to do in this area. For example, between 1987 and 1989, 64.85% of the studies published in *Child Development* (a major research journal in developmental psychology) failed to report the ethnic composition of their samples (Slaughter-Defoe et al., 1990). This continued lack of cross-cultural consideration is indeed a shortcoming. Many consider childhood to be an irrevocable foundation for adult development. We need to consider carefully the diverse ways in which children are raised and socialized throughout the world, particularly because most of them grow up to be healthy, functioning, productive individuals that contribute to their respective societies.

We have much to learn about ourselves as well as others. The excitement of psychology, and especially developmental psychology, is that there will always be new answers that give rise to new questions about which behaviors are shared by all and which are unique to only some.

Glossary

Ambivalent attachment: A bond characterized by children who are uncertain in their responses to their mothers, going back and forth between seeking and shunning the mothers' attention. Mothers, in turn, are characterized as insensitive and less involved.

Attachment: The special bond that develops between the infant and caregiver.

Authoritarian parent: A style of parenting that expects unquestioned obedience and views the child as needing to be controlled.

Authoritative parent: A style of parenting that is firm, fair, and reasonable. This style is seen as promoting psychologically healthy, competent, independent children who are cooperative and at ease in social situations.

Avoidant attachment: A bond characterized by infants who shun their mothers. Mothers, in turn, are suspected of being intrusive and overstimulating.

Conventional morality: An emphasis on conformity to rules that are defined by others' approval or to society's rules.

Difficult temperament: An intense, irregular, withdrawing style that is generally marked by negative moods.

Easy temperament: A very regular, adaptable, mildly intense style of behavior that is positive and responsive.

Goodness of fit: The fit that exists between children's temperament and their parents'.

Permissive parent: A style of parenting that allows children to regulate their own lives and provides few firm guidelines.

Preconventional morality: An emphasis on compliance with rules to avoid punishment and with rules to get rewards.

Postconventional morality: An emphasis on moral reasoning according to individual principles and conscience.

Secure attachment: A bond characterized by mothers who are warm and responsive.

Slow-to-warm-up infants: Infants who need time to make transitions in activity and experiences. Although they may withdraw initially or respond negatively, given time and support they will positively adapt and react.

Temperament: A biologically based style of interacting with the world that exists from birth (for example, easygoing or fussy, active or quiet).

Uninvolved parents: A style of parenting in which parents are often too absorbed in their own lives to appropriately respond to their children and often seem indifferent to them.

References

Ainsworth, M. D., Blehar, M. C., Waters, E., & Wall, S. (1978). *Patterns of attachment: A psychological study of the strange situation.* Hillsdale, NJ: Erlbaum.

Baumrind, D. (1971). Current patterns of parental authority. *Developmental Psychology Monograph, 4* (1, Pt. 2).

Bond, M. H., & Wang, S. (1983). China: Aggressive behavior and the problems of mainstreaming order and harmony. In A. P. Goldstein & M. H. Segall (Eds.), *Aggression in global perspective* (pp. 58–74). New York: Pergamon.

Bowlby, J. (1969). *Attachment and loss, Vol. 1: Attachment.* New York: Basic Books.

Bronstein, P. A., & Paludi, M. (1988). The introductory psychology course from a broader human perspective. In P. A. Bronstein & K. Quina (Eds.), *Teaching a psychology of people: Resources for gender and sociocultural awareness* (pp. 21–36). Washington, DC: American Psychological Association.

Cederblad, M. (1988). Behavioural disorders in children from different cultures. *Acta Psychiatrica Scandinavia Supplementum, 344,* 85–92.

Chisholm, J. (1983). *Navajo infancy.* New York: Aldine.

Durrett, M. E., Otaki, M., & Richards, P. (1984). Attachment and mothers' perception of support from the father. *Journal of the International Society for the Study of Behavioral Development, 7,* 167–176.

Erikson, E.H. (1963). *Childhood and society* (2nd ed.). New York: W. W. Norton.

Freedman, D. (1974). *Human infancy: An evolutionary perspective.* Hillsdale, NJ: Erlbaum.

Garcia Coll, C. T. (1990). Developmental outcomes of minority infants: A process oriented look at our beginnings. *Child Development, 61,* 270–289.

Garcia Coll, C., Sepkoski, C., & Lester, B. M. (1981). Cultural and biomedical correlates of neonatal behavior. *Developmental Psychobiology, 14,* 147–154.

Gilligan, C. (1982). *In a different voice: Psychological theory and women's development.* Cambridge, MA: Harvard University Press.

Grossmann, K., Grossmann, K. E., Spangler, S., Suess, G., & Unzner, L. (1985). Maternal sensitivity and newborn attachment orientation responses as related to quality of attachment in Northern Germany. In I. Bretherton & E. Waters (Eds.), *Growing points of attachment theory. Monographs of the Society of Research in Child Development, 50* (1–2, Serial No. 209).

Harlow, H. F., & Harlow, M. K. (1969). Effects of various mother-infant relationships on rhesus monkey behavior. In B. M. Foss (Ed.), *Determinants of infant behavior* (Vol. 4). London: Methuen.

Harrison, A. O., Wilson, M. N., Pine, C. J., Chan, S. Q., & Buriel, R. (1990). Family ecologies of ethnic minority children. *Child Development, 61,* 347–362.

Kohlberg, L. (1976). Moral stages and moralization: The cognitive-developmental approach. In J. Lickona (Ed.), *Moral development behavior: Theory, research and social issues.* New York: Holt, Rinehart & Winston.

Kohlberg, L. (1984). *The psychology of moral development: The nature and validity of moral stages* (Vol. 2). New York: Harper & Row.

Lamb, M. (1992, June). *Cross-cultural studies in developmental psychology.* Address given at the University of California, Davis, Department of Human Development.

Levine, R. A. (1977). Child rearing as cultural adaptation. In P. H. Leiderman, S. R. Tulkin, & A. Rosenfeld (Eds.), *Culture and infancy* (pp. 15–27). New York: Academic Press.

Maccoby, E. E., & Martin, J. A. (1983). Socialization in the context of the family: Parent-child interaction. In E. M. Hetherington (Ed.), *Handbook of child psychology: Vol. 4. Socialization, personality, and social development* (4th ed.) (pp. 1–101). New York: John Wiley.

Miller, J. G., & Bersoff, D. M. (1992). Culture and moral judgment: How are conflicts between justice and interpersonal responsibilities resolved? *Journal of Personality and Social Psychology, 62,* 541–554.

Miyake, K., Chen, S., & Campos, J. J. (1985). Infant temperament, mother's mode of interaction, and attachment in Japan. An interim report. In I. Bretherton & E. Waters (Eds.), *Growing points of attachment theory. Monographs of the Society of Research in Child Development, 50* (1–2, Serial No. 209).

Morelli, G. A., Oppenheim, D., Rogoff, B., & Goldsmith, D. (1992). Cultural variations in infant sleeping arrangements: Questions of independence. *Developmental Psychology, 28,* 604–613.

Ogbu, J. U. (1981). Origins of human competence: A cultural-ecological perspective. *Child Development, 52,* 413–429.

Sagi, A., Lamb, M. E., Lewkowicz, K. S., Shoham, R., Dvir, R., & Estes, D. (1985). Security of infant-mother, -father, and metapelet attachments among kibbutz reared Israeli children. In I. Bretherton & E. Waters (Eds.), *Growing point in attachment theory. Monographs of the Society for Research in Child Development, 50* (1–2, Serial No. 209).

Shweder, R., Mahapatra, M., & Miller, J. G. (1987). Culture and moral development. In J. Kagan & S. Lamb (Eds.), *The emergence of morality in young children.* Chicago: University of Chicago Press.

Slaughter-Defoe, D. T., Nakagawa, K., Takanishi, R., & Johnson, D. J. (1990). Towards cultural, ecological perspectives on schooling and achievement in African- and Asian-American children. *Child Development, 61,* 363–383.

Snarey, J. R. (1985). Cross-cultural universality of social development: A critical review of Kohlbergian research. *Psychological Bulletin, 97,* 202–232.

Thomas, A., & Chess, S. (1977). *Temperament and development.* New York: Brunner/Mazel.

Trankina, F. J. (1983). Clinical issues and techniques in working with Hispanic children and their families. In G. J. Powell (Ed.), *The psychological development of minority group children* (pp. 307–329). New York: Brunner/Mazel.

Tronick, E. Z., Morelli, G. A., & Ivey, P.K. (1992). The Efe forager infant and toddlers pattern of social relationships: Multiple and simultaneous. *Developmental Psychology, 28,* 568–577.

U. S. Bureau of the Census. (1985). Persons of Spanish origin in the United States: March 1985. *Current Population Reports,* Series P-20, No. 403. Washington, DC: U. S. Government Printing Office.

Walker, L. J. (1984). Sex differences in the development of moral reasoning: A critical review. *Child Development, 57,* 522–526.

Yamamoto, J., & Kubota, M. (1983). The Japanese-American family. In G. J. Powell (Ed.), *The psychological development of minority group children* (pp. 307–329). New York: Brunner/Mazel.

Suggested Readings

Burbank, V. K. (1988). *Aboriginal adolescence.* New Brunswick, NJ: Rutgers University Press.

Chisholm, J. (1983). *Navajo infancy.* New York: Aldine.

Cole, M., & Cole, S. R. (1993). *The development of children* (2nd ed.). New York: Scientific American Books.

Nsamenang, A. B. (1992). *Human development in cultural context: A third world perspective.* Newbury Park, CA: Sage.

Slaughter, D. (Ed.) (1988). *Black children and poverty: A developmental perspective.* San Francisco: Jossey-Bass.

Soyinka, W. (1981). *Ake, the years of childhood.* New York: Random House.

6

Language and Language Acquisition

with

Philip Hull

Center for Psychological Studies

You may wonder why this psychology textbook has a chapter on language. "Isn't that what linguistics textbooks are for?", you may ask. Language is of significant interest to psychologists and psycholinguists because it is an important aspect of human behavior.

Language is the principal means by which we communicate with one another and by which we store information. Language is also the principal means by which each generation receives its cultural inheritance from the previous generation. Indeed, without language, culture as we know it would not exist at all. So it should come as no surprise that language is of particular interest to cross-cultural psychologists.

Language acquisition is an important aspect of the psychology of language because it helps us understand much broader issues of human behavior. For example, by discovering which acquisition processes are universal and which are specific to single cultures, we can better answer an enduring question in psychology: To what extent is our behavior innate (that is, biologically determined) or learned (that is, culturally determined)?

Understanding how language is acquired is also important for practical reasons. As the world increasingly becomes what has been called a "global village" (with greater interdependence among nations), knowledge of more than one language has become a vital tool in understanding and communicating with people from other cultures. This is true both within a pluralistic, multicultural society such as the United States and between people living in different nations. Psychologists can play an important role in facilitating such contact between cultures.

83

The importance of learning about language—and the relationship among language, culture, and behavior—cannot be emphasized enough, especially for psychology students in the United States. In general, Americans are notoriously ignorant of languages other than English, and unfortunately, this ignorance is often accompanied by an ethnocentric view of the need to learn, understand, and appreciate other languages, customs, and cultures. Thus, the study of language in the context of culture and behavior takes on added importance for American psychology students.

In this chapter, we examine some of the ways in which language differences may be related to cognitive differences. We will also address some of the cultural implications of language, with a particular focus on the implications of speaking more than one language. We will examine some similarities and some differences in how languages are acquired in different cultures. In addition, we will discuss what such differences might tell us about the nature of human behavior.

We begin with a brief review of how language itself has typically been defined and some of the traditional ways in which these issues have been addressed. This will help in understanding some of the other issues to be discussed later in this chapter.

Traditional Theories and Views of Language

Language Features

When you think of language, what comes to mind? A junior high school English grammar class? A high school foreign language class? People with "accents"? Struggling to understand what was going on in your first American classroom? Such thoughts all represent aspects of language.

Psycholinguists have typically tried to describe language by using five critical features (which you may already have read about in your psychology textbook):

1. The **lexicon,** or vocabulary, refers to the words contained in a language. For example, the words *tree, eat, how,* and *slowly* are part of the English lexicon.

2. The **syntax and grammar** of a language refer to the system of rules governing word forms and how words should be strung together to form meaningful utterances. For example, English has a grammatical rule that we add *s* to the end of many words to indicate plurality (the plural of *cat* is *cats*) and a syntactic rule that we place adjectives before most nouns, not after (for example, "small dog," not "dog small").

3. **Phonology** refers to the system of rules governing how words should sound (pronunciation or "accent") in a given language. For instance, in English, we don't pronounce *new* the same as *sew*.

4. **Semantics** refers to what words mean. *Table* refers to a physical object that has four legs and a flat horizontal surface.

5. **Pragmatics** refers to the system of rules governing how language is used and understood in given social contexts. For example, the statement "it is cold" could be interpreted as a request to close a window or as a statement of fact about the temperature. How it's interpreted may depend on the social and/or environmental context.

Psycholinguists have also used two other concepts to help explain the structure of language. **Phonemes** are the smallest and most basic units of sound in a language. **Morphemes** are the smallest and most basic units of meaning in a language. Accordingly, phonemes form the base of a language hierarchy, in which the structure language gains is increasingly complex as sounds gain meaning, which in turn produce words, which are strung together in phrases and, finally, sentences.

One of the most important and long-lasting debates in the psychology of language is on the relationship between the kind of language we speak and the kinds of thought processes we have. This is often referred to as the Sapir-Whorf hypothesis. It is particularly important to the cross-cultural psychology of language because each culture is usually associated with a given language as a vehicle for its expression, and each language is usually associated with a given culture. So we may ask ourselves questions such as: How does culture influence language? How does language influence culture?

Another important debate in the psychology of language is on the extent to which the processes of language acquisition are innate (and thus culturally universal) and the extent to which such processes are learned (and thus vary from culture to culture).

Let us now explore each of these debates in turn.

The Sapir-Whorf Hypothesis

The **Sapir-Whorf hypothesis** suggests that speakers of different languages think differently, and they do so because of the differences in their languages. Because different cultures typically have different languages, the Sapir-Whorf hypothesis has particular import for our understanding of cultural differences (or similarities) in thought and behavior as a function of language.

Many studies have looked at several different language cognition issues since Edward Sapir and Benjamin Whorf proposed the hypothesis earlier this century. Such studies are often referred to as studies of the Sapir-Whorf hypothesis, as if there were only one such hypothesis. Actually, there are several different "Sapir-Whorf hypotheses."

In 1960, Joshua Fishman published a comprehensive breakdown of the most important ways in which the Sapir-Whorf hypothesis has been discussed (see Table 6.1). In his description, these different approaches are ordered in increasing levels of complexity. As can be seen in Table 6.1, two factors determine the level at which a given version of the hypothesis might fall. The first factor relates to the particular aspect of language that is of interest—for example, the lexicon or the grammar. The second factor relates to the cognitive behavior of the speakers of a given language—for example, cultural themes or nonlinguistic data such as a decision-making task.

Table 6.1 **Fishman's Sapir-Whorf Hypothesis Schema**

Data of Language Characteristics	Data of Cognitive Behavior	
	Linguistic Data	Nonlinguistic Data
Lexical/Semantic	Level 1*	Level 2
Grammatical	Level 3	Level 4**

*Least sophisticated
**Most sophisticated

Of the four levels, level 1 is the least complex and level 4 is the most complex. Both levels 3 and 4 are actually closer to Whorf's original ideas, in that they have to do with the grammar or syntax of language as opposed to its lexicon. In reviewing the literature on the Sapir-Whorf hypothesis, it is extremely important to keep in mind exactly which level of the hypothesis is being tested.

Cross-Cultural Research on the Sapir-Whorf Hypothesis

In one of the earliest studies on language, Carroll and Casagrande (1958) compared Navaho and English speakers. They examined the relationship between the system of shape classification in the Navaho language and the amount of attention children pay to shape when classifying objects. The Navaho language has the interesting grammatical feature that certain verbs of handling (for example, "to pick up," "to drop") require special linguistic forms depending on what kind of object is being handled. There are 11 such linguistic forms for describing different shapes. There is a form for round spherical objects, one for round thin objects, one for long flexible things, and the like.

Carroll and Casagrande (1958) noted how much more complex this linguistic feature is in Navaho than it is in English. They suggested that such linguistic features might play a role in influencing cognitive processes. In their experiment, they compared Navaho- and English-dominant children to see how often the children used shape, form, or type of material to categorize objects. The Navaho-dominant children were significantly more likely to carry out this task on the basis of shape than were the English-dominant children.

In that same study, Carroll and Casagrande (1958) also reported that the performance of low-income African-American English-speaking children was similar to that of the Anglo children. This is particularly important since the African-American children, unlike the Anglo children, were not accustomed to blocks and form-board type toys. Their finding provided evidence supporting the idea that the type of language we speak may influence the kind of thoughts we have. This suggests that language may act in a mediating role. That is, where prior nonlinguistic experience does not intervene, language may determine the ways in which children conceive of some aspects of their world. In other words, language seems to be one of perhaps several experiences that can influence the way we think.

Carroll and Casagrande's study is one of the few to investigate the Sapir-Whorf hypothesis at Fishman's level 3 or 4. In contrast, there is a considerable amount of research comparing lexical differences and linguistic behavior (Fishman's level 1) or nonlinguistic behavior (Fishman's level 2). Most of this research is at level 2, which typically has compared lexical differences with nonlinguistic behaviors. When such comparisons have shown differences, language is assumed to have caused these differences.

Most of the early work in this area actually focused on color perception. The position of many investigators was stated clearly more than 30 years ago:

> The continuous gradation of color which exists in nature is represented in language by a series of discrete categories. . . . There is nothing inherent either in the spectrum or the human perception of it which would compel its division in this way. The specific method of division is part of the structure of English. (Gleason, 1961)

Studies of language and color perception have typically looked at how colors are categorized and how they are named in different languages. For example, Brown and Lenneberg (1954) found a positive relationship between the codability of a color and the accuracy with which a color could be remembered in a memory task. Codability in their study was defined as how well speakers of English agreed on a name for a given color, the length of the name, and the time taken to name a color.

Thus, if we describe this experiment in terms of Fishman's schema of the Sapir-Whorf hypothesis, color is the nonlinguistic domain, memory is the nonlinguistic behavior, and semantic aspects of language are the linguistic behavior(s). Brown and Lenneberg's results lent support to the Sapir-Whorf hypothesis.

Berlin and Kay (1969) examined 78 languages and found 11 basic color terms that form a universal hierarchy. Some languages such as English and German use all 11 terms, whereas others such as Dani (New Guinea) use as few as 2 terms. Furthermore, Berlin and Kay noticed an evolutionary order in which languages encode these universal categories. For example, if a language is known to have three color terms, then we know that these three terms describe black, white, and red. This hierarchy of color naming in human language is illustrated in Table 6.2.

Table 6.2   **Hierarchy of Color Names (Berlin & Kay, 1969)**

1. All languages contain terms for white and black.

2. If a language contains three terms, then it contains a term for red.

3. If a language contains four terms, then it contains a term for either green or yellow (but not both).

4. If a language contains five terms, then it contains terms for both green and yellow.

5. If a language contains six terms, then it contains a term for blue.

6. If a language contains seven terms, then it contains a term for brown.

7. If a language contains eight or more terms, then it contains a term for purple, pink, orange, gray, or some combination of these.

In order to test such claims as Gleason's, Berlin and Kay (1969) undertook a study of the distribution of color terms in 20 languages. They asked foreign university students in the United States to list the "basic" color terms in each of their native languages. They then asked these foreign students to identify from an array of glass color chips the most typical, or the best examples, of a basic color term that the researchers gave to them. Berlin and Kay found that there are a limited number of basic color terms in any language. They also found that the color chips chosen as best examples of these basic terms tend to fall into clusters that they termed "focal points." Thus, in languages that had a basic term for bluish colors, the best example was found to be the same "focal blue" for speakers of all the languages spoken by these foreign students.

Berlin and Kay's findings suggested that people in different cultures perceive colors in much the same way, despite radical differences in their languages. Many people began to doubt the validity of the Sapir-Whorf hypothesis because it didn't seem to apply in the perceptual domain of color.

Berlin and Kay's findings were later confirmed by a series of experiments conducted by Rosch. In her experiments, Rosch (for example, 1973) set out to test just how culturally universal these focal points are. She compared two languages that differ markedly in the number of their basic color terms: English, with multiple color terms, and Dani, which has only two color terms. Dani is the language spoken by a Stone Age tribe living in the highlands of Irian Jaya, Indonesian New Guinea. One color term, *mili,* was found to include both "dark" and "cold" colors (for example, black, green, and blue), whereas the second color term, *mola,* included both "light" and "warm" colors (white, red, and yellow).

Rosch also explored the relation between language and memory. She argued that if the Whorfian position were correct, Dani's lack of a rich color lexicon would inhibit Dani speakers' ability to discriminate and remember colors. As it happened, Heider and Oliver (1972) found that Dani speakers did not confuse color categories any more than did speakers of English. Neither did Dani speakers perform differently from English speakers on memory tasks.

As mentioned in this and other texts, the way we perceive color is determined to a significant degree by our biological makeup and, in particular, our biological visual system. This system is the same across human cultures. De Valois and his associates (De Valois, Abramov, & Jacobs, 1966; De Valois & Jacobs, 1968) studied a species of monkey with a visual system similar to that of humans. They suggested that we have cells that are stimulated only by two colors (for example, red plus green, blue plus yellow) and that, at any given moment, these cells can be stimulated by only one of the two colors. For example, our red/green cells can only respond to red or to green but not to both simultaneously. This is rather interesting because many people have noticed that while it is possible to mix red and green, it is not possible for humans to perceive such combinations in the same way that we perceive a mixture of blue and green as turquoise or a mixture of red and blue as purple. Thus, a "reddish green" is a perceptual, as well as a semantic, impossibility.

So, it's clear that our biology is very important in how we perceive colors. Given this situation, it would actually be surprising to find language-based differences in color perception. Certainly, we cannot dismiss the Sapir-Whorf hypothesis just because language seems to have little influence on the way we perceive colors. Indeed, if we look at areas of human behavior other than color perception, we find significant evidence to support the Sapir-Whorf hypothesis.

One area of human behavior that appears susceptible to Whorfian effects is that of causality, or how we explain the reasons that things happen the way that they do. Niyekawa-Howard (1968) conducted a study of language and causality—specifically, the relationship between Japanese grammar and Japanese perceptions of what causes events to happen. Traditionally, the Japanese language has an interesting passive form. For instance, because the subject of the phrase "was caused to" takes the action expressed by the main verb, that subject is not responsible for the act nor the outcome. We can convey this information in English but only by using cumbersome extra words and phrases. In contrast, such meaning is conveyed by the Japanese passive form in a subtle way. Niyekawa hypothesized that because of the frequency with which native speakers of Japanese are confronted with this passive form, such speakers would be more likely (as compared to English speakers) to attribute responsibility to others even when the outcome was positive. This is exactly what she found in her study.

More evidence to support the Sapir-Whorf hypothesis appeared in 1981 when Bloom reported his finding that Chinese speakers were less likely than English speakers to give hypothetical interpretations to a hypothetical story. He interpreted these results as constituting strong evidence for the structure of language as a mediator of cognitive processes, because English and Chinese differ in how they convey hypothetical meaning. For example, in English, we usually do this by using the subjunctive tense ("if I were you," not "if I am you"). Chinese has no subjunctive in the sense of a mandatory marking in each verb, (so the grammatical Chinese equivalent of the English example would be, roughly translated, "if I am you"). Although Au (1983, 1984) has contested Bloom's interpretation of his data, Bloom's study remains important as evidence for the importance of the link between language grammar and human cognition.

Yet another source of support for the Sapir-Whorf hypothesis is Kay and Kempton's (1984) finding that at least some differences in cognition depend on differences in linguistic structure. They compared the thought processes of speakers of English with those of speakers of Tarahumara, a language indigenous to the Yucatan peninsula in Mexico, which does not distinguish between blue and green. They had subjects complete two nonlinguistic tasks, both of which involved choosing from a number of color chips the color that was the "most different" from the other(s). They found that color discrimination was better when subjects could use a naming strategy, demonstrating clearly that linguistic differences can affect the performance of a nonlinguistic task.

In summary, we have seen that the most-studied area is lexical differences between languages. The lexicon seems to be only minimally related to our thought processes, which may account for much of the current skepticism about the Sapir-Whorf hypothesis. A less well-studied area, syntactic and grammatical differences between languages, seems to provide stronger evidence for the claim that language influences cognition. Perhaps the strongest evidence will be found in future studies of how the pragmatic systems of different languages influence speakers' thought processes. Take the case of Javanese, for example. This Indonesian language has an elaborate system of different forms of address depending on the social status, age, and sex of the person one is speaking to. Does speaking the Javanese language influence Javanese people to be more precise in their thinking about social and status differences than are speakers of English? Japanese has a similarly complex system of honorifics. Hunt and Agnoli (1991) suggest that such a "Whorfian" process might be operating in Japanese speakers as compared to speakers of English.

In this section we have referred to the Sapir-Whorf hypothesis as it might relate to monolingual speakers of a given language. This is primarily because most, if not all, of the research on this issue has limited itself to the comparison of monolingual populations. What might the Sapir-Whorf hypothesis imply about the behavior of bilingual or multilingual populations? One implication might be that the behavior of bilingual individuals would depend on the language that is in current use. This is not strictly a "Whorfian" issue because it does not necessarily imply that it is any aspect of a bilingual person's two languages that causes language-related changes in bilingual behavior (such as their lexical, syntactic/grammatical, semantic, phonological, or pragmatic systems). It is simply that when we learn a language, we learn it in the context of a culture. When immigrants learn two languages, they often do so in the context of two cultures. So the point here is simply that each language may access a different set of cultural values. In the next section, we explore this issue.

Language and Behavior:
The Special Case of Bilingualism

Earlier this century, many Americans thought that knowledge of more than one language should be avoided. It was commonly believed that humans have only limited "room" to store language; if you learn "too much" language, you take "space" away from other functions such as intelligence. We now know that such notions are wrong and that there is no evidence that bilinguals do worse on intellectual (or other) tasks. On the contrary, there is evidence that knowledge of more than one language may improve cognitive flexibility.

Up to this point in this chapter, we have referred to "speakers of a language" as if most humans speak just one language. Despite the cultural diversity of the United States, we might easily assume both that this is true and that bilingualism is primarily a minority issue. In fact, on a global level, monolinguals (those who speak only one language) are a minority. The majority of the inhabitants of our "global village" speak more than one language.

Besides being an issue of considerable global importance, we in the United States have a large (and growing) number of people who regularly use both English and another language. In fact, in many cases this other language is often their native tongue. Many of these people have come to this country from elsewhere. Such bilingual immigrants pose an especially interesting issue in terms of the psychology of language because their two languages are often associated with two different cultural systems. Moreover, many bilinguals report that they think and/or feel differently, depending on their current linguistic context. This may be thought of as having a different sense of self, depending on which language is being used.

Can we then assume that bilinguals have access, through their two languages, to two culturally different modes of thought? If so, does this imply the existence of two different personalities within the same individual, each associated with one of the bilingual's two languages?

Ervin (1964) compared responses from a sample of English and French bilinguals to pictures from the Thematic Apperception Test (a common test used in many cross-cultural studies). The subjects told their stories in response to the pictures once in English and then another time in French. Ervin found that subjects demonstrated more aggression, autonomy, and withdrawal in French than in English, and that only females demonstrated a greater need for achievement in English than in French. In Ervin's view, these differences were due to the higher value French culture places on verbal prowess in the former case and to greater sex role differences in the latter case.

How might the issue of bilingualism and personality be important in immigrants to the United States? Let us consider an example: a Chinese-English bilingual, who was raised in a monolingual, Chinese-speaking home and who learned English naturalistically only after migrating to the United States from China at age 8. She is a 20-year-old college student, lives with her parents, and has used Chinese as the only language in the home. English is used at school and with most of her peers. One might predict that when using Chinese, she would be likely to behave in ways appropriate to Chinese cultural norms in the home. In English, however, she might be more likely to behave in ways that are shifted away from the Chinese norm to that of the Anglo-American norm.

A "Whorfian" view might account for such language-related behavioral differences in terms of the pragmatic systems of Chinese and English (as well as other linguistic differences). There are at least two other explanations for the mechanisms that might underlie such language-related shifts in personality. These are called the culture-affiliation hypothesis and the minority group-affiliation hypothesis.

The **culture-affiliation hypothesis** is simply that immigrant bilinguals tend to affiliate themselves with the values and beliefs of the culture that is associated with the language in which they are currently operating. When the language is switched, so will the cultural values with which they affiliate. The **minority group-affiliation hypothesis**, in contrast, is that immigrant bilinguals tend to self-identify as members of an ethnic minority group and/or adopt the behavioral stereotypes of the majority culture about their minority as their own when they are operating in the language associated with their minority group. Where such stereotypes are accurate, the minority group-affiliation hypothesis will make the same predictions as does the culture-affiliation hypothesis. That is, when interacting in their first language, people will behave in ways more typical of their culture as well as more consistent with majority-culture stereotypes of that culture. Given that one would expect differences in behavior depending on language context, one would then expect differences in personality in linguistic contexts.

Hull (1987) and Dinges and Hull (1992) report studies in which this prediction was tested. They reasoned that if there were any such differences to be found, they would be most evident among a population of immigrant bilinguals. Such bilinguals are believed to have two clearly distinct cultural affiliations, accessible through the language in which much of this cultural knowledge was learned or is associated. In these studies, Chinese-English and Korean-English immigrant bilinguals were given the California Psychological Inventory (C.P.I.), a widely used personality test. It's a particularly good test for this type of study because it has been translated into many different languages and used in cross-cultural research over many years.

The immigrant bilinguals completed the C.P.I. twice, once in their native language and once in English. The central question was: Would a dual self or dual personality emerge, showing up as between-language, within-group differences in C.P.I. scores? The answer was a resounding yes. In other words, these bilinguals presented different personalities depending on whether they were responding in English (their second language) or in their native language. In a second study, Hull (1990a, 1990b) confirmed these findings using a different measure of personality.

There is also some evidence to suggest that our perceptions of others are dependent on the language we speak when making those judgments. Matsumoto and Assar (1992), for example, asked bilingual observers in India to view a set of 40 different facial expressions of emotion. The observers were asked to judge which emotion was being portrayed in the faces and how intensely. The observers made these judgments twice, a week apart, once in English and a second time in Hindi. The results showed that judgments of which emotion was being portrayed were more accurate when the judgments were made in English. But the emotions were perceived more intensely when the ratings were made in Hindi.

Such research as we have described demonstrates how much language and culture are intertwined with each other. It also demonstrates the importance of language in everyday experience. Such findings also help to dispel the misconception that the existence of two personalities within individuals means that such individuals are suffering from a mental disorder. Such a situation is clearly a natural and healthy part of the bilingual/bicultural experience.

Language Acquisition

As we discussed at the beginning of this chapter, for a considerable period of time, researchers have examined whether the processes of language acquisition are innate (and thus culturally universal) or learned (and thus vary from culture to culture). We do not yet have a clear answer to these questions. The evidence to date suggests that some aspects of language acquisition are learned, whereas others are innate.

How do we learn language? A common myth in many cultures is that children learn their native language by imitating the native language that they hear in their native environment. We now know that imitation is not an important strategy in learning language. In fact, children are far more sophisticated in their learning strategies than we used to believe.

In a now famous study in the 1950s, Jean Berko (Berko, 1958; Berko-Gleason, 1989) showed very cleverly that, rather than simply imitating what they hear, children generate hypotheses about language and then test these hypotheses. This hypothesis generation and testing is a crucial strategy by which children around the world learn their native languages. It thus appears to be a universal strategy for learning language. Berko (1958) showed American children a picture of an imaginary creature. She told them that the picture was of a "wug" (an imaginary creature that she invented for this experiment). She then showed the same children a picture of two such imaginary creatures and asked them what they saw: "Now there are two _____." Most of the children filled in the blank by saying "wugs." Because the word *wugs* is not an English word and is one that the children had never encountered before, this shows very clearly that these children could not have used imitation to produce the word *wugs*. In order to answer "wugs," they had to have prior knowledge of a rule of English grammar—namely that, in English, we often add *s* to nouns to indicate plurality.

Sometimes children's knowledge of grammatical rules causes them to appear to backslide in their language development. Many parents in the United States have been dismayed when their children, who previously used the correct form of the verb "to go," begin to use an "incorrect" form that they may never have used before. For example, after using the standard past tense form "went" in a sentence such as "I went to school," children may suddenly begin to say "I goed to school." Anxious parents may regard such apparent regression as evidence of a learning disability. More often than not, nothing could be further from the truth. The children first learned the form "went" through simple imitation without learning anything about the rules of English grammar. Then later, when their linguistic understanding became more sophisticated, they learned the English grammatical rule to add *ed* to the end of verbs to make them past tense. Using the form "goed" instead of "went" thus shows a higher level of linguistic development since the children are applying a grammatical rule rather than simply imitating a word they have heard. Further in the children's development, they will learn the exceptions to rules previously learned, such as this irregular past tense form, "went." The point here is that knowing a grammatical rule and applying it creatively in new situations shows much greater cognitive sophistication than mere imitation. It is a universal language-learning strategy.

People in different cultures have different beliefs about how children learn language. Cultures also differ in the way they behave toward children learning language. The Kaluli people of Papua New Guinea believe that children need carefully controlled explicit instruction in both the forms of language and conversation skills (Schieffelin, 1981, 1990; Schieffelin & Ochs, 1986). In other words, they believe that children won't learn language and conversational skills unless they are taught to do so explicitly. The Kaluli act on these beliefs and teach their children how to conduct conversations.

Samoan adults typically believe that children's early attempts at language have no meaning and, in any case, that children have nothing to say that is of any importance to adults. Because of these beliefs Samoan adults don't engage their children in formal language training. Nor do they typically engage in conversation with children. In fact, it is the language of elder siblings that Samoan children are mostly exposed to rather than the language of adults (Ochs, 1988; Ochs & Schieffelin, 1979, 1983).

In the United States, there is a curious discrepancy between what adults believe and their actions. On the one hand, most adults believe that children need explicit instruction from caretakers to learn English properly. On the other hand, most American parents actually pay attention to what the children are saying (the content) rather than to how they are saying it (the grammar, syntax, and so on) (Chomsky, 1965, 1967, 1969).

Such differences in cultural beliefs and practices with regard to language learning are fascinating. What is even more fascinating, however, is that in all cultures, regardless of any such beliefs or practices, children learn their native language fluently with or without help from their adults. This implies that all humans have some universal and innate ability to learn language. Chomsky, a renowned linguist, proposed precisely this.

According to Chomsky (1967), humans possess a **Language Acquisition Device** (or LAD). He argues that this LAD enables all normal children to learn language fluently. Although we don't have any direct evidence of the existence of Chomsky's LAD, it is currently one of the best explanations we have for the fact that all normal children learn their native languages fluently regardless of great differences in their environments.

Further evidence to support the existence of a Language Acquisition Device comes from cross-cultural research on pidgins and creoles. (A *pidgin* is a simplified speech used for communication between people with different languages. A *creole* is a language based on two or more languages that serves as the native language of its speakers.) Bickerton (1981), at the University of Hawaii, studied a number of pidgins and their development into creoles. He found that many of the linguistic features found in several unrelated creoles were not present in any of the source languages (from which the original pidgin developed). Where might such features come from? Bickerton suggests that the only plausible explanation for the existence of such features in creoles that have not had contact with other creoles that share those features is that they are "preprogrammed" or "hard-wired" in humans as part of our LAD.

Thus, although it is clear that people of different cultures harbor different opinions and attitudes about language acquisition, it is not clear whether the exact processes of language learning are different across cultures. With the lack of evidence to the contrary, Chomsky's notions of a universal LAD that enables children to learn languages fluently appears to be the best explanation for language acquisition that exists today. Future research may test the limits of this LAD by exploring in more detail exactly how this process occurs. Perhaps then we can uncover some ways in which cultural differences in attitudes and opinions about language learning affect the learning process in specific cultures.

Conclusion

It is true that languages differ enormously from one another, and these differences are related to important differences in the customs and behaviors of the cultures in which those languages reside. Although there has been some skepticism about the strength of the Sapir-Whorf hypothesis, a closer examination of the cross-cultural research testing it tends to support some versions of it and not others. We have also seen that language plays an important and predictive role in the personalities of multilingual people. Finally, although the processes by which we learn language appear to be universal, cultures clearly differ in their attitudes and opinions about language acquisition. It is not yet clear how these attitudes and opinions influence language learning.

As mentioned earlier, our understanding of language and its relationship to behavior and culture is becoming increasingly important in our world today. In our current "global village," knowledge of more than one language has become a vital tool in understanding and communicating with people from other cultures. This is true within a pluralistic, multicultural society such as the United States as well as between people living in different nations. Also, no matter how important multilingualism is now, the future suggests that it will become even more important.

This recognition of the special relationships among language, culture, and behavior cannot be emphasized enough for psychology students in the United States. Our ignorance of languages other than English, and the unfortunate ethnocentrism that often accompanies this ignorance, may be the root of a future downfall. For many of us who have little exposure to these issues in our everyday lives, now is the time to begin our study of language, and culture, for a better understanding of the partners within our global village.

Glossary

Culture-affiliation hypothesis: The hypothesis that immigrant bilinguals will tend to affiliate themselves with the values and beliefs of the culture that are associated with the language in which they are currently operating. When the language is switched, so will the cultural values with which they affiliate.

Language Acquisition Device: A mechanism proposed by Chomsky that enables all normal children to learn language fluently.

Lexicon: The words contained in a language; also called *vocabulary*.

Minority group-affiliation hypothesis: The hypothesis that immigrant bilinguals will tend to self-identify as members of an ethnic minority group and/or adopt the behavioral stereotypes of the majority culture about their minority as their own when they are operating in the language associated with their minority group.

Morphemes: The smallest and most basic units of meaning in a language.

Phonemes: The smallest and most basic units of sound in a language.

Phonology: The system of rules governing how words should sound (pronunciation, accent) in a given language.

Pragmatics: The system of rules governing how language is used and understood in given social contexts.

Sapir-Whorf hypothesis: The hypothesis that the kind of language we speak influences the kinds of thought processes we have.

Semantics: What words mean.

Syntax and grammar: The system of rules governing word forms and how words should be strung together to form meaningful utterances.

References

Au, T. K. (1983). Chinese and English counterfactuals: The Sapir-Whorf hypothesis revisited. *Cognition, 15*, 155–187.

Au, T. K. (1984). Counterfactuals: In reply to Alfred Bloom. *Cognition, 17*, 289–302.

Berko, J. (1958). The child's learning of English morphology. *Word, 14*, 150–177.

Berko-Gleason, J. (Ed.). (1989). *The development of language* (2nd ed.). Columbus, OH: C. E. Merrill.

Berlin, B., & Kay, P. (1969). *Basic color terms: Their universality and evolution.* Berkeley: University of California Press.

Bickerton, D. (1981). *The roots of language.* Ann Arbor, MI: Karoma Publishers, 1981.

Bloom, A. H. (1981). *The linguistic shaping of thought: A study in the impact of language on thinking in China and the West.* Hillsdale, NJ: Erlbaum.

Brown, R., & Lenneberg, E. (1954). A study in language and cognition. *Journal of Abnormal and Social Psychology, 49*, 454–462.

Carroll, J. B., & Casagrande, J. B. (1958). The function of language classifications in behavior. In E. E. Maccoby, T. M. Newcomb, & E. L. Hartley (Eds.), *Readings in social psychology* (pp. 18–31). New York: Holt.

Chomsky, N. (1965). *Aspects of the theory of syntax.* Cambridge, MA: MIT Press.

Chomsky, N. (1967). *Current issues in linguistic theory.* The Hague: Mouton.

Chomsky, N. (1969). *Deep structure, surface structure, and semantic interpretation.* Bloomington, IL: Indiana University Linguistics Club.

De Valois, R. L., Abramov, I., & Jacobs, G. H. (1966). Analysis of response patterns of LGN cells. *Journal of the Optical Society of America, 56*, 966–977.

De Valois, R. L., & Jacobs, G. H. (1968). Primate color vision. *Science, 162*, 533–540.

Dinges, N. G., & Hull, P. (1992). Personality, culture, and international studies. In D. Lieberman (Ed.), *Revealing the world: An interdisciplinary reader for international studies*. Dubuque, IA: Kendall-Hunt, Inc.

Ervin, S. M. (1964). Language and TAT content in bilinguals. *Journal of Abnormal and Social Psychology, 68*, 500–507.

Fishman, J. A. (1960). A systematization of the Whorfian hypothesis. *Behavioral Science, 5*, 323–339.

Gleason, H. A. (1961). *An introduction to descriptive linguistics*. New York: Holt, Rinehart & Winston.

Heider, E. R., & Oliver, D. (1972). The structure of the color space in naming and memory for two languages. *Cognitive Psychology, 3*, 337–354.

Hull, P. V. (1987). *Bilingualism: Two languages, two personalities?* Resources in Education, Educational Resources Clearinghouse on Education. Ann Arbor: University of Michigan Press.

Hull, P. V. (1990a). Bilingualism: Two languages, two personalities? *Dissertation Abstracts International*. Ann Arbor: University of Michigan Press.

Hull, P. V. (August, 1990b). *Bilingualism and language choice*. Paper presented at the Annual Convention of the American Psychological Association. Boston, MA.

Hunt, E., & Agnoli, F. (1991). The Whorfian hypothesis: A cognitive psychology perspective. *Psychological Review, 98*, 377–389.

Kay, P., & Kempton, W. (1984). What is the Sapir-Whorf hypothesis? *American Anthropologist, 86*, 65–89.

Matsumoto, D., & Assar, M. (1992). The effects of language on judgments of universal facial expressions of emotion. *Journal of Nonverbal Behavior, 16*, 85–99.

Niyekawa-Howard, A. M. (1968). *A study of second language learning: The influence of first language on perception, cognition, and second language learning: A test of the Whorfian hypothesis*. Washington, DC: U. S. Dept. of Health, Education, and Welfare, Office of Education, Bureau of Research.

Ochs, E. (1988). *Culture and language development: Language acquisition and language socialization in a Samoan village*. Cambridge, MA: Cambridge University Press.

Ochs, E., & Schieffelin, B. B. (Eds.). (1979). *Developmental pragmatics*. New York: Academic Press.

Ochs, E., & Schieffelin, B. B. (1983). *Acquiring conversational competence*. London & Boston: Routledge & Kegan Paul.

Rosch, E. (1973). On the internal structure of perceptual categories. In T. E. Moore (Ed.), *Cognitive development and the acquisition of language* (pp. 111–144). San Diego, CA: Academic Press.

Schieffelin, B. B. (1981). *How Kaluli children learn what to say, what to do, and how to feel: An ethnographic study of the development of communicative competence*. Unpublished dissertation, University of California, San Diego.

Schieffelin, B. B. (1990). *The give and take of everyday life: Language socialization of Kaluli children.* New York: Cambridge University Press.
Schieffelin, B. B., & Ochs, E. (Eds.). (1986). *Language socialization across cultures.* Cambridge, MA: Cambridge University Press.

Suggested Readings

Bickerton, D. (1981). *The roots of language.* Ann Arbor, MI: Karoma Publishers.
Dinges, N. G., & Hull, P. V. (1993). Personality, culture, and international studies. In D. Lieberman (Ed.), *Revealing the world: An interdisciplinary reader for international studies.* Dubuque, IA: Kendall-Hunt, Inc.
Greenfield, P. M. (1972). Oral and written language: The consequences for cognitive development in Africa, the United States, and England. *Language and Speech, 15,* 169–178.
Hamers, J. F., & Blanc, M. H. A. (1989). *Bilinguality and bilingualism.* New York: Cambridge University Press.
Hunt, E., & Agnoli, F. (1991). The Whorfian hypothesis: A cognitive psychology perspective. *Psychological Review, 98,* 377–389.
Ochs, E. (1988). *Culture and language development: Language acquisition and language socialization in a Samoan village.* New York: Cambridge University Press.
Ristau, C. A., & Robbins, D. (1982). Language in the great apes: A critical review. *Advances in the Study of Behavior, 12,* 141–255.
Rosch, E. (1974). Linguistic relativity. In A. L. Silverstein (Ed.), *Human communication: Theoretical explanations.* New York: Halstead Press.

7

Cognitive Development and Intelligence

with

Philip Hull
Center for Psychological Studies

Psychologists have devoted considerable attention to examining how children learn to think and to defining and measuring intelligence. In many countries, intelligence tests determine whether one goes to college or is eligible for a particular job. Since IQ test scores can be a critical determinant of a person's life, it is important to interpret test results with care. This is particularly true when we attempt to measure intelligence cross-culturally. A person who is considered intelligent in one setting may be judged unfavorably in a context where different skills and behaviors are valued. The way in which mainstream U.S. culture has traditionally defined intelligence has also influenced how many view the process of cognitive development. Unfortunately, it has also sometimes led theorists to propose that people of certain cultures or ethnic groups are more intelligent than others.

In this chapter, we examine how definitions of intelligence vary from culture to culture and how psychologists have compared the thinking and cognitive development of people in different countries and minority groups. We present findings from anthropological, philosophical, and psychological studies across a range of cultures, subcultures, and societies. In reading this chapter, bear in mind the close relationship between the topic of this chapter and issues concerning language—namely, that the language used in the testing situation can influence test results (see Chapter 6 on cultural differences in language). For example, research has shown that some people score higher when tested in English rather than in their native language (Kelly & Philip, 1975); others fare better in their first language (Nyity, 1982). We will conclude this chapter with some thoughts about the need to understand intelligence in a broader sense, to integrate cross-cultural research in a theory that can explain why people around the world think and develop mental skills differently.

We begin by examining what is arguably the most important research on the subject of cognitive development in the 20th century—namely, that of the Swiss psychologist, Jean Piaget (Piaget, 1966, 1970; Piaget & Garcia, 1983). We will then look at recent cross-cultural research in psychology that challenges or enlarges upon some of Piaget's conclusions.

Piaget's Stage Theory of Cognitive Development

An Overview of Piaget's Theory

Cognitive development is a specialty in psychology that studies how thinking skills develop over time. Theories of cognitive development have traditionally focused on the period from infancy to adulthood. One theory has dominated this field for most of the 20th century—Piaget's stage theory of cognitive development.

Piaget based his theories on observations of Swiss children. He found that these children of various ages tended to solve problems quite differently. To explain these differences, Piaget proposed that children progress through four stages as they grow from infancy into adolescence:

1. **Sensorimotor stage:** This stage typically ranges from birth to about 2 years of age. Anxiety in the presence of strangers—stranger anxiety—is common during this period. The most important achievement of this stage is the acquisition of object permanency—that is, knowing that objects exist even when they cannot be seen. Early in this stage, children appear to assume that when a toy or other object is hidden (for example, when a ball rolls under a sofa), it ceases to exist. Later in this stage, children will search under the sofa for the lost ball, demonstrating that they have come to understand that objects exist continuously.

2. **Preoperational stage:** This stage ranges from about 2 to 6 or 7 years of age. Piaget defines this stage in terms of five characteristics: conservation, centration, irreversibility, egocentrism, and animism. *Conservation* is the awareness (or in this stage, the lack of such awareness) that physical quantities remain the same regardless of whether they change shape or appearance. *Centration* is the tendency to focus on a single aspect of a problem. *Irreversibility* is the inability to imagine "undoing" a process. *Egocentrism* is the inability to step into

another's shoes and understand the other person's point of view. *Animism* is the belief that all things, including inanimate things, are alive. For example, children in the preoperational stage might regard a book lying on its side as "tired" or "needing a rest," or they might think that the moon is following them as they walk.

3. **Concrete operations stage:** This stage lasts from about 6 or 7 years until about 11 years of age. During this stage, children acquire new thinking skills to work with actual objects and events. They are able to imagine undoing an action, and they can focus on more than one feature of a problem. Children also begin to understand that there are points of view different from their own. This new awareness helps children master the principle of conservation. A child in the concrete operations stage will understand that six apples are always six apples, regardless of how they are grouped or spaced, and that the amount of clay does not change as a lump is molded into different shapes. However, instead of thinking a problem through, children in this stage tend to rely on trial-and-error strategies.

4. **Formal operations stage:** This stage extends from around 11 years of age through adulthood. During this stage, individuals develop the ability to think logically about abstract concepts such as peace, freedom, and justice. Individuals also become more systematic and thoughtful in their approach to problem solving.

The transition from one stage to another is often gradual, as children develop new abilities alongside earlier ways of thinking. Thus, the behavior of some children may represent a "blend" of two stages during periods when the children are in a state of transition from one stage to another.

Piaget did not merely describe four stages of cognitive development; he also proposed a theory to explain how children progress from one stage to the next. Piaget hypothesized that two primary mechanisms are responsible: assimilation and accommodation. **Assimilation** is the process of fitting new ideas into a pre-existent understanding of the world. **Accommodation** refers to the process of changing one's understanding to accommodate ideas that conflict with existing concepts.

Piaget's Stage Theory in Cross-Cultural Perspective

Piaget's theory contains several assumptions and postulates that can be challenged from a cross-cultural standpoint. These challenges include:

1. Do the four stages according to Piaget always occur in the order in which he postulated? For example, cultures may differ in this ordering.

2. Are the age ranges associated with each stage as postulated by Piaget universal to all cultures? Infants and children from different cultures may enter and leave the different stages at different ages.

3. Are there variations within stages across cultures? It is possible that cultures may differ in the exact content or representation of knowledge in any one given stage.

4. Finally, do all cultures view scientific reasoning as the ultimate end point in development? Cultures may actually differ in their desired end points.

Fortunately, there is sufficient cross-cultural research to help us explore each of these questions.

Do Piaget's stages occur in the same order in different cultures? Studies that have addressed this question have convincingly demonstrated that Piaget's stages occur in the same fixed order in other cultures. For instance, a large cross-cultural survey that tested children in Great Britain, Australia, Greece, and Pakistan demonstrated that schoolchildren in these different societies performed Piagetian tasks within the same stage of concrete operations (Shayer, Demetriou, & Perez, 1988). We do not find cultures where 4-year-olds typically lack an awareness of object permanency or where 5-year-olds understand the principle of conservation. Thus, we know that children from very different cultures do indeed learn groups of Piagetian tasks in a similar order.

Are the ages that Piaget associated with each stage of development the same in all cultures? Cross-cultural research to date has shown that there are surprising cultural variations in the ages at which children in different societies typically reach the third and fourth Piagetian stages. In some cases, there can be differences of as much as five or six years. However, it has often been overlooked that children may have the potential to solve tasks sooner than their answers would indicate. For example, a child in the concrete operations stage will typically give the first answer that comes to mind during a test. If the child comes from a culture in which children practice performing the task in question, then her answer is likely to be correct. If the child has never thought about the concept before, she may well utter the wrong answer and only later realize her mistake. When researchers checked for this possibility by administering tests a second time at the end of testing sessions, they found that many children corrected their previous answers on the second attempt (Dasen, Lavallee, and Retschitzki, 1979; Dasen, Ngini, and Lavallee, 1979; Dasen, 1982). Thus, the important point to remember from such findings is that performance on a task may not reveal actual cognitive potential or ability.

Are there cultural variations within—rather than between—Piaget's stages?
We know from research on several different societies that there is considerable cultural variation in the order in which children acquire specific skills within Piaget's stages. In a comparative study of tribal children (the Inuit of Canada, the Baoule of Africa, and the Aranda of Australia), half of all the Inuit children tested solved a spatial task at the age of 7 years; half of the Aranda solved it at 9 years; the Baoule, however, did not reach the half-point until the age of 12 years (Dasen, 1975). On a test of the conservation of liquids, the order changed dramatically: half of the Baoule children solved the problem when they were 8 years old, the Inuit at 9 years, and the Aranda at 12 years. Why did the ages at which these children could perform the same task vary so much? One reason is that the Inuit and Aranda children live in nomadic societies, where children need to learn spatial skills early because their families are constantly moving. The Baoule children, in contrast, live in a settled society, where they seldom travel but often fetch water and store grain. The skills that these children use in their everyday lives seem to have affected the order in which they were able to solve Piagetian tasks within the concrete operations stage.

Do non-Western cultures also regard scientific reasoning as the ultimate developmental end point? Piaget's theory assumes that the scientific reasoning associated with formal operations is the universal end point of cognitive development. In other words, Piaget assumed that the thinking most valued in Swiss and other Western societies (in formal operations) was the yardstick by which other cultures should be judged. Piaget considered scientific reasoning to be the ultimate achievement. His stage theory, therefore, is designed to retrace the steps by which people arrive at scientific thinking.

Cross-cultural research indicates that the answer to this question is clearly no. Different societies value and reward different skills and behaviors. For example, until recently the most respected scholars in traditional Islamic societies were religious leaders and poets. Although the Islamic educational system included science and mathematics, its primary goal was not to train people in the scientific method, but to transmit faith, general knowledge, and a deep appreciation for poetry and literature. People from such cultures could be expected to be at a disadvantage when confronted with advanced Piagetian tasks, which are drawn almost exclusively from Western physics, chemistry, and mathematics.

Many cultures around the world do not share the conviction that abstract, hypothetical thought processes are the ultimate or desired end point in cognitive development. Many cultures, for example, consider cognitive development to be more relational, involving the thinking skills and processes to engage in successful interpersonal contexts. What

Americans consider to be "common sense," and not cognitive development per se, is often considered a much more desired outcome in many cultures. This is especially true among cultures that are more collectivistic and group oriented than are American and other Western cultures. In fact, high-level, individualistic, abstract thinking is often frowned upon in such collectivistic cultures.

We have seen how important it is to carefully evaluate the meaning of cross-cultural studies of Piaget's stage of formal operations. In some cultures very few people are able to complete fourth-stage Piagetian tasks. Does this mean that entire cultures are suspended at a lower stage of cognitive development? To answer this question, one must first be able to show that Piagetian tasks are a culturally appropriate way of measuring an advanced stage of cognitive development. Unfortunately, such tests may not always be meaningful in a given culture. Besides the issue of cultural appropriateness, there is also the issue of what is being tested. Tests of formal operations can tell us whether people can solve a narrow range of scientific problems, but they do not tell us whether people in different cultures develop advanced cognitive skills in areas other than those selected by Piaget. We can say with certainty, however, that people who have not attended high school or college in a Westernized school system perform very poorly on tests of formal operations (Laurendeau-Bendavid, 1977; Shea, 1985). This again raises the question of the degree to which Piagetian tasks depend on previous knowledge and cultural values rather than on cognitive skills.

It is also important to remember that there are considerable differences in cognitive development within any one culture. These within-culture differences, in turn, make it extremely difficult to draw valid conclusions or inferences about differences in cognitive development between cultures. For example, not only will members of non-Western cultures have difficulty with tests of formal operations; many adults in our own society also have such difficulties. Scientific reasoning does not appear to be as common in Western societies as Piaget thought, and it is frequently limited to special activities. For example, individuals who apply scientific logic to a problem on the job may reason quite differently in other situations.

Given the fact that large numbers of people are unable to complete Piagetian tasks of formal operations, it has not been possible to demonstrate the universality of the fourth stage of Piaget's theory of cognitive development. It is possible that most adults possess the potential to complete Piagetian tasks but fail to do so because they lack either the motivation (or knowledge of how) to demonstrate such ability. To successfully demonstrate success on a task purporting to measure some aspect of cognitive ability or intelligence, the test-taker and the test-maker must agree on what is being assessed. Cultural differences in the ultimate desired end points of cognitive development (as we discussed earlier), as well as cultural differences in definitions of intelligence (discussed later in this chapter), all contribute to this dilemma.

Other Stage Theories of Cognitive Development

In broadening our perspective on Piaget's stage theory of cognitive development, it is important to note that Piaget's theory is only one of several stage theories that have been proposed by social scientists in the West. One of the earliest stage theories, for example, was proposed by the 18th-century German philosopher, Hegel. Hegel ranked all societies on an evolutionary scale based on a classification of religious beliefs with Christianity at the top. Stage theories multiplied in the 19th century after Darwin's theory of evolution became well-known. Several writers (for example, Tylor, 1865; Spencer, 1876) proposed that humanity had progressed from savagery to civilization in a series of stages.

One of the most influential stage theories of the early 20th century was proposed by the French philosopher, Levy-Bruhl (1910, 1922, 1949). As did earlier scholars, Levy-Bruhl drew most of his conclusions from material related to the mystical and religious beliefs of non-Western peoples. Levy-Bruhl proposed the theory that there is a "great divide" between the thought of Westerners and that of people who live in primitive societies. He described non-Western peoples as having a distinct way of thinking, which he attributed to the effects of culture. According to Levy-Bruhl, non-Westerners are not bothered by logical contradictions, and they lack a clear sense of individual identity.

More recently, some scientists have suggested new "great divide" theories (Goody, 1968, 1977; Luria, 1976; Hippler, 1980). Although these researchers have various names for the two groups, their division of humanity breaks down along similar lines. In all these theories, the cultural development or thought of non-Westerners is usually judged to be deficient or inferior to that of Europeans.

Several points need to be made about these other stage theories. It is probably more than coincidence that stage theories produced by Westerners seem to judge people from other cultures (and minorities within Western countries) in terms of how closely they resemble Westerners, thereby placing Westerners at a relatively superior level of development. The popularity of stage theories in the 19th century, for example, coincided with the colonial imperialism of the period. Stage theories provided a justification for the imposition of European rule around the world, because it could be said that scholars had convincingly demonstrated the superiority of European civilization.

Stage theorists also persisted in evaluating the rationality of non-Westerners in terms of their magical and religious beliefs, whereas the rationality of Western beliefs was usually not questioned. Levy-Bruhl's theory has been fiercely attacked over the years by field anthropologists, who object to both his methodology and conclusions. Levy-Bruhl based his work on stories told by missionaries and travelers, many of whom could barely speak the native languages.

To keep things in proper perspective, however, we should note that ethnocentric assumptions are not unique to Westerners. Cross-cultural studies have shown that people from many cultures prefer their own groups and rate them more positively than they rate outsiders. For example, one study compared what people in 30 different East African societies thought of themselves and others. The researchers demonstrated that members of each society rated themselves highly and judged outsiders to be "advanced" when they were culturally similar to their own group (Brewer & Campbell, 1976).

Despite the cross-cultural limitations to Piaget's theory, it is important to keep several strong points in mind. Piaget's theory is considerably more sophisticated than earlier stage theories. By devising tasks to measure concepts in an experimental setting, Piaget established a new standard of proof—one that seems to be much less vulnerable to ethnocentric bias. Piaget's tests can be, and have been, administered cross-culturally, with clear-cut results that do not rest upon the subjective beliefs of the researcher. Still, there are some ethnocentric assumptions in Piaget's theory, which we have discussed, especially regarding the importance he assigned to a handful of specific tasks in establishing his theory of stages. Cognitive development is complicated, and it is unlikely that such tasks can capture all of its complexity. Although such tasks reflect skills that are highly valued in the United States and other Western cultures, it is not clear that they play a significant role in cognitive development in all cultures for all people.

Intelligence: Definitions and Concepts

Traditional Definitions of Intelligence in American Psychology

The English word *intelligence* originates in a Latin word that was coined 2000 years ago by the Roman orator Cicero. In the United States, we use the term **intelligence** to refer to a number of different abilities, skills, talents, and knowledge, generally all referring to mental or cognitive abilities. Thus, we traditionally consider several processes to represent intelligence, such as memory (how well and how much one can remember for how long); vocabulary (how many words one knows and can use properly); comprehension (how well one can understand a passage or set of ideas or statements); mathematical abilities (addition, subtraction, and so on); logical reasoning (how well one can understand underlying logic or sequence among events, things, or objects); and the like.

In recent years, interest in the concept of creativity as a part of intelligence has grown. Until very recently, creativity was not considered a part of intelligence per se. Now, however, psychologists are increasingly considering this important aspect of one's abilities as a type of intelligence.

Likewise, other aspects of intelligence are also coming to the forefront. Gardner and Hatch (1989), for example, suggested that there are really seven different types of intelligence: logical mathematical, linguistic, musical, spatial, bodily-kinesthetic, interpersonal, and intrapersonal. According to this scheme, not only are the core components of each of the seven different types of intelligence different, but so also are sample end states (such as mathematician versus dancer).

Despite the fact that these various types of intelligence have added a new dimension of diversity to our definitions of intelligence, our traditional, mainstream definitions of intelligence still tend to center on cognitive and mental capabilities in verbal and mathematical tasks.

Cultural Differences in the Meaning and Concept of Intelligence

Many languages have no word that corresponds to our idea of intelligence. Definitions of intelligence often reflect cultural values. The closest Mandarin equivalent, for instance, is a Chinese character that means good brain and talented. Chinese people often associate this with traits such as imitation, effort, and social responsibility (Keats, 1982). Such traits do not constitute important elements of intelligence for most mainstream Americans.

The Baganda of East Africa use the word *obugezi* to refer to a combination of mental and social skills that make a person steady, cautious, and friendly (Wober, 1974). The Djerma-Sonhai in West Africa use a term that has an even broader meaning, *lakkal*, which is a combination of intelligence, know-how, and social skills (Bisilliat, Laya, Pierre, & Pidoux, 1967). Still another society, the Baoule, uses the term *n'glouele*, which describes children who are not only mentally alert but also willing to volunteer their services without being asked (Dasen et al., 1985).

Because of such enormous differences in the ways in which cultures define intelligence, it is difficult to make valid comparisons of this notion of intelligence from one society to another. People in different cultures not only disagree about the very nature of what intelligence is, but they also have very different attitudes about the proper way to demonstrate one's abilities. In some cultures such as the mainstream U.S. society, individuals are typically rewarded for displaying knowledge and skills. This same behavior may be considered improper, arrogant, or rude in societies that stress personal relationships, cooperation, and modesty.

These points are important to cross-cultural studies of intelligence because successful performance on a task of intelligence may require behavior that is considered immodest and arrogant in culture A (and therefore only reluctantly displayed by members of culture A) but desirable in culture B (and therefore readily displayed by members of culture B). Clearly, such different attitudes toward the same behavior can result in inaccurate conclusions about differences in intelligence between culture A and culture B.

It is also difficult to compare intelligence cross-culturally for another reason. Namely, because tests of intelligence often rely on knowledge that is particular to a culture, investigators who are based in another culture may not know what to test for. A test designed for one culture is often not suitable for another, even when the test is carefully translated into a second language. For example, one U.S. intelligence test includes the following question: "How does a violin resemble a piano?" Clearly, this question assumes prior knowledge about violins and pianos, which is a reasonable expectation of middle-class Americans, but not of cultures that use other musical instruments.

Much cross-cultural research on intelligence has focused on the issue of testing within multicultural societies, where cultural minorities are evaluated with tests designed for a dominant culture. Cross-cultural research extends, therefore, not only to cultures in different countries, but also to subcultures within Western society. In the next section we will examine some of the problems involved in defining and measuring intelligence cross-culturally.

Cultural Influences on the Measurement of Intelligence

Modern intelligence tests were first developed in the early 1900s for the purpose of identifying mentally retarded children. Intelligence tests provided a way of distinguishing children who were in need of special education from those whose schoolwork suffered for other reasons. In the years that followed, intelligence tests came into widespread use in public schools and other government programs.

Not everyone, however, benefited from the new tests of intelligence. Because such tests relied at least in part on verbal performance and cultural knowledge, immigrants who spoke English poorly and came from different cultural backgrounds were at a disadvantage. For example, when tests of intelligence were administered to immigrants at Ellis Island beginning in 1913, over three-quarters of the Italian, Hungarian, and Jewish immigrants tested as mentally defective. Such low scores for certain immigrant groups provoked a storm of controversy. Some people defended the scientific nature of the new tests, charging that southern

European immigrants were not fit to enter the country. Others responded that intelligence tests were biased and did not accurately measure the mental abilities of people from different cultures. Thus, less than a decade after the invention of intelligence tests, the testing of people from different cultures became a matter of political controversy.

As we approach the end of the 20th century, such controversy has not yet been laid to rest. The debate surrounding the interpretation of test scores of groups who do not belong to the dominant culture continues today, although the groups of people scoring low on standard tests have changed. The average scores of some minority groups in the United States are 12–15% lower than the average observed for Caucasians. This does not mean that *all* the individuals in these groups test poorly; high-scoring individuals can be found in minority subcultures. It simply means that larger percentages of the minority populations score low. In a controversy that has come to be known as the "nature versus nurture" debate, people have sharply differed in their interpretations of these scores. This debate is very important in psychology in general and in cross-cultural psychology in particular.

The nature side of the debate argues that differences in IQ scores among different societies and ethnic groups are mainly due to inborn nature or heredity. Arthur Jensen (1969, 1980, 1981) is one of the most well-known proponents of this position. He believes that about 80% of a person's intelligence is inherited, and he suggests that biological differences explain the gap between the scores of whites and those of ethnic minorities in the United States. Jensen argues that special programs for the underprivileged are a waste of money because inborn intellectual deficiencies of ethnic minorities are the reason for their poor performance on IQ tests.

Studies of twins have provided some evidence for the nature hypothesis. The most important of these studies compared identical twins who grew up in separate homes to fraternal twins raised together (Bouchard & McGue, 1981). If intelligence test scores are determined by heredity, then identical twins raised apart should have very similar scores. But if environment is the primary determinant, then the scores of the fraternal twins raised together should be more similar. These twin studies revealed that the scores of identical twins raised in different environments were significantly more alike than those of fraternal twins raised together. However, the scores of identical twins raised apart varied more than those of identical twins raised together.

These mixed results have been used by both sides. On the nature side, the results have been interpreted to support the claim that as much as 80% of intelligence is genetic, whereas opponents give considerably lower estimates. There is widespread agreement, however, that at least 40% of intelligence can be attributed to heredity (Henderson, 1982; Jencks et al., 1972).

The nurture side of the debate argues that culture and environment fully account for the difference in IQ scores between whites and minorities in the United States. Those who hold this position claim that minorities score lower because most subcultures in this country are economically deprived (Blau, 1981; Wolf, 1965). Advocates of this position have turned to studies showing that IQ scores are strongly related to social class. The average IQ score of poor whites, for instance, is 10–20% lower than the average score of the middle class. The effect of environment on intelligence test scores can be seen most clearly in studies that show that poor whites tested in Southern states scored lower than blacks in Northern states.

As we have seen from our discussion of cognitive development, it is also possible that differences in intelligence scores between groups are the result of (1) different beliefs about what intelligence is or (2) culturally inappropriate measures of intelligence. What we do know is that intelligence tests are a good predictor of the verbal skills necessary for success in the culture that is associated with the formalized educational systems of modern industrial societies and increasingly adopted as a model throughout the world. However, such tests may not measure motivation, creativity, talent, or social skills, all of which are important factors in achievement.

Another view held by some cross-cultural psychologists is that intelligence tests do measure true differences among societies, but that such differences should not be regarded as deficiencies of one culture as compared with another.

Regardless of how we interpret cross-cultural differences in measured intelligence, we should respect the values of other cultures. Indeed, we would be well advised to consider the evaluation of intelligence in another culture according to that culture's own definition of intelligence.

Conclusion

The material presented in this chapter has made it quite clear that cultures differ in their definitions of cognitive development and intelligence. How any one culture may define what is "intelligent" may not be the same as how another culture defines intelligence. For this reason, the signs or behaviors that one can typically use to measure intelligence will differ among cultures. Displaying one's skills, talents, or abilities on some tasks, questions, or activities may be desirable in some cultures. The same behavior, however, may be frowned upon in other cultures as rude, arrogant, inappropriate, or immature.

Cross-cultural research on Piaget's theory, however, has also shown considerable cultural similarities, as well as differences, in the manner by which people progress through the various stages of cognitive development. These similarities have to do with the nature of the stages through which people progress in developing their abstract reasoning skills and in the general age ranges associated with each of the stages. Cross-cultural research, however, has also shown differences within the stages and has questioned whether abstract, scientific reasoning is the ultimate end point of cognitive development.

Issues concerning cultural differences—and similarities—in definitions and processes of intelligence are particularly relevant in certain settings today. Many current curriculum reform movements in the United States, for example, are based on a particular view and definition of intelligence and cognitive development. It is not uncommon to hear allegations of cultural bias in these types of educational reform. Indeed, if sweeping educational changes are implemented without recognition of deeply imbedded cultural differences in the nature and definition of intelligence, even within the United States, then the educational system may see even wider gaps between groups and increasing, rather than decreasing, intergroup conflict on "education."

The material presented in this chapter strongly questions previous conclusions about cultural, racial, or ethnic differences in intelligence. The research makes it clear that many questions about differences in the definitions of intelligence and about the close relationship among culture, language, and intelligence need to be addressed before we can draw valid conclusions about intergroup differences in intelligence. Perhaps we need to consider yet another aspect of intelligence—that is, our attitudes regarding intelligence. A cross-cultural understanding of differences in the definitions and processes of intelligence should help to deepen our appreciation and respect for definitions of intelligence that are different from our own.

Glossary

Accommodation: The process of changing one's understanding to accommodate ideas that conflict with existing concepts.

Assimilation: The process of fitting new ideas into a pre-existent understanding of the world.

Concrete operations stage: The third stage of Piaget's theory of cognitive development, typically ranging from about 6 or 7 years until about 11 years of age. This stage is characterized by the acquisition of new thinking skills to work with actual objects and events, including the concept of conservation and mental undoing.

Formal operations stage: The fourth and last stage of Piaget's theory of cognitive development, extending from around 11 years of age through adulthood. During this stage, individuals develop the ability to think logically .about abstract concepts.

Intelligence: In the United States, intelligence refers to a number of different abilities, skills, talents, and knowledge, generally all referring to mental or cognitive abilities.

Preoperational stage: The second stage of Piaget's theory of cognitive development, typically ranging from about 2 to 6 or 7 years of age. It is characterized by lack of conservation, centration, irreversibility, egocentrism, and animism.

Sensorimotor stage: The first stage of Piaget's theory of cognitive development, typically ranging from birth to about 2 years of age. It is characterized by stranger anxiety and the acquisition of object permanency.

References

Bisilliat, J., Laya, D., Pierre, E., & Pidoux, C. (1967). La notion de lakkal dans la culture Djerma-Songhai [The concept of lakkal in Djerma-Songhai culture]. *Psychopathologie Africaine, 3,* 207–264.

Blau, Z. S. (1981). *Black children–white children: Competence, socialization, and social structure.* New York: Free Press.

Bouchard, T. J., Jr., & McGue, M. (1981). Familial studies of intelligence: A review. *Science, 212,* 1055–1059.

Brewer, M. B., & Campbell, D. T. (1976). *Ethnocentrism and intergroup attitudes.* New York: John Wiley.

Dasen, P. R. (1975). Concrete operational development in three cultures. *Journal of Cross-Cultural Psychology, 6,* 156–172.

Dasen, P. R. (1982). Cross-cultural aspects of Piaget's theory: The competence/performance model. In L. L. Adler (Ed.), *Cross-cultural research at issue* (pp. 163–170). New York: Academic Press.

Dasen, P. R., Dembele, B., Ettien, K., Kabran, K., Kamagate, D., Koffi, D. A., & N'Guessan, A. (1985). N'glouele, l'intelligence chez les Baoule [N'glouele: Intelligence among the Ivory Coast Baoule]. *Archives de Psychologie, 53,* 293–324.

Dasen, P. R., Lavallee, M., & Retschitzki, J. (1979). Training conservation of quantity (liquids) in West African (Baoule) children. *International Journal of Psychology, 14,* 57–68.

Dasen, P. R., Ngini, L., & Lavallee, M. (1979). Cross-cultural training studies of concrete operations. In L. Eckensberger, Y. Poortinga, & W. Lonner (Eds.), *Cross-cultural contributions to psychology* (pp. 94–104). Amsterdam: Swets & Zeitlinger.

Gardner, H., & Hatch, T. (1989). Multiple intelligence go to school: Educational implications of the theory of multiple intelligences. *Educational Researcher, 18,* 4–10.

Goody, J. R. (1968). *Literacy in traditional societies*. Cambridge: Cambridge University Press.

Goody, J. R. (1977). *The domestication of the savage mind*. Cambridge: Cambridge University Press.

Henderson, N. D. (1982). Human behavior genetics. *Annual Review of Psychology, 33*, 403–440.

Hippler, A. E. (1980). Editorial. *International Association of Cross-Cultural Psychology Newsletter, 14*, 2–3.

Jencks, C., Smith, M., Acland, H., Bane, M. J., Cohen, D., Gintis, H., Heyns, B., & Michaelson, S. (1972). *Inequality: A reassessment of the effect of family and schooling in America*. New York: Harper & Row.

Jensen, A. R. (1969). How much can we boost IQ and scholastic achievement? *Harvard Educational Review, 39*, 1–123.

Jensen, A. R. (1980). *Bias in mental testing*. New York: Free Press.

Jensen, A. R. (1981). *Straight talk about mental tests*. London: Methuen.

Keats, D. M. (1982). Cultural bases of concepts of intelligence: A Chinese versus Australian comparison. In P. Sukontasarp, N. Yongsiri, P. Intasuwan, N. Jotiban, & C. Suvannathat (Eds.), *Proceedings of the Second Asian Workshop on Child and Adolescent Development* (pp. 67–75). Bangkok: Burapasilpa Press.

Kelly, M., & Philip, H. (1975). Vernacular test instructions in relation to cognitive task behavior among highland children of Papua New Guinea. *British Journal of Educational Psychology, 45*, 189–197.

Laurendeau-Bendavid, M. (1977). Culture, schooling, and cognitive development: A comparative study of children in French Canada and Rwanda. In P. R. Dasen (Ed.), *Piagetian psychology: Cross-cultural contributions* (pp. 123–168). New York: Gardner/Wiley.

Levy-Bruhl, L. (1910). *Les fonctions mentales dans les societes inferieures*. Paris: Alcan. [Trans., 1928, *How natives think*. London: Allen & Unwin.]

Levy-Bruhl, L. (1922). *Mentalite primitive*. Paris: Alcan. [L. A. Clare, Trans., 1923, *Primitive mentality*. London: Allen & Unwin.]

Levy-Bruhl, L. (1949). *Les carnets de Lucien Levy-Bruhl*. [*The notebooks of Lucien Levy-Bruhl*.] Paris: Presses Universitaires de France.

Luria, A. R. (1976). *Cognitive development: Its cultural and social foundations* (M. Lopez Morillas and L. Solotaroff, Trans.). Cambridge, MA: Harvard University Press. (Original work published 1974)

Nyiti, R. M. (1982). The validity of "cultural differences explanations" for cross-cultural variation in the rate of Piagetian cognitive development. In D. A. Wagner & H. W. Stevenson (Eds.), *Cultural perspectives on child development* (pp. 146–165). San Francisco: W. H. Freeman.

Piaget, J. (1966). Necessite et signification des recherches comparatives en psychologie genetique. *Journal International de Psychologie, 1*, 3–13. [(1974) Need and significance of crosscultural studies in genetic psychology (C. Dasen, Trans.). In J. W. Berry & P. R. Dasen (Eds.), *Culture and cognition* (pp. 299–309). London: Methuen.]

Piaget, J. (1970). Piaget's theory. In P. H. Mussen (Ed.), *Carmichael's manual of child psychology* (Vol. I, 3rd ed.) (pp. 703–732). New York: John Wiley.

Piaget, J. (1972). Intellectual evolution from adolescence to adulthood. *Human Development, 15,* 1–12.

Piaget, J., & Garcia, R. (1983). *Psychogenese et histoire des sciences [Developmental psychology and the history of sciences].* Paris: Flammarion.

Shayer, M., Demetriou, A., & Perez, M. (1988). The structure and scaling of concrete operational thought: Three studies in four countries and only one story. *Genetic Psychology Monographs, 114,* 307–376.

Shea, J. D. (1985). Studies of cognitive development in Papua New Guinea. *International Journal of Psychology, 20,* 33–61.

Spencer, H. (1876). *Principles of sociology.* New York: D. Appleton.

Tylor, E. B. (1865). *Researches into the early history of mankind and development of civilization.* London: John Murray.

Wober, M. (1974). Towards an understanding of the Kiganda concept of intelligence. In J. W. Berry & P. R. Dasen (Eds.), *Culture and cognition* (pp. 261–280). London: Methuen.

Wolf, R. M. (1965). The measurement of environments. In C. W. Harris (Ed.), *Proceedings of the 1964 Invited Conference on Testing Problems.* Princeton, NJ: Educational Testing Service, Inc.

Suggested Readings

Dasen, P. R. (1975). Concrete operational development in three cultures. *Journal of Cross-Cultural Psychology, 6,* 156–172.

Kelly, M., & Philip, H. (1975). Vernacular test instructions in relation to cognitive task behavior among highland children of Papua New Guinea. *British Journal of Educational Psychology, 45,* 189–197.

Nyiti, R. M. (1982). The validity of "cultural differences explanations" for cross-cultural variation in the rate of Piagetian cognitive development. In D. A. Wagner & H. W. Stevenson (Eds.), *Cultural perspectives on child development* (pp. 146–165). San Francisco: W. H. Freeman.

Piaget, J. (1970). Piaget's theory. In P. H. Mussen (Ed.), *Carmichael's manual of child psychology* (Vol. I, 3rd ed.) (pp. 703–732). New York: John Wiley.

Emotion

The importance of emotion in human life and behavior is widely accepted in psychology today. Emotions color life events, giving them meaning. Emotional experiences can also be important motivators of behavior. The display of emotion is important in communication and plays an important role in social interaction.

In this chapter, we examine how the definitions of emotion—as well as the expression, perception, elicitors, and physiological sensations of emotion—vary in people of different cultural backgrounds. We present findings from both anthropological and psychological studies across a wide range of cultures and societies. We also look at studies on cross-racial differences in emotion within the United States. We conclude with a preview of what a cross-cultural theory of emotion would look like and argue its importance in learning about psychology today.

Traditional Theories and Views of Emotion

When we think of emotion, one or two things usually come to mind. One is the experience of emotion—that is, our subjective, inner feeling state. The second is our expressions of emotion, through voice, face, language, or gestures. In fact, these two aspects of emotion are usually how the psychological study of emotion is introduced to psychology students. One focuses on the *experience* or *feeling* of emotion and how it is elicited or brought forth. The second focuses on the *expression* or *display*

117

of emotion—that is, how the experience is shown. Let us briefly examine some of the major characteristics of these two approaches.

There are several major theories of emotional experience, many of which are presented in introductory psychology. One of the most prevalent theories, for example, is the **James/Lange theory**. This theory suggests that the experience of emotion results from one's perception of physiological (autonomic) arousal and overt behavior. Thus, you see a bear and run; your interpretation of your running (breathing, heart rate, and so on) produces the emotional experience of fear.

In contrast, the **Cannon/Bard theory** of emotion argues that autonomic arousal is too slow to account for changes in emotional experience. Instead, conscious emotional experience results from direct stimulation of brain centers in the cortex.

The **Schachter/Singer theory** of emotion is a commonly presented theory that focuses on the role of cognitive interpretation. This theory suggests that emotional experiences depend solely on one's interpretation of the environment in which one is being aroused. According to this theory, emotions are not differentiated physiologically. Instead, what is important in the production of emotional experience is how one interprets the events around oneself. Emotion is the labeling of the arousal or behavior in that situation.

Several theories on the expression of emotion are generally presented in introductory psychology, including Ekman's, Izard's, Tomkins's, and Plutchik's. Tomkins's theory, for example, suggests that emotions are evolutionarily adaptive and that their expression is biologically innate and universal to all people of all cultures and ethnicities. Research done by Ekman (1972) and Izard (1971) has shown how at least six facial expressions of emotion are pancultural or universal—anger, disgust, fear, happiness, sadness, and surprise.

Despite differences among these theories, there is considerable similarity across them in their *implied* view of emotion. All, for example, suggest a central role for the subjective experience of emotion—one's inner feelings. The James/Lange, Cannon/Bard, and Schachter/Singer theories are all attempts to explain the nature of that subjective, inner state we call emotion. Evolutionary theories based on emotional expressions also posit a central role for inner feelings, as emotional expressions are outward displays of that inner experience.

Another common theme across emotion theories is the importance of emotion labeling, or what we call an emotion. The James/Lange, Cannon/Bard, and Schachter/Singer theories, for example, all suggest that the labeling process is an important and integral part of emotion. Evolutionary theories of emotion are, for the most part, based on studies relying on the labeling of facial expressions of emotion as evidence for universality.

These two similarities—the focus on inner, subjective experience and the importance of labeling—are "givens" in the way American academics and laypersons alike speak of emotion. These issues "define" emotions in two important ways—what it is and what we call it. This view of emotions probably makes good, intuitive sense to many of us. Still, this way of understanding emotion may be a particularly Western—or even more specifically, an American—way of understanding emotions. Not all cultures view emotions this way.

Cultural Differences in Defining and Understanding Emotion

Even before we examine how people of different cultures may be similar or different in their emotions, we need to consider whether different cultures define and understand emotion in the same way. Recently, Russell (1991) reviewed much of the cross-cultural and anthropological literature on emotion concepts and concluded that cultures do indeed differ, sometimes considerably, in their definitions and understanding of emotion. Russell's excellent review of this topic provides a strong basis by which to address this question.

The Concept and Definition of Emotion

When we discuss human emotions in American psychology, we often presuppose that what we are talking about is the same for all people. Indeed, studies spanning many, different cultures suggest that most cultures have a concept of emotion. Brandt and Boucher (1986), for example, studied the concepts of depression in eight different cultures. The languages studied included Indonesian, Japanese, Korean, Malaysian, Spanish, and Sinhalese. Each of the languages had a word for emotion, suggesting cross-cultural existence of the concept of emotion.

But not all cultures of the world have the concept of emotion. Levy (1973, 1983), for example, suggests that Tahitians do not have a word for emotion. Lutz (1980, as reported in Russell, 1991, and Lutz, 1983) also suggests that the Ifaluks of Micronesia do not have a word for emotion. Perhaps the word for, and thus concept of, emotion is particular only to certain types of cultures.

Even among cultures that have a word for emotion, the word may not have the same meaning as the English word. For example, Matsuyama, Hama, Kawamura, and Mine (1978) analyzed emotional words in the Japanese language, including some words that are typically considered emotions (such as *angry* and *sad*). Some words included in the study, however, are words that Americans might question as to whether they denote emotion (such as *considerate* and *lucky*). Samoans do not have a word for emotion, but do have a word (*lagona*) that refers to feelings and sensations (Gerber, 1975, as reported in Russell, 1991).

Thus, not all cultures in the world have a word representing the concept of emotion, and even among those that do, not all concepts of emotion are equivalent.

The Categorization or Labeling of Emotion

People in different cultures also categorize or label emotions differently. Some English words, such as *anger, joy, sadness, liking,* and *loving,* have equivalents in different languages and cultures. But there are many English words that have no equivalents in another culture. There are also emotion words in other languages that have no exact English equivalents.

In German, for example, the word *schadenfreude* refers to pleasure derived from another's misfortunes. There is no exact English translation of this word. The Japanese language includes words such as *itoshii, ijirashii,* and *amae.* These also have no exact English translation but are loosely translated, respectively, as longing for an absent loved one, a feeling associated with seeing someone praiseworthy overcoming an obstacle, and dependence.

Conversely, some African languages have one word that covers what the English language suggests are two emotions—anger and sadness (Leff, 1973). Likewise, Lutz (1980) suggests that the Ifaluk word *song* can be described sometimes as anger and sometimes as sadness.

Some English words have no equivalents in other languages. The English words *terror, horror, dread, apprehension,* and *timidity* are all referred to by a single word (*gurakadj*) in Gidjingali, an Australian aboriginal language (Hiatt, 1978). This aboriginal word also refers to the English concepts of shame and fear. *Frustration* is a word that may have no exact equivalent in Arabic languages (Russell, 1991).

Such language differences across cultures suggest that different cultures divide the world of emotion differently. Thus, not only are the concepts of emotion culture bound, but so also are the ways in which each culture attempts to frame and label its emotion world.

The Location of Emotion

One of the most important components of emotion in American psychology is the inner, subjective experience of emotion. But the importance placed on inner feelings, and the importance of introspection (looking inside oneself), may be culture bound by American psychology. Other cultures can, and do, view emotions as originating or residing somewhere else.

For example, emotion words in the languages of several Oceanic peoples, such as the Samoans (Gerber, 1975), Pintupi Aborigines (Myers,

1979), and Solomon Islanders (White, 1980), are statements about relationships among people or between people and events. Likewise, Riesman (1977) suggests that the African Fulani's concept of *semteende*, which is commonly translated as shame or embarrassment, refers more to a situation than to a feeling. That is, someone is in a state of *semteende* if the situation is appropriate to *semteende*, regardless of what one feels (Russell, 1991).

In the United States, we place matters of emotion and inner feelings in the heart. Even among cultures that do locate emotions within the body, the exact location differs. The Japanese, for example, identify many of their emotions in the *hara*—the gut or abdomen. The Chewong of Malay group feelings and thoughts in the liver (Howell, 1981). Levy (1984) suggests that Tahitians believe emotions arise from the intestines. Lutz (1982) suggests that the closest Ifaluk word to the English *emotion* is *niferash*, which she translates as "our insides."

Thus, our understanding of even the location of emotions seems to be bound by culture. Cultural differences in concept, definition, labeling, and location of emotions all produce differences in the meaning of emotion to people and in their behaviors across cultures.

Cultural Differences in the Meaning of Emotions to People and in Behavior

In American psychology, emotions have enormous *personal* meaning, perhaps because American psychology views inner, subjective feelings as the major defining characteristic of emotion. Once one defines emotions in such a way, a major role of emotion is to inform oneself about oneself. Our self-definitions—that is, the ways by which we define and identify ourselves—are all informed by our emotions, as they are personal, private, inner experiences.

Cultures differ, however, in the role played by the emotions. Many cultures, for example, consider emotions as statements of the relationship between people and their environment; the environment includes both things and social relationships with other people. Emotions for both the Ifaluks of Micronesia (Lutz, 1982) and the Tahitians (Levy, 1984), for instance, denote statements of social relationships and the physical environment. The Japanese concept of *amae*, which is typically considered a central emotion in the Japanese culture, specifies an interdependent relationship between two people. Views of emotion as social constructions have not been totally absent in American psychology (for example, Averill, 1980), but they have received considerably less attention in mainstream academic psychology than views that center on the introspection of subjective feeling states.

Cross-Cultural Psychological Research on Emotion

The previous section made it clear that, although there is considerable consistency across cultures in the concept, labeling, location, and meaning of emotion, there are also many cultural differences as well. Most of that evidence came from the anthropological literature and in-depth ethnographies of individual cultures and societies. In this section, we examine some findings from cross-cultural research in psychology on the emotions.

Psychological research on emotion across cultures differs from anthropological studies and ethnographies in several important ways. One of the major differences is that psychologists generally define *beforehand* what constitutes an emotion and what aspect of that definition they will study. If, for example, a researcher studies the expression of anger across cultures, he or she must assume that anger is an emotion in all the cultures to be studied and that the expressive aspect of that emotion is equivalent across cultures.

Cultural differences in the concept and definition of emotion, as we saw in the previous section, place limitations on this line of inquiry. In a study of anger, for instance, it is entirely possible that the cultures included in the study have different definitions of anger or express anger differently. The expression of anger may have different meanings in different cultures.

Still, despite these difficulties, psychological research on emotion represents an important line of inquiry into cultural influences on emotion. Most of the studies have been conducted by Western (or more specifically, American) psychologists. These studies are by no means "complete" in the sense that *all* emotions for *all* people of *all* cultures have been studied. They do, however, *exemplify* how culture can mold emotion, and in so doing, raise awareness of the importance of these sociocultural influences. The studies are also important because they show that there are considerable cultural differences in emotion, even when the aspect of emotion studied is defined by mainstream, Western views of emotion.

Emotional Expression

Cross-cultural research on emotional expressions has generally centered on the study of facial expressions—for good reason. Facial expressions of emotion are the most well-studied aspect of emotional expression, and cross-cultural research on facial expressions provided much of the impetus for current work on emotions in American psychology.

Although the universality of some facial expressions of emotion is now well accepted in psychology, social scientists and laypersons alike have long recognized that people of different cultures can, and do, differ in their emotional expressions. In fact, the differences provide the forum for a long-standing debate about the universality versus cultural specificity of emotional expression. This debate led to the groundbreaking research by Paul Ekman and Carroll Izard presented in most introductory courses.

Ekman and Izard provided the first systematic and conclusive evidence for the universal expressions of anger, disgust, fear, happiness, sadness, and surprise. The universality of these emotions means that their facial configurations are biologically inborn or innate, similar across all people regardless of culture or ethnicity. Thus, when people have these emotions, they should express them in exactly the same ways across cultures.

Still, these findings run counter to what we intuitively feel about the existence of cultural differences in emotional expression. Certainly, the universality of emotional expression per se cannot account for cultural differences. Instead, cultures differ in their *rules* governing *how* the universal emotions can be expressed. These rules center on the appropriateness of displaying each of these emotions, depending on social circumstances. We call these rules **cultural display rules** (Ekman, 1972).

Actually, the existence of cultural display rules governing the display of emotion was demonstrated over two decades ago in a study comparing the facial behaviors of American and Japanese people (Friesen, 1972). In this study, members of both cultures viewed highly stressful films (showing burns, amputations, sinus surgery, childbirth with forceps) in two different social conditions. In the first condition, the participants viewed the films alone; in the second, they viewed the films while in the full view of a higher-status experimenter. Throughout the experiment, their facial expressions were videorecorded without their knowledge. When alone, both the Americans and the Japanese displayed the same expressions of disgust, anger, fear, and sadness at the same times. When the higher-status experimenter was present in the second condition, however, there were considerable cultural differences. The Americans continued to show their negative emotions, whereas the Japanese invariably smiled in every instance.

These findings showed how universal, biologically innate emotional expressions interact with culturally defined rules of display in producing emotional expressions in interaction. In the first condition, display rules did not operate, so the Americans and the Japanese exhibited the same expressions. In the second condition, display rules were operative, forcing the Japanese to smile in order not to offend the experimenter, despite their obvious negative feelings.

Other studies have documented how display rules differ across cultures (Matsumoto, 1990; Matsumoto & Hearn, 1993). In one of these (Matsumoto & Hearn, 1993), participants in the United States, Poland,

and Hungary reported the appropriateness of expressing each of the six universal emotions in three different social situations: (1) by yourself, (2) with others considered "ingroup" members (for example, close friends, family members), and (3) with others considered "outgroup" (for example, in public, with casual acquaintances). The Poles and Hungarians reported displaying fewer negative and more positive emotions in ingroups than did the Americans, and more negative emotions in outgroups. Americans, in contrast, were more likely than the Poles or Hungarians to display negative emotions to ingroup members and positive emotions to outgroup members. The Poles also reported that the display of negative emotions was less appropriate even when they were alone!

Research has also found some ethnic differences in display rules within the United States (Matsumoto, in press). American subjects were self-classified into one of four major ethnic categories: Caucasian, black, Asian, and Hispanic/Latino. As in the study of ingroups and outgroups, the subjects rated the appropriateness of displaying the universal emotions in different social situations. The findings showed that Caucasians rated contempt more appropriate than did Asians, disgust more appropriate than did blacks and Hispanics, fear more appropriate than did Hispanics, and sadness more appropriate than did blacks and Asians. In addition, Caucasians rated the expression of emotions in public and with children more appropriate than did Hispanics; with casual acquaintances more appropriate than did blacks, Asians, and Hispanics; and with lower-status others more appropriate than did blacks or Hispanics. Interestingly, however, in another part of the experiment, blacks reported expressing anger more often than did Caucasians, Asians, and Hispanics.

Thus, although the universal facial expressions are biologically innate and stored in the brain as facial prototypes from birth in all people, cultures do exert considerable influence over emotional expressions via culturally learned display rules. Given that most interactions among people are social by definition, we should expect that cultural differences via display rules are operative most, if not all, of the time. People of different cultural backgrounds can, and do, express emotions differently.

Emotional Perception

Because the expression of certain emotions is universal, it follows that the *recognition* of these same emotions is also universal. That is exactly what the early research by Ekman and Izard found, and what most introductory textbooks traditionally report. Since the original publication of these studies in the early 1970s, these findings were unchallenged until cross-cultural research in the 1980s began to document ways in which cultures influence the perception of emotion as well.

Ekman et al. (1987) conducted one of the first studies to show that cultures differ in emotional perception. They presented observers in ten different cultures with photographs depicting each of the six universal emotions. The subjects not only labeled each emotion by selecting an emotion word from a predetermined list, but they also rated *how intensely* they perceived the emotion expressed. The subjects in the ten cultures agreed on what emotion was being displayed, highlighting the universality of recognition. But there was disagreement across the cultures on how intensely they perceived the emotions. Follow-up tests showed that Asian cultures rated the emotions less intensely than did non-Asian cultures. Matsumoto and Ekman (1989) replicated these findings, showing that cultural differences in perceived intensity existed regardless of whether the subjects rated someone of their own or of another culture.

There also appears to be cross-racial differences within the United States in attributions of intensity to emotional stimuli. In another part of the cross-racial study conducted with American subjects (Matsumoto, in press), Caucasian, black, Asian, and Hispanic/Latino subjects viewed examples of the universal facial expressions of emotion and made a scalar rating of how intensely they perceived each face. The findings showed that blacks perceived anger and fear more intensely than did Asians, disgust more intensely than did Caucasians and Asians, Caucasian faces more intensely than did Caucasians and Asians, and female expressions more intensely than did Asians. Hispanics also perceived fear more intensely than did Asians.

Cultures also influence the *labeling* of emotion. Cultures generally agree on which emotions are being displayed in a facial expression, but there is some variability in the *level* of agreement. For example, even though most of the subjects in Indonesia, Japan, France, Brazil, and the United States may agree that a face expresses a certain emotion (such as fear), there will be some differences across the cultures in how many subjects in each culture agree that the expression depicts fear (for example, 90% of the subjects in the United States, Brazil, and France may label the expression as fear, whereas only 70% of the subjects in Japan and Indonesia may label it as fear). This type of cultural difference in the labeling of emotions is exactly what two recent studies found (Matsumoto, 1989, 1992).

In fact, cultural differences in the degree to which members of different cultures label emotions existed in the data collected for the original universality research conducted by Ekman and Izard (for example, see Ekman, 1972; Izard, 1971). Cultural differences were simply not tested then because the goals of these studies were to uncover cultural similarities, not differences. Actually, one of the studies documenting cultural differences in the labeling of emotion (Matsumoto, 1989) involved a re-analysis of the original data collected by Ekman and Izard.

Other studies have documented cultural differences in the perception and interpretation of emotion. For example, one study showed cultural differences between American and Japanese children as young as 3 years old in the labeling of emotions from nonverbal vocal cues (Matsumoto & Kishimoto, 1983). Other studies have reported cultural differences in the interpretation of other nonverbal behaviors such as postures (Kudoh & Matsumoto, 1985; Matsumoto & Kudoh, 1987). Finally, a small but growing number of studies suggest that people perceive emotions more accurately when judging others of the same ethnicity as themselves, as opposed to judging others of different ethnicities (Shimoda, Argyle, & Ricci Bitti, 1978; Wolfgang & Cohen, 1988).

How do cultures influence the perception and interpretation of emotion? Some psychologists believe that cultures have *rules* that govern the perception of emotion, much like the display rules that govern their expression. Rules governing the interpretation and perception of emotion are called **decoding rules** (Buck, 1984). These are learned, culturally based rules that shape how people of each culture view and interpret the emotional expressions of others. Like display rules, decoding rules are learned early in life, and learned sufficiently well so that we are not completely conscious of their influence. Decoding rules, then, are like a cultural *filter* that affects how we perceive the emotional expressions of others.

Emotional Experience

In the last few years, several research programs have begun to study how people of different cultures experience emotions differently (for example, see Scherer, Summerfield, & Wallbott, 1986; Wallbott & Scherer, 1986). These studies, taken together, have involved thousands of respondents in over 30 different cultures around the world, who completed questionnaires about the emotions they experience in their everyday lives. The findings from these studies collectively suggest that cultures exert considerable influence over how people experience emotions.

One of the studies (Scherer, Matsumoto, Wallbott, & Kudoh, 1988) tested differences among Europeans, Americans, and Japanese on the relative incidence of emotions. Although you may think that people in these areas of the world experience emotions at about the same frequency, the data suggested otherwise. The Japanese reported experiencing all emotions—including joy, sadness, fear, and anger—more often than did either the Americans or the Europeans. The Americans, in turn, reported experiencing joy and anger more often than did the Europeans.

Respondents in this study also rated how *strongly* they experienced their emotions (intensity) and for how *long* (duration). The results again showed some differences. Americans reported feeling their emotions for longer durations and at greater intensities than did the Europeans or the Japanese.

Emotion Antecedents

Several studies have examined whether the *antecedents* of emotion—that is, what triggers an emotion—are different in different cultures. Do the same types of events bring about the same types of emotions, at about the same frequency, across cultures? Researchers interested in this question a decade or more ago (for example, Boucher, 1979) suggested that the antecedents of emotion *had* to be similar across cultures because emotions themselves are universal. More recent studies, however, suggest considerable cultural differences not only in the types of events that trigger emotions, but also in the *degree* to which they bring forth emotions.

For example, cultural events, the birth of a new family member, body-centered "basic pleasures," and achievement-related situations were more important antecedents of joy for Europeans and Americans than for the Japanese. Death of family members or close friends, physical separation from loved ones, and world news were more frequent triggers of sadness for the Europeans and Americans than for the Japanese. Problems in relationships, however, produced more sadness for the Japanese than for Americans or Europeans. Strangers and achievement-related situations elicited more fear for Americans, whereas novel situations, traffic, and relationships were more frequent elicitors of fear for the Japanese. Finally, situations involving strangers were frequent elicitors of anger for the Japanese but not for the Americans or Europeans. Situations involving relationships brought about more anger for Americans than for the Japanese.

The Cognitive Evaluation of Emotion Antecedents

How do people in different cultures evaluate emotion antecedents? Do emotions and their eliciting situations have commonalities across cultures in how people think about them? Or do people in different cultures think about emotion-eliciting situations differently? One study comparing Americans with Japanese has examined these questions (Matsumoto, Kudoh, Scherer, & Wallbott, 1988). Its findings demonstrate considerable cultural differences in the ways people in different cultures evaluate emotion-eliciting situations.

For example, there were cultural differences in self-esteem resulting from emotion-eliciting events; emotions had a more positive effect on self-esteem and self-confidence for Americans than they did for the Japanese. There were also cultural differences in attributions of causality of emotions, with Americans attributing the cause of sadness-producing events to others, and Japanese attributing the cause of sadness to themselves. Americans are also more likely to attribute the causes of joy, fear, and shame to other people, whereas the Japanese tend to attribute the causes of these emotions to chance or fate. Japanese believe more than Americans that no action or behaviors are necessary *after* an emotion is elicited. For emotions such as fear, more Americans than Japanese believe they can do something to influence the situation positively. For anger and disgust, more Americans believe they are powerless and dominated by the event and its consequences. For shame and guilt, more Japanese than Americans pretend that nothing has happened and try to think of something else.

The Physiology of Emotion

To this date, there are no studies that have formally tested cultural differences in physiological reactions to emotions. Several studies, however, have tested cultural differences in physiological and behavioral reactions *reported* by people in different cultures (Matsumoto et al., 1988; Scherer et al., 1988). Although these data cannot speak to actual physiology and behavior per se, they do raise some interesting speculations about possible cultural differences.

On the whole, Japanese respondents reported fewer hand and arm gestures, whole body movements, and vocal and facial reactions to emotions than did the Americans or Europeans. Americans reported the highest degree of expressivity in both facial and vocal reactions. Americans and Europeans also reported more purely physiological sensations than did the Japanese. These sensations included changes in temperature (becoming flushed, hot, and so on), cardiovascular changes (heart racing, pulse changing), and gastric disturbances (stomach problems).

Toward a Cross-Cultural Theory of Emotion

Culture is extremely important in the shaping of human emotions. This evidence comes from anthropological and ethnographic studies of emotions across different cultures, psychological research on emotions across cultures, and psychological research on emotions across racial groups within the United States. As psychologists continue to explore the roles and contributions of culture in human emotion, other studies will no doubt increasingly document other cultural differences as well.

Before this occurs, however, we need to search *now* for ways of better organizing and understanding cultural influences on emotion. The information available is already mind-boggling, and the future promises an even greater number of findings. Before we merely uncover more and more "facts" about cultural differences on emotion, we need to adopt meaningful ways of understanding, predicting, and interpreting cultural differences. Searching for, and adopting, theoretically relevant approaches to culture and emotion will aid us in understanding culture and emotion. It will also guide us in our research efforts to unravel their relationship in important ways.

Where do we start? There is a growing consensus among psychologists and other social scientists that we need to define cultures by ways other than ethnicity or nation. As discussed in Chapter 1, culture is not biology; rather, it is a sociopsychological construct. As a result, we need to move away from classifying people as Caucasian, black, Hispanic, and Asian, or Americans, French, Japanese, and British. Instead, we need to find psychologically meaningful ways of defining culture that ignore ethnicity or nationality.

Some psychologists have made attempts to do just that in the study of culture and emotion (for example, Gudykunst & Ting-Toomey, 1988; Matsumoto, 1989, 1990, 1991). These approaches have focused on the sociopsychological construct known as "individualism versus collectivism" as a meaningful measure of culture. *Individualism* refers to the degree to which a culture fosters individual needs, wishes, and desires over group needs. *Collectivism* refers to the degree to which a culture emphasizes the sacrifice of individual wishes for the sake of the group. One major advantage to defining cultures according to individualism versus collectivism is that it is a totally sociopsychological construct, not bound by ethnicity or nationality. Using this dimension, we can examine how groups (African Americans, Hispanics, Asians, and so on) differ from one another and how individuals *within* these groups differ among themselves.

Central to a cross-cultural theory of emotion is the suggestion that emotional expressions differ as a function of individualism or collectivism, rather than as a function of being black, Japanese, or Egyptian (Matsumoto, 1991). People who are individualistic, for example, should be more likely to express negative emotions (anger, disgust) toward their friends and family than would collectivistic people. Individualists should also be more likely than collectivists to express positive emotions (happiness, interest) toward strangers and in public. Collectivists should be more likely than individualists to express positive emotions toward their friends and family and negative emotions toward people they don't know. Findings from many of the latest studies on emotion appear to support the usefulness of this cultural characterization in understanding cultural differences in emotion (for example, Gudykunst & Ting-Toomey, 1988; Matsumoto, 1989, 1990, 1992; Matsumoto & Hearn, 1993; Matsumoto & Kudoh, in press).

This approach is not the answer to end all questions in our attempts to understand the influence of culture on emotion. As future cross-cultural research on emotion in psychology occurs, more such theories will undoubtedly be developed, tested, and probably revised. Ways to characterize cultures that are more meaningful than individualism and collectivism may be developed, and researchers may find other cultural dimensions more relevant to understanding cultural differences in emotion.

Nevertheless, we need to consider cultural influences on emotion in our theories of emotion. The contemporary student of psychology in the near future should recognize cross-cultural approaches to emotion just as he or she recognizes other theories prevalent in American psychology, such as the James/Lange, Cannon/Bard, and Schachter/Singer theories. The existing data from cross-cultural studies and the diversity of the people of the world and their emotions not only warrant the existence of a cross-cultural theory, they mandate it.

Conclusion

In this chapter, we have seen that sociocultural factors exert considerable influence on all components of emotion, including emotional expression; emotional perception, experience, and antecedents; and self-reported physiological reactions. We have also seen that cultures differ in the concepts of emotion. These factors have been demonstrated as important not only in cross-cultural research across different countries, but also in cross-racial research within the United States. Future research promises an increase not only in the number but also the complexity of findings. The sociocultural diversity of people across the world, and within our own country, ensures this increase.

As we continue in our study of emotion, psychology, and people in general, perhaps it is most important for us to recognize that, although emotions are a universally important aspect of human behavior, sociocultural factors can, and do, influence emotions quite considerably. People of different cultures, ethnicities, and societies differ emotionally. One of the first tasks in learning about psychology is to recognize, and more importantly, respect those differences.

Glossary

Cannon/Bard theory: This theory suggests that conscious emotional experience results from direct stimulation of brain centers in the cortex.

Cultural display rules: Culturally based rules that people learn to modify their emotional expressions based on social situations.

Decoding rules: Culturally based rules that shape how people of each culture view and interpret the emotional expressions of others.

James/Lange theory: This theory suggests that the experience of emotion results from one's perception of physiological (autonomic) arousal and overt behavior.

Schachter/Singer theory: This theory suggests that emotional experiences depend solely on one's interpretation of the environment in which one is being aroused.

References

Averill, J. R. (1980). Emotion and anxiety: Sociocultural, biological, and psychological determinants. In A. O. Rorty (Ed.), *Explaining emotions* (pp. 37–72). Berkeley: University of California Press.

Boucher, J. D. (1979). Culture and emotion. In A. J. Marsella, R. G. Tharpl, & T. V. Ciborowski (Eds.), *Perspectives on cross-cultural psychology* (pp. 159–178). San Diego, CA: Academic Press.

Brandt, M. E., & Boucher, J. D. (1986). Concepts of depression in emotion lexicons of eight cultures. *International Journal of Intercultural Relations, 10*, 321–346.

Buck, R. (1984). *The communication of emotion.* New York: Guilford Press.

Ekman, P. (1972). Universal and cultural differences in facial expression of emotion. In J. R. Cole (Ed.), *Nebraska Symposium on Motivation, 1971* (pp. 207–283). Lincoln: University of Nebraska Press.

Ekman, P., Friesen, W. V., O'Sullivan, M., Chan, A., Diacoyanni-Tarlatzis, I., Heider, K., Krause, R., LeCompte, W. A., Pitcairn, T., Ricci-Bitti, P. E., Scherer, K., Tomita, M., & Tzavaras, A. (1987). Universals and cultural differences in the judgment of facial expressions of emotion. *Journal of Personality and Social Psychology, 53*, 712–717.

Friesen, W. V. (1972). *Cultural differences in facial expressions in a social situation: An experimental test of the concept of display rules.* Unpublished doctoral dissertation, University of California, San Francisco.

Gerber, E. (1975). *The cultural patterning of emotions in Samoa.* Unpublished doctoral dissertation, University of California, San Diego.

Gudykunst, W. B., & Ting-Toomey, S. (1988). Culture and affective communication. [Special issue: *Communication and affect.*] *American Behavioral Scientist, 31*, 384–400.

Hiatt, L. R. (1978). Classification of the emotions. In L. R. Hiatt (Ed.), *Australian aboriginal concepts* (pp. 182–187). Princeton, NJ: Humanities Press.

Howell, S. (1981). Rules not words. In P. Heelas & A. Lock (Eds.), *Indigenous psychologies: The anthropology of the self* (pp. 133–143). San Diego, CA: Academic Press.

Izard, C. E. (1971). *The face of emotion.* New York: Appleton-Century-Crofts.

Kudoh, T., & Matsumoto, D. (1985). A cross-cultural examination of the semantic dimensions of body postures. *Journal of Personality and Social Psychology, 48,* 1440–1446.

Leff, J. (1973). Culture and the differentiation of emotional states. *British Journal of Psychiatry, 123,* 299–306.

Levy, R. I. (1973). *Tahitians.* Chicago: University of Chicago Press.

Levy, R. I. (1983). Introduction: Self and emotion. *Ethos, 11,* 128–134.

Levy, R. I. (1984). The emotions in comparative perspective. In K. Scherer and P. Ekman (Eds.), *Approaches to emotion* (pp. 397–412). New York: Erlbaum.

Lutz, C. (1980). *Emotion words and emotional development on Ifaluk Atoll.* Unpublished doctoral dissertation, Harvard University.

Lutz, C. (1982). The domain of emotion words in Ifaluk. *American Ethnologist, 9,* 113–128.

Lutz, C. (1983). Parental goals, ethnopsychology, and the development of emotional meaning. *Ethos, 11,* 246–262.

Matsumoto, D. (1989). Cultural influences on the perception of emotion. *Journal of Cross-Cultural Psychology, 20,* 92–105.

Matsumoto, D. (1990). Cultural similarities and differences in display rules. *Motivation and Emotion, 14,* 195–214.

Matsumoto, D. (1991). Cultural influences on facial expressions of emotion. *Southern Communication Journal, 56,* 128–137.

Matsumoto, D. (1992). American-Japanese cultural differences in the recognition of universal facial expressions. *Journal of Cross-Cultural Psychology, 23,* 72–84.

Matsumoto, D. (in press). Ethnic differences in affect intensity, emotion judgments, display rules, and self-reported emotional expression. *Motivation and Emotion.*

Matsumoto, D., & Ekman, P. (1989). American-Japanese cultural differences in intensity ratings of facial expressions of emotion. *Motivation and Emotion, 13,* 143–157.

Matsumoto, D., & Hearn, V. (1993). *Culture and emotion: Display rule differences between the United States, Poland, and Hungary.* Manuscript submitted for publication.

Matsumoto, D., & Kishimoto, H. (1983). Developmental characteristics in judgments of emotion from nonverbal vocal cues. *International Journal of Intercultural Relations, 7,* 415–424.

Matsumoto, D., & Kudoh, T. (1987). Cultural similarities and differences in the semantic dimensions of body postures. *Journal of Nonverbal Behavior, 11,* 166–179.

Matsumoto, D., & Kudoh, T. (in press). Cultural differences in social judgments of facial expressions of emotion: What's in a smile? *Journal of Nonverbal Behavior.*

Matsumoto, D., Kudoh, T., Scherer, K., & Wallbott, H. (1988). Emotion antecedents and reactions in the U.S. and Japan. *Journal of Cross-Cultural Psychology, 19,* 267–286.

Matsuyama, Y., Hama, H., Kawamura, Y., & Mine, H. (1978). Analysis of emotional words. *The Japanese Journal of Psychology, 49*, 229–232.

Myers, F. R. (1979). Emotions and the self: A theory of personhood and political order among Pintupi aborigines. *Ethos, 7*, 343–370.

Riesman, P. (1977). *Freedom in Fulani social life: An introspective ethnography* (M. Fuller, Trans.). Chicago: University of Chicago Press. (Original work published 1974)

Russell, J. A. (1991). Culture and the categorization of emotion. *Psychological Bulletin, 110*, 426–450.

Scherer, K., Matsumoto, D., Wallbott, H., & Kudoh, T. (1988). Emotional experience in cultural context: A comparison between Europe, Japan, and the USA. In K. Scherer (Ed.), *Facets of emotion: Recent research* (pp. 5–30). Hillsdale, NJ: Erlbaum.

Scherer, K. R., Summerfield, A., & Wallbott, H. (1986). Cross-national research on antecedents and components of emotion: A progress report. *Social Science Information, 22*, 355–385.

Shimoda, K., Argyle, M., & Ricci Bitti, P. (1978). The intercultural recognition of facial expressions of emotion. *European Journal of Social Psychology, 8*, 169–179.

Wallbott, H., & Scherer, K. (1986). How universal and specific is emotional experience? Evidence from 27 countries on five continents. *Social Science Information, 25*, 763–795.

White, G. M. (1980). Conceptual universals in interpersonal language. *American Anthropologist, 88*, 759–781.

Wolfgang, A., & Cohen, M. (1988). Sensitivity of Canadians, Latin Americans, Ethiopians, and Israelis to interracial facial expressions of emotions. *International Journal of Intercultural Relations, 12*, 1–13.

Suggested Readings

Ekman, P. (1973). *Darwin and facial expressions*. New York: Academic Press.

Matsumoto, D. (in press). *Unmasking Japan: The feelings and emotions of the Japanese*. Stanford, CA: Stanford University Press.

Scherer, K. R. (Ed.). (1988). *Facets of emotion: Recent research*. Hillsdale, NJ: Erlbaum.

9

Abnormal Psychology

with
Dawn Terrell
San Francisco State University

One of the most active areas of cross-cultural inquiry is the examination of the role of culture in understanding, assessing, and treating abnormal behavior. Several major themes have guided research and thinking in abnormal psychology. First and foremost are questions concerning definitions of abnormality: What is abnormal behavior? A second set of questions relates to the expression of abnormal behavior and our ability to detect it (assessment). A third question concerns how we are able to treat abnormal behavior when it is detected.

These questions have special significance in relation to culture, as culture adds an important wrinkle in approaches to abnormality and treatment (Marsella, 1979). Do definitions of normality and abnormality vary across cultures, or are there universal standards of abnormality? Do cultures vary in rates of abnormal behavior? Is abnormal behavior expressed in the same way across cultures, or can we identify culturally distinct patterns of abnormal behavior?

The answers to these questions have gained importance in the last two decades as psychologists and other mental health professionals have questioned the cultural sensitivity of traditional methods of assessing and treating individuals with psychological disorders. Indeed, as this chapter will illustrate, the answers to these questions have important implications for how we identify and intervene to change abnormal behavior.

In this chapter, we will review studies of the prevalence and course of psychological disorders, such as schizophrenia and depression, across

135

cultures and also discuss some culture-specific disorders. We will also briefly examine the different treatment implications offered by cultural variations in definitions of abnormality. The research and theory presented here indicate that culture plays a role in shaping not only an individual's experience of psychological disorder, but also his or her response to assessment and treatment techniques.

Defining Abnormality

Consider the following scenario:

> A woman is in the midst of a group of people but seems totally unaware of her surroundings. She is talking loudly to no one in particular, often using words and sounds the people around her find unintelligible. When questioned later about her behavior, she reports that she had been possessed by the spirit of an animal and was talking with a man who had recently died.

Some Traditional Viewpoints

Is this woman's behavior abnormal? In defining abnormal behavior, psychologists usually adopt one of several different approaches. These include a statistical approach and applications of criteria of impairment or inefficiency, deviance, and subjective distress.

From a **statistical-comparison approach**, the woman's behavior could be defined as abnormal because its occurrence is rare or infrequent. Being out of touch with one's surroundings, having delusions (mistaken beliefs) that one is an animal, and talking with the dead are not common experiences. One of the problems with this approach to defining abnormality, however, is that not all rare behavior is disordered, nor is all disordered behavior rare! Composing a concerto and speaking four languages are behaviors that are uncommon yet are generally viewed as highly desirable. Conversely, drinking to the point of drunkenness occurs quite often in the United States (and in many other countries), but drunkenness is nevertheless widely recognized as a sign of a possible substance abuse disorder.

Another approach for defining abnormality focuses on whether an individual's behavior is associated with impairment or inefficiency in carrying out customary roles. It may be hard to imagine the woman described in the scenario carrying out normal daily functions—caring for herself and working—while she believes herself to be an animal. In many instances, psychological disorders do involve serious impairments or a reduction in an individual's overall functioning. This, however, is not always the case. Some people suffering from **bipolar disorder** (manic–depressives) report enhanced productivity during manic episodes.

If we examine the woman's behavior in terms of deviance, we might also conclude that it is abnormal because it seems to go against social norms. But not all behavior that is socially deviant can be considered abnormal or psychologically disordered. For example, many people continue to believe that homosexuality is deviant, although it is no longer classified as a mental disorder (American Psychiatric Association, 1987). Also, although some in this culture may view homosexuality as abnormal, in other cultures and at various periods in history homosexuality has been widely practiced and tolerated. Using societal norms as a criterion for abnormality is thus difficult not only because norms change over time, but because they are subjective. What one member of a society or culture considers deviant, another may accept.

Reliance on reports of **subjective distress** to define abnormal behavior is also problematic. Whether a person experiences distress as a consequence of abnormal behavior may depend on how others treat him or her. For example, if the woman in the scenario is ridiculed, shunned, and viewed as "sick" because of her behavior, she may well experience distress. Conversely, if she is seen as having special powers and is part of an accepting circle, she may not be distressed at all.

As can be seen, each of the more or less traditional viewpoints used by psychologists has advantages as well as disadvantages. These issues become even more complex when culture is considered. Definitions of abnormality may vary both within and across cultures.

Cross-Cultural Viewpoints of Abnormality

Dissatisfaction with traditional definitions of abnormality has led some cross-cultural investigators to argue that we can understand and identify abnormal behavior only if we take the cultural context into account. This viewpoint suggests that we must apply a principle of cultural relativism to abnormality. For example, the woman's behavior in the scenario might appear disordered if it occurred on a street corner in a large U.S. city. It could, however, appear appropriate and understandable if it occurs in the context of a shamanistic ceremony in which she is serving as healer. Cultures that hold beliefs in supernatural interventions are able to clearly distinguish when trance states and talking with spirits are an acceptable part of a healer's behavioral repertoire and when the same behaviors would be considered a sign of disorder (Murphy, 1976). Examples of such cultures include the Yoruba in Africa and an Eskimo tribe in Alaska.

Some behaviors, particularly those associated with **psychosis** (such as delusions and hallucinations), are universally recognized as abnormal

(Murphy, 1976). However, some investigators (for example, Kleinman, 1988; Marsella, 1979, 1980) argue that abnormality and normality are culturally determined concepts. These investigators point to the fact that cultures differ in their beliefs about and attitudes toward abnormal behavior.

Reliance on reports of subjective distress to define abnormal behavior is also problematic when considering abnormality across cultures. There is some indication that cultural groups vary in the degree of distress they report experiencing in association with psychological disorders. For example, Kleinman (1988) describes research indicating that depressed Chinese and African individuals report less guilt and shame than do depressed Euro-American and European individuals. The Chinese and African individuals, however, do report more somatic complaints. These findings may reflect cultural variations in response set, discussed in Chapter 1. Some cultural groups may have values that prohibit reporting or focusing on subjective distress, in contrast to Western notions of the importance of self-disclosure.

Whether to accept universal or culturally relative definitions of abnormality is a source of continuing controversy in the field of cross-cultural psychology. This tension can be seen as well in considering the expression of abnormality across cultures.

Expression of Abnormality Across Cultures

The focus of much of the cross-cultural study of abnormality has been on determining whether the rates and manifestations of psychological disorders vary across cultures. The two disorders studied most extensively are schizophrenia and depression, typically using diagnostic criteria and assessment procedures developed in Western psychology and psychiatry. This approach can be characterized as basically an "etic" approach that assumes universally accepted definitions of abnormality and methodology (review Chapter 1 for a definition of *emic* and *etic*).

In contrast to this etic approach to cross-cultural study of abnormality, there have also been some ethnographic reports of **culture-bound syndromes.** These are forms of abnormal behavior observed only in certain sociocultural milieus. Findings concerning different rates and courses of disorder across cultures, and of culturally distinct forms of disorder, suggest the importance of culture in shaping the expression of abnormal behavior.

Cultural Variations in Schizophrenia

Traditional views of schizophrenia. **Schizophrenia** is part of a "group of psychotic disorders characterized by gross distortions of reality; withdrawal from social interaction; and disorganization of perception, thought, and emotion" (Carson, Butcher, & Coleman, 1988, p. 322). Some theories concerning the etiology (causes) of schizophrenia give primacy to biological factors (for example, excess dopamine or some other biochemical imbalance). Others emphasize family dynamics (for example, expression of hostility to ill person). The **diathesis-stress model of schizophrenia** suggests that individuals with a biological predisposition to the disorder (diathesis) may develop the disorder following exposure to environmental stressors.

Cross-cultural studies of schizophrenia. The World Health Organization (WHO, 1973, 1979, 1981) sponsored the International Pilot Study of Schizophrenia (IPSS) to compare the prevalence and course of the disorder in several countries: Columbia, Czechoslovakia, Denmark, England, India, Nigeria, the Soviet Union, Taiwan, and the United States. Following rigorous training in using the research assessment tool, psychiatrists in each of the countries achieved good reliability in diagnosing schizophrenia in patients included in the study. As a result, WHO investigators were able to identify a set of symptoms that were present across all cultures in the schizophrenic samples. These symptoms include lack of insight, auditory and verbal hallucinations, and ideas of reference (assuming one is the center of attention) (Leff, 1977).

The WHO studies are widely cited to bolster arguments for the universality of schizophrenia. But some important cross-cultural differences were found as well. In a finding that took the investigators by surprise, the course of the illness was shown to progress better for patients in developing countries compared to those in highly industrialized countries. Patients in Columbia, India, and Nigeria recovered at faster rates than those in England, the Soviet Union, or the United States. These differences were attributed to cultural factors such as extended kin networks and the tendency to return to work in developing countries.

The researchers also noted differences in symptom expression across cultures. Patients in the United States were less likely to demonstrate lack of insight and auditory hallucinations than were Danish or Nigerian patients. These findings may be related to cultural differences in values associated with insight and self-awareness, which are highly regarded in the United States, but not as much so in the other countries. Also, there may have been cultural differences in the tolerance for these types of symptom profiles; the Nigerian culture as a whole is more accepting of the presence of voices. Nigerian and Danish patients, however, were more likely to demonstrate **catatonia** (extreme withdrawal or agitation).

Kleinman (1988) and Leff (1981) discussed some of the methodological problems that plagued the WHO studies. For instance, the assessment tool failed to tap culturally unique experiences and expressions of disorder. Kleinman also noted that the samples were made artificially homogenous because of the selection criteria. He argued that the findings of cross-cultural differences might have been greater still had not the heterogeneity of the sample been reduced.

Other cross-cultural comparisons of rates and expression of schizophrenia (Leff, 1977; Murphy, 1982) have also found evidence of cultural variations. Murphy (1982) found that rates of admission for schizophrenia are four times higher in Ireland compared to England and Wales. These findings suggested that some features of Irish culture (sharp wit, ambivalence toward individuality) may have accounted for the cultural differences. In an early study of New York psychiatric cases, Opler and Singer (1959) found that Irish-American schizophrenic patients were more likely to experience paranoid delusions than were Italian-American schizophrenic patients. The authors cited cultural variations in parenting to account for the difference. A study of Japanese schizophrenics (Sue & Morishima, 1982) indicated that they are more likely than Euro-American counterparts to be withdrawn and passive, in conformity to cultural values.

Recent studies of schizophrenics have tested the theory that expressed emotion—family communication characterized by hostility and overinvolvement—increases the risk of relapse. The expressed-emotion construct is important because it suggests that family and social interactions influence the course of schizophrenia. These interactions are in turn influenced by cultural values. Research indicates that expressed emotion predicts relapse in Western samples (Mintz, Mintz, & Goldstein, 1987). Kleinman (1988), however, notes the difficulties in using this construct in other cultures, particularly in those that emphasize nonverbal communication. Karno and associates (1987) reported that expressed emotion also predicts relapse in Mexican Americans, but Kleinman (1988) questions whether measures of expressed emotion developed in one cultural context have validity in another.

Reports of cultural differences in diagnosis have also raised questions about the validity of assessment techniques used in cross-cultural comparisons of schizophrenia and other disorders (Kleinman, 1988; Leff, 1977). In a reanalysis of some of the early WHO data, Leff (1977) found that U.S. psychiatrists were more likely to give diagnoses of schizophrenia than were psychiatrists in England, and less likely to give diagnoses of depression. Abebimpe (1981) and others (Thomas & Sillen, 1972) have documented that African Americans are more likely than Euro-Americans to receive diagnoses of schizophrenia rather than depression, even when the symptom picture is the same. Racial bias seems to account for some of the differential pattern (Thomas & Sillen, 1972), and cultural differences in expression of symptomatology may also be important.

Cultural Variations in Depression

Traditional views of depression.   All of us have experienced moods of depression, sadness, or the blues in our lives. We may have these feelings in response to a death in the family, a breakup of a relationship, falling short of a goal, and the like. The presence of a **depressive disorder** involves the symptoms of "intense sadness, feelings of futility and worthlessness, and withdrawal from others" (Sue, Sue, & Sue, 1990, p. 325). Depression is often also characterized by physical changes (such as sleep and appetite disturbances) as well as emotional and behavioral changes (Berry, Poortinga, Segall, & Dasen, 1992).

Like schizophrenia, depression is one of the most common psychological disorders in the United States. In a large-scale study, Myers et al. (1984) found that 3% of the adult male population and 7% of the adult female population had experienced a depressive disorder in the previous six-month period. Lifetime prevalence rates for depression are also high, sometimes as high as 26% for women and 12% for men (American Psychiatric Association, 1987, cited in Sue et al., 1990). There is also some evidence to suggest that the incidence rate for depression has risen over the last few decades (Robins et al., 1984).

Cross-cultural views of depression.   In cross-cultural studies of depression, variations in symptomatology have been widely documented. Some cultural groups (such as the Nigerians) are less likely to report extreme feelings of worthlessness. Others (such as the Chinese) are more likely to report somatic complaints (Kleinman, 1988). As with schizophrenia, rates of depression also vary from culture to culture (Marsella, 1980).

Leff (1977) argues that cultures vary in terms of their differentiation and communication of emotional terminology, and hence in how they experience and express depression. In Chapter 8, we saw that some cultures have few words to convey emotions such as sadness or anger. We also saw that some cultures locate feeling states in various parts of the body. This may explain why some cultural groups emphasize somatic complaints in the expression of depression.

In arguing for a culturally relative definition of depression, Kleinman (1988, p. 25) writes that

> depression experienced entirely as low back pain and depression experienced entirely as guilt-ridden existential despair are such substantially different forms of illness behavior with distinctive symptoms, patterns of help seeking, and treatment responses that although the disease in each instance may be the same, the illness, not the disease, becomes the determinative factor. And one might well ask, is the disease even the same?

Earlier, Kleinman (1978) argued that depressive disease reflects a biologically based disorder, whereas depressive illness refers to the personal and social experience of depression. Although Kleinman accepts the idea that depressive disease is universal, he argues that the expression and course of the illness are culturally determined.

Marsella (1979, 1980) also argues for a culturally relative view of depression. He states that depression takes a primarily affective form in cultures with strong objective orientations (that is, cultures that emphasize individualism). In these cultures, feelings of loneliness and isolation would dominate the symptom picture. Somatic symptoms such as headaches would be dominant in subjective cultures (those having a more communal structure). Marsella (1979) has also proposed that depressive symptom patterns will differ across cultures due to cultural variations in sources of stress as well as in resources for coping with the stress.

Culture-Bound Syndromes

Perhaps the strongest evidence for applying cultural relativism to abnormality comes from ethnographic reports of culture-bound syndromes. Using primarily emic (culture-specific) approaches involving ethnographic examination of behavior within a specific cultural context, anthropologists and psychiatrists have identified several apparently unique forms of psychological disorders. Some similarities between symptoms of these culture-specific disorders and those recognized across cultures have been observed. The particular patterning of culture-specific symptoms, however, typically does not fit the diagnostic criteria of psychological disorders recognized in Western classification schemes.

The most widely observed culture-bound syndrome has been identified in several countries in Asia (Malay, Philippines, Thailand). *Amok* is a disorder characterized by sudden rage and homicidal aggression. It is thought to be brought on by stress, sleep deprivation, and alcohol consumption (Carson et al., 1988) and has been primarily observed in males. Several stages of the disorder have been identified, ranging from extreme withdrawal prior to the assaultive behavior to exhaustion and amnesia after the rage. The term "running amok" derives from observations of this disorder.

Witiko (also known as *windigo*) is a disorder that has been identified in Algonquin Indians in Canada. It involves the belief that one has been possessed by the witiko spirit—a man-eating monster. Cannibalistic behavior may result, along with suicidal ideation to avoid acting on the cannibalistic urges (Carson et al., 1988).

Anorexia nervosa is a disorder that has been identified in the West but has not been observed in Third World countries (Swartz, 1985). The disorder is characterized by a distorted body image, fear of becoming fat, and a serious loss of weight associated with food restraining or purging. Several factors have been cited as possible causes of this disorder, including cultural emphasis on thinness as an ideal for women, constricted sex roles, and an individual's fears of being out of control or of taking on adult responsibilities.

Kiev (1972) and Yap (1974) reviewed the literature on these and other culture-bound syndromes, including *latah* (characterized by hysteria and echolalia, observed primarily in women in Malay); *koro* (impotence resulting from fear that the penis is retracting, observed in Southeast Asian men); and *susto* (characterized by depression and apathy thought to reflect "soul loss," observed in Indians of the Andean highlands). Yap (1974) has attempted to organize information concerning culture-bound syndromes into a classification scheme that parallels Western diagnostic schemes. Thus, latah and susto are viewed as unique cultural expressions of universal primary fear reactions. Amok is similarly viewed as a unique cultural expression of a universal rage reaction. Yap recognizes that his attempt to subsume culture-bound syndromes into a universal classification scheme may be premature, particularly since Western clinical tools and methods of research may make it difficult to assess culturally diverse expressions of abnormal behavior.

Pfeiffer (1982) has identified four dimensions for understanding culture-bound syndromes. He argues that culture-specific areas of stress may contribute to the syndromes. Such areas of stress include family and societal structure and ecological conditions. For example, koro might be best understood as resulting from the unique cultural emphasis on potency in certain cultures that emphasize paternal authority. Culture-specific shaping of conduct and interpretations of conduct may also account for the development of culture-bound syndromes. Pfeiffer suggests that cultures may implicitly approve patterns of exceptional behavior, as in the case of amok, in which aggression against others "broadly follows the patterns of societal expectations" (p. 206). Finally, Pfeiffer argues that how a culture interprets exceptional behavior will be linked to culture-specific interventions. For example, interventions to heal the soul loss associated with susto will involve sacrifices carried out by a native healer to appease the earth so that it will return the soul.

Pfeiffer (1982) and others (Kleinman, 1988; Marsella, 1979) argue that it is impossible to use current Western classification schemes to understand culture-bound syndromes because the latter are experienced from a qualitatively different point of view. They argue that culture shapes the experience of psychological disorder, both in determining the expression of symptoms of universal disorders and in contributing to the emergence of culture-specific disorders. Kleinman and Marsella go a step further, arguing that recognition of the role of culture in shaping abnormal behavior requires that we reexamine the way we assess and treat individuals with psychological disorders.

Assessment and Treatment of Abnormal Behavior Across Cultures

Assessment of abnormal behavior involves identifying and describing an individual's symptoms "within the context of his or her overall level of functioning and environment" (Carson et al., 1988, p. 531). The tools and methods of assessment should be sensitive to cultural and other environmental influences on behavior and functioning. The literature involving standard assessment techniques, however, indicates that there may be problems of bias or insensitivity when psychological tests and other methods developed in one cultural context are used to assess behavior in other cultures.

Tseng and McDermott (1981) write that the goal of treatment of abnormal behavior is to "relieve symptoms and help the patient become a healthier, more mature person . . . better able to deal with life and the problems it presents" (p. 264). They note that while there may be widespread agreement concerning the general goal of treatment, cultures will vary in their definitions of what is considered "healthy" or "mature." There also may be cultural differences in perceptions of problems and in preferred strategies for coping with problems (Terrell, 1992). As Berry et al. (1992) note, cultural beliefs and practices influence treatment because they shape both the therapist's and the client's definitions and understandings of the problem. As with assessment, however, traditional approaches to treatment of abnormal behavior may prove insensitive or inappropriate when applied across cultures.

Most psychology texts do a good job of describing traditional methods of assessment: various psychological tests, classification and diagnostic schemes, interview procedures, and observations. Similarly, different approaches to treatment of psychological disorders are amply covered, including psychoanalytic, behavioral, and humanistic approaches to therapy. In this section, we briefly review the literature on assessment and treatment across cultures, paying attention to models proposed to address cultural issues in assessment and treatment.

Issues in Cross-Cultural Assessment of Abnormal Behavior

We have seen how the definition and expression of abnormal behavior may vary within and across cultures. Traditional tools of clinical assessment, however, are primarily based on a standard definition of abnormality and use a standard set of classification criteria for evaluating problematic behavior. Therefore, the tools may have little meaning in cultures with varying definitions, however well translated they are into the native language, and they may mask or fail to capture culturally specific expressions of disorder (Marsella, 1979). The assessment problems encountered in studying schizophrenia and depression across cultures illustrate the limitations of traditional assessment methods.

Leff (1986) commented on the ethnocentric bias of such clinical interview procedures as the Present State Examination and the Cornell Medical Index. The Present State Examination was used to diagnose schizophrenia in the WHO studies described earlier. In a psychiatric survey of the Yoruba in Nigeria, investigators had to supplement the latter instrument to include culture-specific complaints such as feeling "an expanded head and goose flesh."

Standard diagnostic instruments to measure depressive disorder may also miss important cultural expressions of the disorder in Africans (Beiser, 1985) and Native Americans (Manson, Shore, & Bloom, 1985). In an extensive study of depression among Native Americans (Manson & Shore, 1981; Manson et al., 1985), the American Indian Depression Schedule (AIDS) was developed to assess and diagnose depressive illness. The investigators found that depression among Hopi Indians includes symptoms not measured by standard measures of depression such as the Diagnostic Interview Schedule (DIS) and the Schedule for Affective Disorders and Schizophrenia (SADS). These measures, based on diagnostic criteria found in the Diagnostic and Statistical Manual of Mental Disorders (APA, 1987), failed to capture the short, but acute dysphoric moods sometimes reported by the Hopi (Manson et al., 1985).

In reviewing the limitations of standard assessment techniques, several authors (Higginbotham, 1979; Marsella, 1979; Lonner & Ibrahim, 1989) have offered guidelines for developing measures to be used in cross-cultural assessment of abnormal behavior. They suggest that sensitive assessment methods examine sociocultural norms of healthy adjustment as well as culturally based definitions of abnormality. Higginbotham (1979) also suggests the importance of examining culturally sanctioned systems of healing and influence on abnormal behavior. There is evidence that people whose problems match cultural categories of abnormality are more likely to seek folk healers (Leff, 1986). Failure to examine indigenous healing systems would thus overlook some expressions of disorders. Assessment of culturally sanctioned systems of cure should also enhance the planning of treatment strategies, one of the major goals of traditional assessment (Carson et al., 1988).

Issues in the Treatment of Abnormal Behavior Across Cultures

In the last two decades, there has been a growing literature indicating that culturally diverse clients may be underserved or inappropriately served by traditional treatment methods. In a pioneering study of ethnic differences in response to standard mental health services in the Seattle area, Sue (1977) found lower rates of utilization of services among Asian Americans and Native Americans compared to Euro-Americans and African Americans. More dramatically, he found that all the groups except Euro-Americans had high dropout rates and relatively poorer treatment outcomes. A later study in the Los Angeles area showed similar findings (Sue, 1991). Sue (1977; Sue & Zane, 1987) concluded that low utilization and high attrition rates were due to the cultural insensitivity of standard treatment methods.

In efforts to fashion more culturally sensitive services, Sue and others (Comas-Diaz & Jacobsen, 1991; Higginbotham, 1979; Sue & Zane, 1987; Tseng & McDermott, 1981) suggest that treatment methods should be modified to improve their fit with the worldviews and experiences of culturally diverse clients. For example, psychoanalytic approaches are derived from a worldview assuming that unconscious conflicts (probably sexual) give rise to abnormal behavior. This worldview may reflect the experience of the well-to-do Austrian women whom Freud treated and based many of his theoretical assumptions on. A therapeutic approach based on such a worldview, however, may prove inappropriate in cultures that attribute abnormality either to natural factors (for example, physical problems or being out of harmony with one's environment) or supernatural causes (for example, spirit possession). Cultural systems of cure and healing may be effective precisely because they operate within a particular culture's worldview (Tseng & McDermott, 1981). Thus, a spiritual ceremony performed by native shaman (priest or healer) might prove to be a more effective treatment of the culture-bound syndrome of susto than would a cognitive behavioral approach.

A long line of research on preferences for therapeutic approaches in ethnically different populations in the United States indicates that non–Euro-American clients tend to prefer action-oriented therapy rather than the non-directive approaches characteristic of psychoanalytic and humanistic therapy (Sue & Zane, 1987). There is also some indication that culturally diverse clients prefer to see therapists who are similar in terms of cultural background and gender. More recent research, however, indicates that similarity of worldviews and attitudes to treatment between client and therapist may be more important than ethnic similarity (Atkinson, Ponce, & Martinez, 1984). Acculturation status may also determine client responses to treatment (Atkinson, Casa, & Abreu, 1992). "Culture-sensitive" counselors have been rated as being more credible and competent to conduct treatment across cultures by African Americans (Atkinson, Furlong, & Poston, 1986), Asian Americans (Gim, Atkinson, & Kim, 1991), and Mexican Americans (Atkinson et al., 1992).

Several authors (for example, Higginbotham, 1979; Sue, Akutsu, & Higashi, 1985; Sue & Zane, 1987; Tseng & McDermott, 1981) have outlined the competencies and knowledge base necessary for therapists to conduct sensitive and effective treatment across cultures. For example, Sue et al. (1985) suggest that the culturally sensitive therapist has acquired (1) knowledge of diverse cultures and lifestyles, (2) skill and comfort in using innovative treatment methods, and (3) actual experience working with culturally diverse clients. It is also critically important for the culturally sensitive therapist to be aware of his or her own cultural background and its influences on definitions and perceptions of abnormal behavior. Furthermore, the therapist must be aware of how cultural beliefs and experiences influence the course of treatment. Comas-Diaz and Jacobsen (1991) have outlined several ways in which ethnocultural factors may shape therapy. These include eliciting strong transference reactions (unconscious projections onto the therapist) and barriers to empathy (understanding of another's experience).

A focus of recent discussions of cross-cultural treatment of abnormal behavior has been culture-specific interventions. Several culture-specific forms of treatment have been identified in the literature, including Naikan and Morita therapy in Japan and espiritismo practiced among some Puerto Ricans. These approaches are generally very "foreign" to many Americans. Naikan therapy, for example, involves a "process of continuous medication based upon highly structured instruction in self-observation and self-reflection" (Murase, 1986, p. 389). Patients, usually placed in a small sitting area, practice their meditations from early in the morning (about 5:30 A.M.) until the evening (9:00 P.M. or so). Interviewers visit every 90 minutes to discuss progress, usually for about five minutes. Patients are instructed to examine themselves severely, much like a prosecutor would examine an accused prisoner.

Prince (1980) argues that what is common to treatment across cultures is the mobilization of healing forces within the client. Several others (such as Torrey, 1972; Tseng & McDermott, 1981) have also attempted to determine universal features of culture-specific systems of treatment. Although there may well be universal elements underlying systems of cure, culture-specific systems alone appear to address the unique definitions and expressions of abnormal behavior in a given culture.

Conclusion

In this chapter, we have seen that traditional definitions of abnormality may be limited. When the experiences of individuals from other cultures are studied, traditional definitions are not as useful in identifying, assessing, and treating abnormal behavior. There is a continuing controversy about whether to accept universal or culturally relative definitions of abnormal behavior. It seems clear, however, that there are cultural differences in both rates and expressions of major psychological disorders such as schizophrenia and depression. It also seems clear that some forms of abnormal behavior are not universal, but rather are unique to certain cultural settings.

Recognition of the role of culture in influencing the definition and expression of abnormality suggests that we must modify our methods of assessing and treating abnormal behavior. To develop adequate assessment and treatment strategies, we must take into account knowledge of culturally based definitions of normality and abnormality and culture-specific systems of healing. Research indicates that culturally sensitive assessment and treatment methods are vital to appropriately and effectively meet the mental health needs of culturally diverse populations.

Glossary

Bipolar disorder: A mood disorder characterized by alternating bouts of mania and depression.

Catatonia: A form of schizophrenia characterized by extreme withdrawal or agitation.

Culture-bound syndromes: Forms of abnormal behavior observed only in certain sociocultural milieus.

Depressive disorder: A mood disorder that involves the symptoms of "intense sadness, feelings of futility and worthlessness, and withdrawal from others" (Sue, Sue, & Sue, 1990, p. 325). Depression is often also characterized by physical changes (such as sleep and appetite disturbances) as well as emotional and behavioral changes (Berry, Poortinga, Segall, & Dasen, 1992).

Diathesis-stress model of schizophrenia: A model of schizophrenia that suggests that individuals with a biological predisposition to the disorder (diathesis) may develop the disorder following exposure to environmental stressors.

Psychosis: A class of abnormal behavior that is usually characterized by a loss of touch with reality. These may include delusions or hallucinations.

Schizophrenia: Part of a "group of psychotic disorders characterized by gross distortions of reality; withdrawal from social interaction; and disorganization of perception, thought, and emotion" (Carson, Butcher, & Coleman, 1988, p. 322).

Statistical-comparison approach: An approach to defining behavior as abnormal as a function of the frequency of its occurrence.

Subjective distress: One's individual feelings of distress of negative emotions.

References

Abebimpe, V. R. (1981). Overview: White norms and psychiatric diagnosis of black patients. *American Journal of Psychiatry, 139*, 888–891.

American Psychiatric Association. (1987). *Diagnostic and statistical manual of mental disorders* (3rd ed.) [DSM-III-R]. Washington, DC: APA.

Atkinson, D. R., Casa, A., & Abreu, J. (1992). Mexican American acculturation, counselor ethnicity and cultural sensitivity, and perceived counselor competence. *American Psychologist, 39*, 515–520.

Atkinson, D. R., Furlong, M. J., & Poston, W. C. (1986). Afro-American preferences for counselor characteristics. *Journal of Counseling Psychology, 33*, 326–330.

Atkinson, D. R., Ponce, F. Q., & Martinez, F. M. (1984). Effects of ethnic, sex, and attitude similarity on counselor credibility. *Journal of Counseling Psychology, 31*, 588–590.

Beiser, M. (1985). A study of depression among traditional Africans, urban North Americans, and Southeast Asian refugees. In A. Kleinman & B. Good (Eds.), *Culture and depression: Studies in the anthropology and cross-cultural psychiatry of affect and disorder* (pp. 272–298). Berkeley: University of California Press.

Berry, J. W., Poortinga, Y. H., Segall, M., & Dasen, P. R. (1992). *Cross-cultural psychology: Research and applications*. Cambridge: Cambridge University Press.

Carson, R. C., Butcher, J. N., & Coleman, J. C. (1988). *Abnormal psychology and modern life* (8th ed.). Glenview, IL: Scott, Foresman.

Comas-Diaz, L., & Jacobsen, F. M. (1991). Ethnocultural transference and countertransference in the therapeutic dyad. *American Journal of Orthopsychiatry, 61*, 392–402.

Gim, R. H., Atkinson, D. R., & Kim, S. J. (1991). Asian-American acculturation, counselor ethnicity and cultural sensitivity, and ratings of counselors. *Journal of Counseling Psychology, 38*, 57–62.

Higginbotham, H. N. (1979). Culture and mental health services. In A. J. Marsella, G. DeVos, & F. L. K. Hsu (Eds.), *Perspectives on cross-cultural psychology* (pp. 307–332). New York: Academic Press.

Karno, M., Jenkins, J. H., De la Selva, A., Santana, F., Telles, C., Lopez, S., & Mintz, J. (1987). Expressed emotion and schizophrenic outcome among Mexican-American families. *Journal of Nervous and Mental Disease, 175*, 145–151.

Kiev, A. (1972). *Transcultural psychiatry*. New York: Free Press.

Kleinman, A. (1978). Culture and depression. *Culture and Medical Psychiatry, 2*, 295–296.

Kleinman, A. (1988). *Rethinking psychiatry: From cultural category to personal experience*. New York: Free Press.

Leff, J. (1977). International variations in the diagnosis of psychiatric illness. *British Journal of Psychiatry, 131*, 329–338.

Leff, J. (1981). *Psychiatry around the globe: A transcultural view*. New York: Marcel Dekker.

Leff, J. (1986). The epidemiology of mental illness. In J. L. Cox (Ed)., *Transcultural psychiatry* (pp. 23–36). London: Croom Helm.

Lonner, W. J., & Ibrahim, F. A. (1989). Assessment in cross-cultural counseling. In P. B. Pedersen, J. Dragus, W. Lonner, & J. E. Trimble (Eds.), *Counseling across cultures* (3rd ed.) (pp. 299–334). Honolulu: University of Hawaii Press.

Manson, S. M., & Shore, J. H. (1981). Psychiatric epidemological research among American Indian and Alaska Natives: Some methodological issues. *White Cloud Journal, 2,* 48–56.

Manson, S. M., Shore, J. H., & Bloom, J. D. (1985). The depressive experience in American Indian communities: A challenge for psychiatric theory and diagnosis. In A. Kleinman & B. Good (Eds.), *Culture and depression: Studies in the anthropology and cross-cultural psychiatry of affect and disorder* (pp. 331–368). Berkeley: University of California Press.

Marsella, A. J. (1979). Cross-cultural studies of mental disorders. In A. J. Marsella, G. DeVos, & F. L. K. Hsu (Eds.), *Perspectives on cross-cultural psychology* (pp. 233–262). New York: Academic Press.

Marsella, A. J. (1980). Depressive experience and disorder across cultures. In H. C. Triandis & J. Dragus (Eds.), *Handbook of cross-cultural psychology. Vol. 6, Psychopathology* (pp. 237–289). Boston: Allyn & Bacon.

Mintz, J., Mintz, L., & Goldstein, M. (1987). Expressed emotion and relapse in first episodes of schizophrenia. *British Journal of Psychiatry, 151,* 314–320.

Murase, T. (1986). Naikan therapy. In T. S. Lebra and W. P. Lebra (Eds.), *Japanese culture and behavior* (pp. 388–398). Honolulu: University of Hawaii Press.

Murphy, H. B. M. (1982). Culture and schizophrenia. In I. Al-Issa (Ed.), *Culture and psychopathology* (pp. 221–249), Baltimore, MD: University Park Press.

Murphy, J. M. (1976). Psychiatric labeling in cross-cultural perspective. *Science, 191,* 1019–1028.

Myers, J. K., Weissman, M. M., Tischler, G. L., Holzer, C. E., Leaf, P. J., Orvaschel, H., Anthony, J. C., Boyd, J. H., Burke, J. D., Kramer, M., & Stolzman, R. (1984). Six-month prevalence of psychiatric disorders in three communities: 1980 to 1982. *Archives of General Psychiatry, 41,* 959–967.

Opler, M. K., & Singer, J. L. (1959). Ethnic differences in behavior and psychopathology. *International Journal of Social Psychiatry, 2,* 11–23.

Pfeiffer, W. M. (1982). Culture-bound syndromes. In I. Al-Issa (Ed.), *Culture and psychopathology* (pp. 201–218). Baltimore, MD: University Park Press.

Prince, R. (1980). Variations in psychotherapeutic procedures. In H. C. Triandis & J. Dragus (Eds.), *Handbook of cross-cultural psychology. Vol. 6, Psychopathology* (pp. 291–349). Boston: Allyn & Bacon.

Robins, L. N., Helzer, J. E., Weissman, M. M., Orvaschel, H., Gruenberg, E., Burke, J. D., & Reiger, D. (1984). Lifetime prevalence of specific psychiatric disorders in three sites. *Archives of General Psychiatry, 41,* 949–958.

Sue, D., Sue, D., & Sue, S. (1990). *Understanding abnormal behavior* (3rd ed.). Boston: Houghton Mifflin.

Sue, S. (1977). Community mental health services to minority groups: Some optimism, some pessimism. *American Psychologist, 32,* 616–624.

Sue, S. (1991, August). *Ethnicity and mental health: Research and policy issues.* Invited address presented at the Annual Meeting of the American Psychological Association, San Francisco, CA.

Sue, S., Akutsu, P. O., & Higashi, C. (1985). Training issues in conducting therapy with ethnic minority group clients. In P. Pedersen (Ed.), *Handbook of cross-cultural counseling and therapy* (pp. 275–280). Westport, CT: Greenwood.

Sue, S., & Morishima, J. K. (1982). *The mental health of Asian Americans.* San Francisco: Jossey-Bass.

Sue, S., & Zane, N. (1987). The role of culture and cultural techniques in psychotherapy: A reformation. *American Psychologist, 42,* 37–45.

Swartz, L. (1985). Anorexia nervosa as a culture-bound syndrome. *Social Science and Medicine, 20,* 725–730.

Terrell, M. D. (1992, August). *Stress, coping, ethnic identity and college adjustment.* Paper presented at the Annual Meeting of the American Psychological Association, Washington, DC.

Thomas, A., & Sillen, S. (1972). *Racism and psychiatry.* New York: Brunner/Mazel.

Torrey, E. F. (1972). *The mind game: Witchdoctors and psychiatrists.* New York: Emerson Hall.

Tseng, W., & McDermott, J. F. (1981). *Culture, mind and therapy: An introduction to cultural psychiatry.* New York: Brunner/Mazel.

World Health Organization. (1973). *Report of the International Pilot Study of Schizophrenia* (Vol. 1). Geneva: WHO.

World Health Organization. (1979). *Schizophrenia: An international follow-up study.* New York: John Wiley.

World Health Organization. (1981). *Current state of diagnosis and classification in the mental health field.* Geneva: WHO.

Yap, P. M. (1974). *Comparative psychiatry. A theoretical framework.* Toronto: University of Toronto Press.

Suggested Readings

Berry, J. W., Poortinga, Y. H., Segall, M. H., & Dasen, P. R. (1992). *Cross-cultural psychology: Research and applications.* New York: Cambridge University Press.

Sue, D., Sue, D., & Sue, S. (1990). *Understanding abnormal behavior* (3rd ed.). Boston: Houghton Mifflin.

Sue, S., & Zane, N. (1987). The role of culture and cultural techniques in psychotherapy: A reformation. *American Psychologist, 42,* 37–45.

10 *Social Psychology*

Humans are social animals, and our everyday lives involve many interactions with and influences by others. It is probably very difficult to think of an existence that is devoid of any contact with others. Social psychology is the branch of psychology concerned with individual behavior in social context—the way our thoughts, feelings, and behaviors influence, and are influenced by, others.

Psychologists have typically considered many varied topics and issues that are relevant to the study of social psychology. These include attribution, aggression, altruism, conformity, psychopathology, love, and the like. Because social psychology spans such a broad range of topics, it is perhaps one of the broadest branches of psychology.

It is probably fair to say that in the history of psychology, social psychology as a discipline has not enjoyed the same degree of interest or value among scientists as other fields of psychology. Much of the bias against social psychology in the past was influenced by the belief that anything "social" cannot be "scientific." Unfortunately, this belief still exists today, although not so much within psychology as outside.

Another factor contributing to social psychology's relative lack of popularity in the United States is the American culture's emphasis on the individual. The cultural value that Americans place on unique individualism has often been considered contradictory to the discipline engendered by social psychology. In studying social psychology, one can almost sense a negative bias against certain topics, such as conformity, that is undoubtedly related to our own culture's bias against "groupism."

This negative bias is not found in many other countries and cultures. In many other countries (but not all), social psychology enjoys a healthy reputation among the psychological and scientific communities. We find the bias in some countries and not in others because different cultures view the relationship between individuals and groups in different ways. Many other cultures consider groups to be a necessary and positive aspect of human functioning. (Indeed, many cultures consider groups to be the *sole* mechanism by which society exists!) Fortunately, there is a lot of research from other cultures that can be compared with traditional research findings generated in our own culture.

As mentioned, social psychology is not a single topic, but many separate, albeit interrelated, topics. A few of them are presented in this chapter: attributions; interpersonal attraction and love; conformity, compliance, and obedience; group productivity and social loafing; and person perception and impression formation. These topics are covered by most introductory courses and typically fall under the rubric of social psychology. Because each is a separate topic, it is difficult to make global, summary statements about all of them in a single section. Instead, each section begins with a brief definition of the topic, describes some of the major findings obtained in research in the United States, and then concludes with findings from cross-cultural research on that topic that may challenge the traditional notions. This chapter ends with a summary of the points in relation to cultural stereotypes and ethnocentrism.

Attributions

Attributions are the inferences that people draw about the causes of events and their own and others' behaviors. The study of attributions is important in social psychology because they tell us how people explain behaviors. Studying attributions also allows us to examine the biases that operate as people explain others' behaviors, which, in turn, affect their own behavior.

Research on attributions in the United States has centered on several issues. One issue concerns the *types* of attributions that people make, especially in relation to the locus of their attributions of causality. A popular concept in attribution research, for example, involves the distinction between internal and external attributions. **Internal attributions** are those that specify the cause of behavior within a person; **external attributions** are those that locate the cause of behavior outside a person.

Attributions have been widely studied in achievement situations, ranging from academic settings to sports to occupational contexts. These studies, in turn, have led to the development of several major theories of attribution. Research on **attribution bias**—the tendency to make certain types of attributions despite lack of evidence—has led to several popular concepts in social psychology, including fundamental attribution error, defensive attributions, and self-serving bias.

Knowledge Based on Research in the United States

One popular model of attribution is Kelley's covariation model (1967, 1973). This model assumes that people attribute behavior to causes that are present when the behavior occurs and absent when the behavior does not occur. According to this theory, people usually consider three types of information—consistency, distinctiveness, and consensus—when making attributions. *Consistency* refers to whether a person's behavior in a situation is the same over time. *Distinctiveness* refers to whether a person's behavior is unique to the specific target of the behavior. *Consensus* refers to whether other people in the same situation tend to respond in the same manner. Behaviors that have high consistency but not distinctiveness or consensus produce internal attributions. Behaviors that have high consistency, high distinctiveness, and high consensus, however, produce external attributions.

Another major theory of attribution is Weiner's theory (1974). This theory focuses on the concept of stability. According to Weiner, stability cuts across the internal-external dimension, creating four types of attributions for success and failure: stable and unstable internal and external attributions. For example, if you fail to get a job you wanted, you might attribute your failure to stable, internal factors (such as lack of ability or initiative); stable, external factors (too much competition); unstable, internal factors (lack of effort); or unstable, external factors (bad luck).

Research on attributional bias is informative about the culture-bound nature of attributions in this country. **Fundamental attribution error**, for example, refers to the tendency to explain the behavior of others using internal attributions, but to explain one's own behaviors using external attributions (Jones & Nisbett, 1971; Watson, 1982). For example, you might attribute a friend's poor grade to low intelligence or ability (internal attribution). At the same time, however, you might attribute your own poor grade to the teacher's bias or bad luck (external attribution).

Self-serving bias is the tendency to attribute one's successes to personal factors and one's failures to situational factors (Bradley, 1978). If you fail an exam, for instance, you may attribute your failure to a poorly constructed test, lousy teaching, distractions, or a bad week at home (external attribution). If you ace an exam, however, you are more likely to attribute that to effort, intelligence, or ability (internal attribution).

Defensive attribution refers to the tendency to blame victims for their misfortune, so that one feels less likely to be victimized in a similar way (Thornton, 1984). If you attribute another's misfortunes (burglary, rape, getting fired from a job, or the like) to the victim rather than to circumstance, then you will find it easier *not* to consider that the same misfortune may occur to you.

These attributional styles and theories affect our behaviors and our understanding of others' behaviors. However, this knowledge is derived from research conducted almost exclusively in the United States. Cross-cultural research on attributions helps us question the limitations of this knowledge.

Cross-Cultural Findings on Attributions

Cross-cultural research on attributions is especially important in furthering our understanding of intercultural interactions. The consequences for incorrect attributions are potentially severe. Interpreting the causes of behavior accurately, especially with regard to intentions and goodwill, is important to the success of *any* type of social interaction. Intercultural interactions are no exception. For instance, an individual may be too quick to attribute another person's behavior to ill will or negative feelings when actually the behavior is rooted in a cultural dynamic that fosters such behavior. If this happens, the relationship may suffer drastically. In our attributions of others' behaviors, as well as our own, we should allow for the influence of cultural factors. By doing so, we take an important step toward improving intercultural understanding and relationships.

There are many examples of how people of other cultures differ from Americans in their attributions. Several studies, for instance, have shown that the self-serving bias found in studies with American students is not always found in students from other cultures. For instance, Hau and Salili (1991) asked junior and senior high school students in Hong Kong to rate the importance and meaning of 13 specific causes of academic performance. Effort, interest, and ability all were rated the most important causes, regardless of success or failure. These are all internal attributions. Likewise, Moghaddam, Ditto, and Taylor (1990) showed that Indian women who had immigrated to Canada were more likely to attribute both successes *and* failures to internal causes.

Two studies with Taiwanese subjects also challenge our notions about self-serving attributions. Crittenden (1991) showed that Taiwanese women used more external and self-effacing attributions about themselves than did American women. Crittenden suggested that the Taiwanese women did this to enhance their public and private self-esteem by using an attributional approach that conformed to a feminine gender role. Earlier, Bond, Leung, and Wan (1982) showed that self-effacing Chinese students were better liked by their peers than those who adopted this attributional style to a lesser degree.

Other cross-cultural studies on attribution pepper the literature with findings that challenge our traditional notions of attribution. Kashima and Triandis (1986), for example, showed that Japanese used a much more group-oriented, collective approach to attributional styles with regard to attention and memory achievement tasks. Unlike their American counterparts, Japanese subjects attributed failure to themselves more, and success to themselves less. Kashima and Triandis interpreted this finding as suggestive of American and Japanese cultural differences in the degree to which members of each culture take responsibility.

Forgas, Furnham, and Frey (1989) documented broad cross-national differences in the importance of different types of specific attributions for wealth. Their study included 558 subjects from the United Kingdom, Australia, and the Federal Republic of Germany. The British considered family background and luck as the most important determinants of wealth. The Germans also considered family background as the most important determinant. The Australians, however, rated individual qualities as the most important determinant of wealth.

Duda and Allison (1989) have provided a framework to consider limits to attribution theories based on cross-cultural research. They have suggested that theories are limited in cross-cultural application because of ethnocentric notions on three important issues. The first concerns the impact of culture on definitions of success and failure. How Americans view success and failure is often not how people of other cultures define them. The second issue concerns cultural differences in the meanings of the specific elements in attribution theories (effort, work, luck, and so on). Different meanings of these elements have different implications for the meanings of the attributions associated with them. Finally, the third issue has to do with limitations in the use of bipolar dimensions in research. Cultural differences in the dimensions that are important in understanding and predicting attributions may lead to entirely different expectations of attribution styles.

Several studies highlight the possible negative consequences of cultural differences in attributions. Wong, Derlaga, and Colson (1988), for example, asked 40 white and 40 black undergraduates to read stories about the performance of either a black or a white child. The students were then asked to (1) explain why the child failed or succeeded, (2) describe their own questions concerning the child's performance, and (3) predict the child's performance on other tasks. All subjects, regardless of their race, generated more questions and causal explanations for the performance of a black rather than a white target. All subjects also expected the white student to do better than the black counterpart on other tasks.

Tom and Cooper (1986) examined the attributions of 25 white elementary school teachers for the performance of students varying in social class, race, and gender. The results indicated that the teachers were more likely to take into account the successes of middle-class, white students, and discount their failures, relative to students of other social classes or races.

Other findings also exist. Hall, Howe, Merkel, and Lederman (1986), for example, asked teachers to make causal attributions about the performance of black and white students. Their findings suggested that the teachers all believed that the black females exerted the greatest amount of effort (although the teachers also believed that the black males exerted the least). Graham and her colleagues (for example, Graham, 1984; Graham & Long, 1986) have also shown that there is considerable overlap in the attributions of black and white subjects in their studies and that these attributions are often equally adaptive. In addition, these researchers have found that attributions are also influenced by social factors such as class, as well as by race and culture.

Cross-cultural research on attributions *in toto* does not yet provide a clear, consistent picture of the nature of attributions or the attributional processes across all cultures and races. But its message to date is quite clear: People of different cultures do have different attributional styles, and these differences are deeply rooted in cultural background and upbringing. A sufficient number of studies question the cross-cultural applicability of many of the popular notions about attributions found to be true in the United States. Self-serving biases, defensive attributions, and fundamental attribution error do not exist in the same way, or have the same meaning, in other cultures.

Interpersonal Attraction and Love

Interpersonal attraction refers to positive feelings toward others and is an important dimension of social psychology. Psychologists use this term broadly to encompass a variety of experiences, including liking, friendship, admiration, lust, and love. Research on interpersonal attraction and love in the United States has produced a number of interesting findings, mainly focusing on the key factors that contribute to attraction. Unfortunately, there is not much cross-cultural research on these topics in the literature. The findings from those few studies that have been published, however, give important clues to cultural differences in attraction and love.

Knowledge Based on Research in the United States

Several studies have shown that proximity influences attraction. Early research (for example, Festinger, Schachter, & Back, 1950) showed that people who lived closer to one another were more likely to like one another. Despite the amount of time that has passed since this study, findings from some recent studies still support this notion. In the late 1970s, for instance, Ineichen (1979) showed that people who lived closer together were more likely to get married.

Physical attractiveness has been shown to be quite influential in interpersonal relationships (Patzer, 1985). This attractiveness, however, may be more important for females than for males (Buss, 1988). Although people prefer physically attractive partners in romantic relationships, the **matching hypothesis** suggests that people of approximately equal physical characteristics are likely to select each other as partners. Likewise, the **similarity hypothesis** suggests that people similar in age, race, religion, social class, education, intelligence, attitudes, and physical attractiveness tend to form intimate relationships (Brehm, 1985; Hendrick & Hendrick, 1983). The **reciprocity hypothesis** suggests that people tend to like others who like them.

Among the prevalent theories of love and attachment in American psychology are Hatfield and Berscheid's and Sternberg's. Hatfield and Berscheid's theory proposes that romantic relationships are characterized by two kinds of love (Berscheid & Walster, 1978; Hatfield, 1988). One is **passionate love**, involving an absorption of another that includes sexual feelings and intense emotion. The second is **companionate love**, involving warm, trusting, and tolerant affection for another whose life is deeply intertwined with one's own.

Sternberg's (1988) theory is similar but further divides companionate love into two components: intimacy and commitment. **Intimacy** refers to warmth, closeness, and sharing in a relationship. **Commitment** refers to an intention to maintain a relationship in spite of the difficulties that arise. In Sternberg's theory, eight different forms of love can exist, depending on the presence or absence of each of the three factors. When all three exist, Sternberg calls that relationship **consummate love**.

Cross-Cultural Findings on Interpersonal Attraction and Love

Before reviewing cross-cultural studies on interpersonal attraction and love, we should note that cross-cultural research on these topics is not as abundant as on other topics. This may reflect a difference on the part of psychologists (and the lay public) of other cultures that love, attraction, and liking do not fall within the purview of science to the degree that they do for Americans and American psychologists. Or perhaps this belief is also held by American scientists who plan to do cross-cultural research.

Interestingly, the cross-cultural studies that do exist seem to support this speculation. Ting-Toomey (1991), for example, compared ratings of love commitment, disclosure maintenance, ambivalence, and conflict expression by 781 subjects from France, Japan, and the United States.

Love commitment was measured by ratings of feelings of attachment, belonging, and commitment to the partner and relationship; disclosure maintenance by ratings of feelings concerning private self in the relationship; ambivalence by ratings of feelings of confusion or uncertainty regarding the partner or the relationship; and conflict expression by ratings of frequency of overt arguments and seriousness of problems. The French and the Americans gave significantly higher ratings than did the Japanese on love commitment and disclosure maintenance. The Americans also gave significantly higher ratings than did the Japanese on relational ambivalence. The Japanese and the Americans, however, had significantly higher ratings than did the French on conflict expression.

Simmons, vomKolke, and Shimizu (1986) examined attitudes toward love and romance among American, German, and Japanese students. The results indicated that romantic love was valued more in the United States and Germany than in Japan. These authors suggested that this cultural difference arose because romantic love is more highly valued in less traditional cultures with few strong, extended-family ties, and less valued in cultures where kinship networks influence and reinforce the relationship between marriage partners.

In another study, Furnham (1984) administered the Rokeach Value Survey to groups of South Africans, Indians, and Europeans. The Europeans valued love more than did the South Africans and the Indians. The South Africans, however, placed higher value on equality and peace.

Again, cross-cultural research on interpersonal attraction and love does not enjoy as broad an empirical base as other topics within social psychology. The lack of studies, and the findings that do exist in the studies presented in this section, suggest considerable cultural differences in the values and attitudes concerning love and romance from traditional American culture.

Conformity, Compliance, and Obedience

Conformity refers to the yielding of people to real or imagined social pressure. **Compliance** is generally defined as the yielding of people to social pressure regarding their public behavior, even though their private beliefs may not have changed. **Obedience** is a form of compliance that occurs when people follow direct commands, usually from someone in a position of authority.

Each of these topics is an important issue in social psychology. In American psychology, there is an underlying negative bias against them. These terms no doubt contradict some values traditionally thought to be American, such as uniqueness, individualism, and freedom. Research on these issues in the United States has shown that they can have considerable effects on individual behaviors.

Knowledge Based on Research in the United States

Two of the most well-known studies in American psychology on conformity, compliance, and obedience are the Asch and Milgram studies. Asch's studies (1951, 1955, 1956) examined subjects' responses to a simple judgment task when experimental confederates responding before the subject all give the incorrect response. Across studies and trials, group size and group unanimity were major influencing factors. Conformity would peak when the groups included seven people and the group was unanimous in their judgments (even though the judgments were clearly wrong). Compliance in Asch's studies resulted from subtle, implied pressure. But in the real world, compliance can occur in response to explicit rules, requests, and commands.

In Milgram's studies (1963, 1964, 1974), subjects were brought into a laboratory presumably to study the effects of punishment on learning. Subjects were instructed to provide shocks to another subject (actually an experimental confederate) when the latter gave the wrong response or no response. The apparent shock meter was labeled from "slight shock" to "DANGER: Severe Shock," and the confederate's behaviors ranged from simple utterances of pain through pounding on the walls, pleas to stop, and then deathly silence. Despite these conditions, 65% of the subjects obeyed the commands of the experimenter and administered the most severe levels of shock.

The Asch experimenters were rather innocuous in the actual content of the compliance (for example, judgments of the length of lines). The Milgram studies, however, clearly highlighted the potential negative and harmful effects of compliance and obedience. To this day, they stand among the most well-known studies in American psychology. Today, such experiments are unlikely to be attempted again because of current restrictions based on ethics and university standards of conduct.

Cross-Cultural Findings on Conformity, Compliance, and Obedience

Many cross-cultural studies, particularly with Asian cultures, indicate that not only do people of other cultures engage in conforming, compliant, and obedient behaviors to a greater degree than do Americans, but that they also value conformity to a greater degree. For example, Punetha, Giles, and Young (1987) administered an extended Rokeach Value Survey to three groups of Asian subjects and a group of British subjects. The British clearly valued individualistic items, such as independence and freedom, whereas the Asian subjects endorsed societal values including conformity and obedience.

Studies involving other Asian versus American comparisons have generally produced the same results. Hadiyono and Hahn (1985), for example, showed that Indonesians endorsed conformity more than did Americans. Argyle, Henderson, Bond, Iizuka, and Contarello (1986) showed that the Japanese and Hong Kong Chinese endorsed obedience more than did British and Italian subjects. Buck, Newton, and Muramatsu (1984) showed that the Japanese were more conforming than were Americans.

Some studies have shown that these differences are not limited to Asian cultures. Cashmore and Goodnow (1986), for example, demonstrated that Italians were more conforming than Anglo-Australians. El-Islam (1983) documented cultural differences in conformity in an Arabian sample.

These findings are undoubtedly related to cultural differences in values regarding "groupism" versus individualism. Traditional American culture fosters individualistic values, thus endorsing behaviors and beliefs contrary to conformity. To conform in American culture is to be weak or deficient somehow. But this is not true in other cultures. Many cultures foster more collective, group-oriented values, and concepts of conformity, obedience, and compliance enjoy much higher status and positive orientation than in the United States. In these cultures, conformity is not only viewed as "good," it is necessary for the successful functioning of the culture, its groups, and the interpersonal relationships of the members of that culture.

Cross-cultural studies on child-rearing values speak to the strength of these values in socialization. Two studies have shown that not only Asians but also Puerto Rican subjects value conformity and obedience as a child-rearing value (Burgos & Diaz-Perez, 1986; Stropes-Roe & Cochrane, 1990). A number of anthropological works on the Japanese culture (for example, Benedict, 1946; Doi, 1985) indicate the importance of obedience and compliance in child-rearing in that culture.

Group Behavior: Productivity versus Social Loafing

Research on groups, and not individuals within groups per se, also falls under the purview of social psychology. Research on group behavior has received considerable attention in the literature, covering such topics as the bystander effect and altruistic behaviors, group decision-making processes, and productivity. Each of these areas affects real-life settings and issues and forms the basis for many intervention techniques, especially in organizational and industrial psychology.

In this section, we focus on the study of individual and group productivity. Much of what is reported about this topic in social psychology concerns the opposite of productivity: social loafing.

Knowledge Based on Research in the United States

Research on group productivity has typically shown that individual productivity often declines in larger groups (Latane, Williams, & Harkins, 1979). These findings have contributed to the coining of the term, *social loafing*. Two factors appear to contribute to this phenomenon. One is the reduced efficiency resulting from the loss of coordination among workers' efforts. As group membership increases, presumably the lack of coordination among the people tends to reduce efficiency, resulting in lack of activity or duplicate activity. This consequently results in loss of productivity.

The second factor typically identified as a contributor to lack of group productivity involves the reduction in effort by individuals when they work in groups as compared to when they work by themselves (**social loafing**). Latane and his colleagues (Latane, 1981; Latane, Williams, & Harkins, 1979) have conducted a number of studies investigating group size, coordination, and effort. They have found that larger groups produced lack of both coordination and effort, resulting in decreased productivity. Latane (1981) attributed these findings to a diffusion of responsibility in groups. That is, as group size increases, the responsibility for getting a job done is divided among more people, and many group members slack off because their individual contribution is less recognizable.

Cross-Cultural Findings on Group Productivity

Several cross-cultural studies suggest that social loafing is definitely *not* generalizable across other cultures. Earley (1989), for example, examined social loafing in an organizational setting among managerial trainees in the United States and the People's Republic of China. Subjects in both cultures worked on a task under conditions of low or high accountability and low or high shared responsibility. The results were clear, indicating that social loafing was observed only among the American subjects, whose individual performances in a group were less than when working alone, but not among the Chinese.

Shirakashi (1985) and Yamaguchi, Okamoto, and Oka (1985) conducted studies involving Japanese participants in several tasks. They showed that not only did social loafing not occur, but exactly the opposite occurred. That is, being in a group enhanced individual performance of their subjects rather than diminished it. Gabrenya, Wang, and Latane (1985) also demonstrated this **social striving**, not social loafing, in a sample of Chinese schoolchildren.

Several authors have offered some speculations concerning why social striving has been observed in other cultures. These explanations center on the culture's degree of collectivism, or group orientation. Cultures that are more collectivistic—such as China and Japan—foster interpersonal interdependence and group collective functioning more than does the individualistic American culture. As a result, groups tend to be more productive in these cultures, precisely because they foster coordination among ingroup members. They also place higher value on individual contributions in group settings.

Interestingly, a trend toward social striving may also be occurring within the United States. Several studies involving American subjects have begun to challenge the traditional notions of social loafing (for example, Harkins, 1987; Harkins & Petty, 1982; Shepperd & Wright, 1989; Weldon & Gargano, 1988; Zaccaro, 1984). Jackson and Williams (1985), for instance, showed that Americans working collectively indeed improved performance and productivity. Thus, our notions of social loafing and group productivity are challenged not only cross-culturally, but within our own American culture as well. With increased American interest in the organizational and management styles of other countries, particularly Japan, this topic is sure to gain even more attention in the future.

Person Perception and Impression Formation

Person perception refers to the process of forming impressions of others. This area is important in social psychology because psychologists have long realized the influence of impressions and perceptions of others in our interactions and dealings with them. Questions concerning the degree to which impressions influence our actual behaviors, and the extent to which people's expectations color their impressions of others, fall within the purview of person perception. Psychologists are also concerned with questions concerning whether bad first impressions can be overcome.

This topic is discussed last in this chapter because it is influenced by *all* the areas previously discussed—attribution, interpersonal relationships, conformity, and group behavior. In addition, our understanding of cultural influences on person perception is informed by other aspects of psychology throughout this book.

In general, the areas of person perception and impression formation in American social psychology have encumbered their own specific lines of interest. Research in the United States on person perception has outlined several key factors that contribute to the formation of our impressions of others, including appearance, schemas, stereotypes, and selectivity in person perception.

Knowledge Based on Research in the United States

Appearance, especially physical attractiveness, influences judgments of personality. Research with American subjects has consistently shown that, in general, people tend to ascribe desirable personality characteristics to those who are good looking, seeing them as more sensitive, kind, sociable, pleasant, likable, and interesting than those who are unattractive (Dion, 1986; Patzer, 1985). Attractive people are also judged as more competent and intelligent (Ross & Ferris, 1981).

Other aspects of appearance also influence our perceptions of others. For example, greater height has been associated with perceptions of leadership ability, competence, and salary (Deck, 1968; Patzer, 1985). Adults with baby-face features tend to be judged as more warm, kind, naive, and submissive; adults with more mature facial features tend to be judged as strong, worldly, and dominant (Berry & McArthur, 1985, 1986). People who are neat dressers are thought to be conscientious (Albright, Kenny, & Malloy, 1988). People with poor eye contact are often judged as dishonest (DePaulo, Stone, & Lassiter, 1985).

Research on person perception in the United States has also focused on the ways in which impressions are formed and information about others is stored. Much attention has been given to the study of cognitive or social schemas as organizational tools. **Social schemas** are organized clusters of ideas about categories of social events and people and have been shown to widely influence person perceptions (Zajonc, 1985). Much attention has also been given to the study of stereotypes and their influence on our impressions of others. **Stereotypes** are widely held beliefs that people have certain characteristics because of their membership in a particular group. Finally, social psychologists have studied the influence of *selectivity* of our perceptions of others to either confirm or disconfirm beliefs and stereotypes.

Cross-Cultural Findings on Person Perception and Impression Formation

Many cross-cultural studies challenge our traditional notions of person perception in American psychology. For example, cross-cultural studies of nonverbal behavior—including gaze, proximity, touching behaviors, verbal utterances, and facial expressions—all speak to the impact of culture on communication. Differences in these behaviors arising from differences in cultural upbringing undoubtedly affect our perception of people of different cultures. We are often unaware of the existence of cultural differences or are unprepared to deal with them. Thus, it is easy to form negative perceptions of others because of cultural differences in these nonverbal behaviors.

Although the effects of attractiveness and physical appearance on the formation of positive impressions are well documented, cultures clearly differ on the meaning and definition of attractiveness. Beauty can be a quite relative judgment, and people of different cultures can have quite different, and distinct, concepts of what is beautiful and what is not. Cultural differences in the definition of attractiveness can clearly affect its influence on the formation of impressions.

Cultural differences in facial expressions also speak to the impact of cultures on person perception. In one study (Matsumoto & Kudoh, in press), for example, American and Japanese subjects were asked to judge Caucasian and Japanese faces that were either smiling or neutral on three dimensions: attractiveness, intelligence, and sociability. The Americans consistently rated the smiling faces higher on all three dimensions, congruent with our traditional notions of person perception and impression formation. The Japanese, however, rated the smiling faces only as more sociable. There was no difference in their ratings of attractiveness between smiling and neutral expressions, and they rated the neutral faces as more intelligent!

Even when different cultures agree on overall dimensional judgments of others, they may disagree on what kinds of behavioral consequences those judgments may have. For example, Bond and Forgas (1984) presented Chinese and Australian subjects with a description of a target person varying across dimensions such as extroversion, agreeableness, conscientiousness, and emotional stability. Across both cultures, target-person conscientiousness was linked with intentions of trust, whereas extroversion and agreeableness were linked to intentions of association. However, the Chinese subjects were much more likely than were the Australians to form behavioral intentions of trust and to form behavioral associations based on agreeableness.

Thus, ample evidence exists to suggest that cultures differ in both the process and meaning of person perception and impression formation. This area of social psychology is indeed germane to our understanding of cultures, stereotypes, and ethnocentrism.

Conclusion: Cultures, Stereotypes, and Ethnocentrism

Although only a few cross-cultural studies have focused directly on the issues of appearance, schemas, stereotypes, or selectivity in perception, the entire field of cross-cultural psychology speaks strongly to our overall understanding of person perception. This area is particularly germane to intergroup relationships.

Improving our understanding of the dynamics of person perception and its influence on the development and maintenance of stereotypes is extremely important in today's world. Despite the steps that we have taken to close the gap between different groups of people in the last few decades, especially between the races, the 1992 riots in Los Angeles and the cries to "Buy American!" in the last few years both speak to the pervasive and strong sentiments of "groupism" that can have negative, and positive, effects.

As discussed throughout this book, culture influences behavior, thoughts, and feelings and produces differences that challenge our preconceived notion of psychology in the United States. These differences are especially applicable to the area of person perception. Cultural differences in behaviors can lead to misperceptions, and misjudgments, of people.

The first way in which cross-cultural psychology impacts on our knowledge and understanding of person perception and intergroup relationships is by improving our understanding of "culture." Most cross-cultural psychologists would agree that culture is a sociopsychological phenomenon—the shared attitudes, beliefs, values, and behaviors communicated from one generation to the next via language (Barnouw, 1985). This definition of culture is "fuzzy," not clear, soft, not hard. Culture is *not* race, per se, although a race in general may embrace a particular culture. Culture is *not* nation per se, although people of different nations in general embrace their own cultures. In this light, many of the behaviors we observe in people of other races or nations seem different because of differences in culture, not necessarily differences in race or nationality.

Ironically, however, it is precisely these cultural differences in behavior that give rise to stereotypes. We often observe people of different races engaging in behavior that we may not deem appropriate or acceptable given a certain situation or context. Many times we interpret these behaviors within *our own* cultural background and upbringing, and *attribute* those behaviors to reasons that make sense only within our own cultural understanding. We may do this automatically, without pause or consideration of the different cultural backgrounds or circumstances that may have brought about the behavior in the first place. This type of nonrecognition of a cultural viewpoint other than our own may lay the foundation for *ethnocentrism*—the tendency to interpret the behaviors and events around us through our own cultural filter. We may become selective in the events that we perceive and in the attributions that we assign to them.

Improving our understanding of culture, however, helps us to bridge the gap between groups and to begin to break away from the bonds of ethnocentrism. By recognizing that culture is neither race nor nation, we can begin to break persistent racial stereotypes and to search for cultural—that is, sociopsychological—reasons for differences in behavior. At the same time, we need to search our own culture to find reasons why these stereotypes have persisted and how our own culture may be fostered or facilitated by their maintenance.

Cross-cultural psychology also informs us about *variability* within groups and cultures. No single score on any scale can describe or define a culture in its broadest sense. Culture is much too grand and rich to be defined by one component. Culture is not the *average* across a set of people; all the people, their diversity as well as their homogeneity, contribute to that culture. Improving our understanding of the great diversity and variability that exists within any culture will help to release us from stereotypes that we may carry in our interactions with people of different cultures. By recognizing that this degree of diversity exists in all cultures, we are free to allow ourselves to engage with people on their grounds, rather than by predetermining their actions, behaviors, and reasons via stereotype.

Finally, cross-cultural psychology informs us about the importance of cultural background, upbringing, and heritage and their impact on our present-day behaviors. Many of our behaviors as adults are not only shaped by culture, but also draw their meaning from culture. Recognizing the important contributions of culture to behaviors and reasons for these behaviors helps us to understand, respect, and appreciate the differences when we observe them in real life.

Glossary

Attribution bias: The tendency to make certain types of attributions despite the lack of evidence to support such attributions.

Attributions: The inferences that people draw about the causes of events and their own and others' behaviors.

Commitment: An intention to maintain a relationship in spite of the difficulties that arise.

Companionate love: Love characterized by warm, trusting, and tolerant affection for another whose life is deeply intertwined with one's own.

Compliance: The yielding of people to social pressure in their public behavior, even though their private beliefs may not have changed.

Conformity: The yielding of people to real or imagined social pressure.

Consummate love: In Sternberg's theory of love, this type of love is characterized by the existence of passionate love, intimacy, and commitment.

Defensive attributions: The tendency to blame victims for their misfortune, so that one feels less likely to be victimized in a similar way.

External attributions: Attributions that locate the cause of behavior outside a person.

Fundamental attribution error: The tendency to explain the behavior of others using internal attributions, but to explain one's own behaviors using external attributions.

Internal attributions: Attributions that specify the cause of behavior within a person.

Interpersonal attraction: Positive feelings toward others.

Intimacy: Warmth, closeness, and sharing in a relationship.

Matching hypothesis: The hypothesis about interpersonal attraction that suggests that people of approximately equal physical characteristics are likely to select each other as partners.

Obedience: A form of compliance that occurs when people follow direct commands, usually from someone in a position of authority.

Passionate love: Love characterized by an absorption of another that includes sexual feelings and intense emotion.

Person perception: The process of forming impressions of others.

Reciprocity hypothesis: The hypothesis about interpersonal attraction that suggests that people tend to like others who like them.

Self-serving bias: The tendency to attribute one's successes to personal factors and one's failures to situational factors.

Similarity hypothesis: The hypothesis about interpersonal attraction that suggests that people similar in age, race, religion, social class, education, intelligence, attitudes, and physical attractiveness tend to form intimate relationships.

Social loafing: A term coined to describe findings that suggest that individual productivity often declines in larger groups.

Social schemas: Organized clusters of ideas about categories of social events and people.

Social striving: A term coined to describe findings from cross-cultural research that suggest that being in a group enhances individual performance rather than diminishes it.

Stereotypes: Widely held beliefs that people have certain characteristics because of their membership in a particular group.

References

Albright, L., Kenny, D. A., & Malloy, T. E. (1988). Consensus in personality judgements at zero acquaintance. *Journal of Personality and Social Psychology, 55,* 387–395.

Argyle, M., Henderson, M., Bond, M. H., Iizuka, Y., & Contarello, A. (1986). Cross-cultural variations in relationship rules. *International Journal of Psychology, 21,* 287–315.

Asch, S. E. (1951). Effects of group pressure upon the modification and distortion of judgments. In H. Guetzkow (Ed.), *Groups, leadership and men: Research in human relations* (pp. 177–190). Pittsburgh: Carnegie Press.

Asch, S. E. (1955). Opinions and social pressures. *Scientific American, 193,* 31–35.

Asch, S. E. (1956). Studies of independence and conformity: A minority of one against a unanimous majority. *Psychological Monographs, 70*(9, Whole No. 416).

Barnouw, V. (1985). *Culture and personality.* Chicago: Dorsey Press.

Benedict, R. (1946). *The chrysanthemum and the sword.* Boston: Houghton Mifflin.

Berry, D. S., & McArthur, L. Z. (1985). Some components and consequences of a babyface. *Journal of Personality and Social Psychology, 48,* 312–323.

Berry, D. S., & McArthur, L. Z. (1986). Perceiving character in faces: The impact of age-related craniofacial changes in social perception. *Psychological Bulletin, 100,* 3–18.

Berscheid, E., & Walster, E. (1978). *Interpersonal attraction.* Reading, MA: Addison-Wesley.

Bond, M. H., & Forgas, J. P. (1984). Linking person perception to behavior intention across cultures: The role of cultural collectivism. *Journal of Cross-Cultural Psychology, 15,* 337–352.

Bond, M. H., Leung, K., & Wan, K. C. (1982). The social impact of self effacing attributions: The Chinese case. *Journal of Social Psychology, 118,* 157–166.

Bradley, G. W. (1978). Self-serving biases in the attribution process: A re-examination of the fact or fiction question. *Journal of Personality and Social Psychology, 35,* 56–71.

Brehm, S. S. (1985). *Intimate relationships.* New York: Random House.

Buck, E. B., Newton, B. J., & Muramatsu, Y. (1984). Independence and obedience in the U. S. and Japan. *International Journal of Intercultural Relations, 8,* 279–300.

Burgos, N. M., & Diaz-Perez, Y. I. (1986). An explanation of human sexuality in the Puerto Rican culture. [Special issue: *Human sexuality, ethnoculture, and social work.*] *Journal of Social Work and Human Sexuality, 4,* 135–150.

Buss, D. M. (1988). The evolution of human intrasexual competition: Tactics of mate attraction. *Journal of Personality and Social Psychology, 54,* 616–628.

Cashmore, J. A., & Goodnow, J. J. (1986). Influences on Australian parents' values: Ethnicity versus sociometric status. *Journal of Cross-Cultural Psychology, 17,* 441–454.

Crittenden, K. S. (1991). Asian self-effacement or feminine modesty? Attributional patterns of women university students in Taiwan. *Gender and Society, 5,* 98–117.

Deck, L. P. (1968). Buying brains by the inch. *Journal of College and University Personnel Associations*, *19*, 33–37.

DePaulo, B. M., Stone, J., & Lassiter, G. D. (1985). Deceiving and detecting deceit. In B. R. Schlenker (Ed.), *The self and social life* (pp. 323–370). New York: McGraw-Hill.

Dion, K. K. (1986). Stereotyping based on physical attractiveness: Issues and conceptual perspectives. In C. P. Herman, M. P. Zanna, & E. T. Higgins (Eds.), *Ontario symposium on personality and social psychology* (Vol. 3). Hillsdale, NJ: Erlbaum.

Doi, T. (1985). *The anatomy of self.* Tokyo: Kodansha.

Duda, J. L., & Allison, M. T. (1989). The attributional theory of achievement motivation: Cross-cultural considerations. *International Journal of Intercultural Relations*, *13*, 37–55.

Earley, P. C. (1989). Social loafing and collectivism: A comparison of the United States and the People's Republic of China. *Administrative Science Quarterly*, *34*, 565–581.

El-Islam, M. F. (1983). Cultural change and intergenerational relationships in Arabian families. *International Journal of Family Psychiatry*, *4*, 321–329.

Festinger, L., Schachter, S., & Back, K. (1950). *Social pressures in informal groups: A study of human factors in housing.* New York: Harper.

Forgas, J. P., Furnham, A., & Frey, D. (1989). Cross-national differences in attributions of wealth and economic success. *Journal of Social Psychology*, *129*, 643–657.

Furnham, A. F. (1984). Value systems and anomie in three cultures. *International Journal of Psychology*, *19*, 565–579.

Gabrenya, W. K., Jr., Wang, Y., & Latane, B. (1985). Social loafing on an optimizing task: Cross-cultural differences among Chinese and Americans. *Journal of Cross-Cultural Psychology*, *16*, 223–242.

Graham, S. (1984). Communicating sympathy and anger to Black and White children: The cognitive (attributional) consequences of affective cues. *Journal of Personality and Social Psychology*, *47*, 40–54.

Graham, S., & Long, A. (1986). Race, class, and the attributional process. *Journal of Educational Psychology*, *78*, 4–13.

Hadiyono, J. E. P., & Hahn, M. W. (1985). Personality differences and sex similarities in American and Indonesian college students. *Journal of Social Psychology*, *125*, 703–708.

Hall, V. C., Howe, A., Merkel, S., & Lederman, N. (1986). Behavior, motivation, and achievement in desegregated junior high school science classes. *Journal of Educational Psychology*, *78*, 108–115.

Harkins, S. G. (1987). Social loafing and social facilitation. *Journal of Experimental Social Psychology*, *23*, 1–18.

Harkins, S. G., & Petty, R. E. (1982). Effects of task difficulty and task uniqueness on social loafing. *Journal of Personality and Social Psychology*, *43*, 1214–1229.

Hatfield, E. (1988). Passionate and companionate love. In R. J. Sternberg & M. L. Barnes (Eds.), *The psychology of love* (pp. 191–217). New Haven, CT: Yale University Press.

Hau, K., & Salili, F. (1991). Structure and semantic differential placement of specific causes: Academic causal attributions by Chinese students in Hong Kong. *International Journal of Psychology, 26,* 175–193.

Hendrick, C., & Hendrick, S. (1983). *Liking, loving, and relating.* Pacific Grove, CA: Brooks/Cole.

Ineichen, B. (1979). The social geography of marriage. In M. Cook & G. Wilson (Eds.), *Love and attraction.* New York: Pergamon Press.

Jackson, J. M., & Williams, K. D. (1985). Social loafing on difficult tasks: Working collectively can improve performance. *Journal of Personality and Social Psychology, 49,* 937–942.

Jones, E. E., & Nisbett, R. E. (1971). The actor and the observer: Divergent perceptions of the causes of behavior. In E. E. Jones, D. E. Kanouse, H. H. Kelley, R. E. Nisbett, S. Valins, & B. Weiner (Eds.), *Attribution: Perceiving the causes of behavior.* Morristown, NJ: General Learning Press.

Kashima, Y., & Triandis, H.C. (1986). The self-serving bias in attributions as a coping strategy: A cross cultural study. *Journal of Cross-Cultural Psychology, 17,* 83–97.

Kelley, H. H. (1967). Attributional theory in social psychology. *Nebraska Symposium on Motivation, 15,* 192–241.

Kelley, H. H. (1973). The processes of causal attribution. *American Psychologist, 28,* 107–128.

Latane, B. (1981). The psychology of social impact. *American Psychologist, 36,* 343–356.

Latane, B., Williams, K., & Harkins, S. (1979). Many hands make light the work: The causes and consequences of social loafing. *Journal of Personality and Social Psychology, 37,* 322–332.

Matsumoto, D., & Kudoh, T. (in press). Cultural differences in social judgments of facial expressions of emotion: What's in a smile? *Journal of Nonverbal Behavior.*

Milgram, S. (1963). Behavioral study of obedience. *Journal of Abnormal and Social Psychology, 67,* 371–378.

Milgram, S. (1964). Issues in the study of obedience. *American Psychologist, 19,* 848–852.

Milgram, S. (1974). *Obedience to authority.* New York: Harper & Row.

Moghaddam, F. M., Ditto, B., & Taylor, D. M. (1990). Attitudes and attributions related to psychological symptomatology in Indian immigrant women. *Journal of Cross-Cultural Psychology, 21,* 335–350.

Patzer, G. L. (1985). *The physical attractiveness phenomena.* New York: Plenum Press.

Punetha, D., Giles, H., & Young, L. (1987). Ethnicity and immigrant values: Religion and language choice. *Journal of Language and Social Psychology, 6,* 229–241.

Ross, J., & Ferris, K. R. (1981). Interpersonal attraction and organizational outcome: A field experiment. *Administrative Science Quarterly, 26,* 617–632.

Shepperd, J., & Wright, R. (1989). Individual contributions to a collective effort: An incentive analysis. *Personality and Social Psychology Bulletin, 15,* 141–149.

Shirakashi, S. (1985). Social loafing of Japanese students. *Hiroshima Forum for Psychology, 10,* 35–40.

Simmons, C. H., vomKolke, A., & Shimizu, H. (1986). Attitudes toward romantic love among American, German and Japanese students. *Journal of Social Psychology, 126,* 327–336.

Sternberg, R. J. (1988). Triangulating love. In R. J. Sternberg and M. L. Barnes (Eds.), *The psychology of love* (pp. 119–138). New Haven, CT: Yale University Press.

Stropes-Roe, M., & Cochrane, R. (1990). The child-rearing values of Asian and British parents and young people: An inter-ethnic and inter-generational comparison in the evolution of Kohn's 13 qualities. *British Journal of Social Psychology, 29,* 149–160.

Thornton, B. (1984). Defensive attribution of responsibility: Evidence for an arousal-based motivational bias. *Journal of Personality and Social Psychology, 46,* 721–734.

Ting-Toomey, S. (1991). Intimacy expressions in three cultures: France, Japan, and the United States. *International Journal of Intercultural Relations, 15,* 29–46.

Tom, D., & Cooper, H. (1986). The effect of student background on teacher performance attributions: Evidence for counterdefensive patterns and low expectancy cycles. *Basic and Applied Social Psychology, 7,* 53–62.

Watson, D. (1982). The actor and the observer: How are their perceptions of causality divergent? *Psychological Bulletin, 92,* 682–700.

Weiner, B. (1974). *Achievement motivation and attribution theory.* Morristown, NJ: General Learning Press.

Weldon, E., & Gargano, G. M. (1988). Cognitive loafing: The effects of accountability and shared responsibility on cognitive effort. *Personality and Social Psychology Bulletin, 14,* 159–171.

Wong, P. T. P., Derlaga, V. J., & Colson, W. (1988). The effects of race on expectancies and performance and attributions. *Canadian Journal of Behavioral Science, 20,* 29–39.

Yamaguchi, S., Okamoto, K., & Oka, T. (1985). Effects of coactor's presence: Social loafing and social facilitation. *Japanese Psychological Research, 27,* 215–222.

Zaccaro, S. J. (1984). The role of task attractiveness. *Personality and Social Psychology Bulletin, 10,* 99–106.

Zajonc, R. (1985). Cognitive theories in social psychology. In G. Lindzey & E. Aronson (Eds.), *Handbook of social psychology* (Vol. 1) (pp. 320–411). New York: Random House.

Suggested Readings

Asante, M., & Gudykunst, W. (1989). *Handbook of intercultural and international communication.* Beverly Hills: Sage.

Bond, M. H. (1988). *The cross-cultural challenge to social psychology.* Newbury Park: Sage.

Ferrante, J. (1992). *Sociology: A global perspective.* Belmont, CA: Wadsworth.

Worchel, S., & Austin, W. G. (1986). *Psychology of intergroup relations.* Chicago: Nelson Hall.

11 *Conclusion*

This book has tried to show you how culture influences so much of our daily lives. Across many of the topics traditionally covered in psychology today, culture plays a major, albeit sometimes silent and invisible, role in determining how we act and perceive the actions of others.

Chapters 1 and 2 laid the foundations of much of the message throughout the book. Chapter 1 presented a definition of culture and discussed some of the special issues concerning cross-cultural research that are pertinent to most, if not all, of the studies cited in the book. We also discussed the definition of etics and emics and how these terms play a part in the development of ethnocentrism and stereotyping.

In Chapter 2, we saw how culture can influence our fundamental views of ourselves. We also examined how these views of ourselves, in turn, can influence how we think, act, and feel.

Chapters 3 through 10 dealt with specific content areas of psychology. In all of these chapters, we reviewed not only what is traditionally covered in psychology courses, but also cross-cultural studies that challenge the notions of "truth" that we have developed from that traditional knowledge. In Chapter 3, for example, we discussed how culture can influence the way we perceive the world around us. In Chapter 4, we discussed how culture seems to influence the way we think. However, we also saw how education and other environmental factors play a big part in the development of many psychological skills.

In Chapter 5, we learned how cultures differ in their attitudes and behaviors toward child-rearing, parenting, and socialization, and how these differences affect such development processes as moral reasoning. In Chapter 6, we discussed how cultures influence language and language acquisition. We also studied how culture, language, and personality interact in bilingual individuals.

In Chapter 7, we reviewed cross-cultural studies of Piaget's theory of cognitive development. We briefly discussed other theories of cognitive development, uncovering the possible biases that underlie them. In this chapter, we also talked about cultural differences in the definition of intelligence and some of the difficulties in measuring it.

In Chapter 8, we reviewed anthropological as well as psychological studies on emotion. We saw how the concept and meaning of emotion can differ across cultures and how culture can influence other aspects of emotion, such as the expression, perception, experience, and antecedents of emotion.

In Chapter 9, we discussed some of the major issues regarding the interaction between culture and abnormal psychology. This discussion covered cultural differences in the definitions of abnormality. We also looked at findings from major, cross-national studies of schizophrenia and depression as well as some culture-specific disorders. These, of course, have varied treatment implications, which also differ across cultures.

Finally, in Chapter 10, we reviewed the cross-cultural literature on various topics of social psychology, including attribution, attraction, group productivity, and conformity. Here again, we saw how cultures can influence such social processes, highlighting the limitations of knowledge that is based solely on studies within this culture.

This book does not focus only on cultural differences. Indeed, several topics within psychology appear to be pancultural or universal. Some processes of perception, for example, may very well have a universal base. Some types of cognition and thinking skills and strategies may share pancultural elements. Processes of language acquisition may be universal, as are the expressions of certain emotions in the face.

Across all the chapters, we have learned that human behavior is just too rich and complex to be "captured" by studies that are conducted in only a single culture. One of the major goals of this book has been to make exactly this point, exposing psychology students to the breadth of human behavior that exists. Another goal has been to challenge the truths that have been typically presented as such in this field. The many cross-cultural studies that we covered in this book, and the many, many more that are in the literature, attest to the diversity of human behavior—and to the need to allow for this diversity as we develop psychological truths.

Still, we have so much more to learn. As time progresses, the need to learn increases. Improvements in communications technologies that bring previously distant points on the globe close together further enmesh our global village. The opening of national borders and the infusion of people from all walks of life and cultures into the workplace and family ensure that cross-cultural issues will remain a high priority in the years to come. Can psychology keep up?

Further cross-cultural research will help to continue uncovering both universal and culture-specific aspects of human behavior and psychology. Writers will increasingly include culture as a major determinant in their theories of human behavior. As new information is uncovered, we can and will improve our thinking about the nature of culture and cultural influences on the behaviors of others as well as ourselves.

In closing this book, we offer some guiding principles by which we can welcome the uncertainty brought by the further discovery of knowledge in future research. We hope that these brief statements will aid in developing not only better critical thinking skills about culture and psychology, but better critical behavioral skills as well.

Culture Is a Psychological Construct

As we discussed throughout this book, culture is a *psychological* construct. It refers to the degree to which a group of people share attitudes, values, beliefs, and behaviors. It is communicated from one generation to the next via language or observation. As such, culture is a functional entity—one that you cannot see, but can only infer from observations of human behavior.

Culture is not race. Being of African, Asian, or whatever descent does not mean that one is automatically associated with a particular culture. Culture is not nationality. Being a citizen of the United States, France, or China does not mean that one automatically adopts an American, French, or Chinese culture. Culture is not birthplace. Being born in Canada, Mexico, or Egypt does not automatically mean that one harbors the culture of that country.

As we learn more about cultural influences on human behavior, we must also learn more about what culture is and is not. In doing so, we need to recognize the fuzzy nature of the definition of culture, based in functional psychology. By defining cultures in this way, we can avoid using stereotypes and anecdotes based on race and other aspects of biology in understanding cultural differences among people.

Recognize Individual Differences Within a Culture

Defining culture as a sociopsychological construct is not enough. With a functional definition of culture, we also need to recognize individual differences within cultural groups. That is, within any cultural group that we can identify (or that identifies itself as a culture), there are bound to be individual differences. For example, consider a culture that is quite individualistic (like our own American culture). Most members of this culture may be quite individualistic. Some, however, may be *very* individualistic, even according to their own culture's standards. Yet other members in the same culture may be relatively collectivistic. Certainly, describing all individuals within this cultural group as individualistic ignores actual cultural differences among the individual members.

These types of individual differences will exist given any definition of culture and for any group that identifies itself as a culture. The existence of these individual differences seriously challenges our ability, and the wisdom, of using global, stereotypic statements and beliefs to describe all of the members of any culture, including our own.

Understand Our Own Filters and Ethnocentrism

We hope that this book has been able to show you that culture is truly an important determinant of human behavior. As we discussed throughout, and especially highlighted in Chapter 2, however, culture is a silent and invisible determinant. We are not always aware of our own cultural filters as we perceive, think about, and interpret events and behaviors of others. We are not always aware of the cultural bases of our own behaviors and actions.

One important first step in gaining an understanding of cultural influences on behavior is to recognize that we have our own filters for perception and bases for behavior. We need to stop and think about how our own cultural upbringing contributed to how we ourselves interact with the world and others. This comparison comes to the forefront when we travel outside our own culture. In encounters with the cultures of others, we are forced to think about differences in cognition and behavior. In thinking about these differences, we have to reach a better understanding of our own filters and biases.

Allow for the Possibility That Conflicts Are Cultural

In interacting with others, conflicts and misunderstandings will occur. Unfortunately, we are often too quick to attribute the cause of the conflict or misunderstanding to a difference of opinion or to a fault or shortcoming in the other person. With a better understanding of cultural influences on behavior, however, we can allow for the possibility that much of the conflict and misunderstanding is due to cultural differences. This is especially true when interacting with people of different cultural backgrounds. By allowing for this possibility, we can avoid personalizing the source of conflict and misunderstanding in our interactions and instead focus on why the conflict arose.

Recognize That Differences May Occur Because of Legitimate Differences in Culture

Simply allowing for conflicts and misunderstandings to be attributed to culture is not enough. Indeed, we need to recognize, and respect, legitimate differences between our cultural upbringing and that of others. This is often a very difficult task because we typically perceive transgressions of our own ways of behaving as "bad" or "wrong" when the transgression occurs within our own cultural context. Thus, it is easy to label the behaviors of others as "bad" or "wrong."

However, a person from another culture may view those same behaviors as "good," "acceptable," or "normal." In fact, another's behavior that we label "bad," "ignorant," or "stupid" may in fact be grounded in sincerity and trustworthiness. No matter how much we want to attach a negative label, the other person's cultural ways, values, and beliefs have just as much legitimacy to that person as ours have to us.

A step in the right direction is to respect that legitimacy and that difference and find a way to work from that level of respect.

Learn More about Cultural Influences on Behavior

Our final prescription for our work as we turn toward the future is to continue to learn about how culture influences human behavior. As we come in contact with people of different cultures from around the world, either through our own travels or through theirs, we are exposed to many different ways in which culture manifests itself in behavior. As our understanding of these manifestations grows, we will come to appreciate even more the important role that culture plays, not only in providing us with a way in which to live, but also in helping all of us find a way to survive. Indeed, culture provides people with the rules by which survival can be ensured, given that resources are available for that survival.

Another reason to continue learning about cultures is that cultures continue to change. Culture is not a static, fixed entity. With our functional definition of culture, we know that cultures can change over time. We are witnessing today changes in the cultures and the people of Europe, Asia, and the United States. Such changes ensure that there will never be a shortage of things to learn about cultural influences on human behavior. But we have to want to learn them.

Conclusion

We recognized from the start that this book would not be a primary source of learning basic truths in psychology; that should be accomplished by other texts. Instead, we wanted to raise questions about the traditional knowledge, to determine whether what we know as truth is applicable to people of *all* cultural backgrounds. We sought answers to our questions in the cross-cultural literature.

In challenging the traditional knowledge, we cannot, and should not, disregard its importance or the work that was involved in producing it. Indeed, to disregard that material or the work that produced it would be insensitive, and insensitivity has no place in academic work.

We have offered this book to you as a way to seek alternatives to the material typically presented in psychology. In offering these alternatives, we have sought to accomplish two goals:

1. By seeing alternative ways of observing and understanding people, you will be able to choose a viewpoint or perspective of psychology and human behavior that is right for you.

2. Through exposure to these alternatives, you will be able to recognize, understand, and most importantly, appreciate the psychology of people of diverse backgrounds, some of which will be very, very different from your own.

We hope that we have achieved these goals.

Index